WHAT THE CHURCH
TEACHES

WHAT THE CHURCH TEACHES

BY J. D. CONWAY

HARPER & BROTHERS
Publishers, New York

NIHIL OBSTAT: A. J. Burke, *Censor Librorum*
IMPRIMATUR: ✠ Ralph L. Hayes, *Episcopus Davenportensis*
January 11, 1962

Library of Congress catalog card number: 62-11125

CONTENTS

CONTENTS CONTINUED

INTRODUCTION

This book is not a complete presentation of Catholic doctrine; it did not develop from a theological outline. Rather, it grew from the interest of inquirers, hardly any of them Catholic. But it has grown into a fairly integral summary of Church teaching, with typical examples in various areas such as the sacraments and morality—areas too vast for complete treatment in a brief survey.

Our story starts with God: His existence; it ends with God: our union with Him in heaven; its prevalent theme is the relationship of God to man: in creation, in man's sin and punishment, in revelation and religion, in the Redemption and our sanctification.

The Church of Jesus Christ has an essential and pervasive part in our sanctification, and most inquirers who are not Catholic are concerned with various features of Church teaching, practice, and discipline. So the major portion of the book answers questions on these subjects.

All but one of the articles in this book have appeared in the *Catholic Digest,* in a monthly feature entitled "What Would You Like to Know about the Church?" The questions are real, sincere, and authentic; and the answers seek rather to explain than to convince: to show what we believe and our sensible reasons for believing; to set forth truth plainly rather than to argue. Possibly none of my inquirers has been persuaded to agree with me; but I hope all have learned what we believe and why.

The chapter on Natural Law is not a reply to a specific question. It first appeared in the *Catholic Messenger* and is presented here to show the rational basis of Catholic morality, of which we then see a few typical examples. There could be a hundred more.

The chapter on Secularism has been revised to relieve it of its involvement in a particular problem. Otherwise, except for some slight changes in dates, tenses, and statistics in order to make them current as of their publication in book form, the material remains as it originally appeared, with occasional specific references to the persons who asked the questions.

The general outline of the Catholic catechism is fairly evident in the arrangement of the chapters of this book. We start with the existence of God and the creation of the world; then there is the creation and fall of man with its sequel, the evil in the world.

Next come questions about religion in general, and various religions in particular; and about sacred Scripture and tradition, the inspired and living source of Catholic teaching.

Following that are questions about our Lord Jesus Christ and about the graces He obtained for the salvation of men.

Then we consider the Church: her foundation and some of her salient characteristics; her Pope, priests, and sisters; the Mass and one of her sacraments—the one of greatest popular interest; the Blessed Virgin Mary and the Saints.

Next there is a brief bit about the moral law and four facets of the Church's relation with those who are outside her fold.

The final chapters deal with various aspects of the supernatural: its reality, and its relation to natural phenomena which bear resemblance to it. These chapters culminate in the resurrection and eternal life.

I am very grateful to the publisher and editors of the *Catholic Digest,* first, for their invitation to write the articles, and second, for permission to use them here. I am particularly grateful to Father Paul Bussard for his personal interest and encouragement and to Father Kenneth Ryan, who chose the questions, assigned me my monthly theme, and helped greatly with his comments and evaluations. In these and in all my writings I owe much to my lifelong friend and confrere, Monsignor Barnes, the editor of the *Catholic Messenger*. He first challenged, encouraged, and published my answers to questions, and he has continued to publish my weekly column for fourteen years.

J. D. CONWAY

WHAT THE CHURCH
TEACHES

1

THE EXISTENCE OF GOD

THE QUESTION

I was interested in the response you made in regard to comparative modern religions in a recent issue of the *Catholic Digest*. It brings to mind a further question.

A group of us are studying comparative religion, and we are using historical charts, maps, and the like. We have observed that from a historical perspective many of the ancient (as well as the modern) religions, at least in their origins, were not theistically oriented. You have even admitted this in regard to Shinto, Confucianism, and Buddhism; and it is certainly true of all the survivals of totemism, animism, and fetishism which existed in primitive societies. Would not these observations make invalid one of the principal arguments for theism: that men in all places and all times believed in a supreme power?

We would be most interested in your reply.

R. Brooks Manley

THE ANSWER

It would seem, Brooks, that you are immersed in evolutionary theories of the origin and growth of man's religious beliefs. It will help our dialogue if we realize that your friends and I view this question from opposite poles. I believe that God created man; the evolutionists are likely to hold, rather, that man created God.

I hold that man can know of God's existence by studying the works of creation, as you might know an author by read-

1

ing his book. But God exists whether I know it or not, and my rude ideas about Him do not mar His actual perfection. Your friends would rather hold that God emerges from the instinctive needs of man, and grows to greater excellence as man's mind molds the crude creature of his fears into an eventual paragon of Being.

I have another belief, too, which we should not ignore or try to conceal, even though it does not enter directly into this discussion. I hold that God revealed Himself directly to the first man He created. Adam knew God better than a modern theologian does.

In spite of this belief, I do not find your evolutionary theories particularly disturbing. When Adam got himself expelled from the garden of God's intimacy, he deprived the whole human race of all but a lingering thread of vague tradition about that primitive revelation. So in spite of man's early heritage his practical knowledge of God had to be obtained by his own efforts. Like most things of nature, it tended to evolve.

Some books on the history of primitive religions hold my view of God's primitive revelation of Himself to man. They emphasize evidence that earliest man started out with notions of monotheism and then degenerated into superstition. The Pygmies of Africa and some tribes of the South Pacific seem to bolster this deduction.

Books of your evolutionists, on the contrary, tend to fit all the facts they find into their picture of the gradual development of man's theistic concepts. As I said, these theories do not trouble me as long as we admit that God exists. It sounds quite reasonable that He has made Himself known to man in an obscure way through His creation, and that man's comprehension of Him has been progressive. Our knowledge of God's creation has been a long time growing. Why should our knowledge of the Creator Himself be acquired more rapidly?

I think, then, that we may agree on the general evidence of your historical charts and maps. Man has gradually acquired greater knowledge. He has advanced toward the truth of theism. My argument with your friends would begin only

2

when they step out of their historical field and into philosophy. I must disagree when they try to tell me that God is nothing more than a social and psychological phenomenon: a concept, at first confused, which man's mind has gradually clarified through progressive phases of fear and rationalization.

Why do we believe that God is a reality? I think you know well that the so-called universality of man's belief in a supreme power is merely a persuasive argument. We do not claim it to be a conclusive proof. If we do not create God, neither do we elect Him by majority vote. His existence is not the result of a popularity contest conducted through the ages. The fact that "men in all places and at all times" have believed in some sort of god or gods merely gives added assurance to convictions we have formed on other grounds. It is nice to have people agree with us; and the notion is persistent that surely all men everywhere cannot be completely deluded in their common consent.

We should be careful not to overstate this argument— though I suspect that you have found it overstated in some polemic books. We do not claim that all men in all times and places have been monotheist, or even theist, in the sense we are using the word. We do not say that they have always believed in a supreme power—to use your own expression— but rather in some superior forces or persons above, beyond, and behind perceptible nature. Not all persons would hold these superior powers to be apart from the world, but at least they are potencies hidden beneath the surface of sensible reality.

I willingly concede to you that these universal beliefs of mankind have sometimes been rank superstition, groveling nature worship, or credulous fetishism. But I do wonder if we are not inclined, in our modern superiority, to judge our primitive ancestors a bit harshly. It is possible that fantastic external practices sometimes conceal discerning spiritual concepts of personal gods, creative powers, and lawgiving authority.

Why do we have to go back to the primitives? Just how many full-fledged theists do you think we have with us today?

3

Theism is a term hard to define, but we seem to be restricting it to belief in some intelligent, personal, active Being (or beings) apart from the world and responsible for the world.

Several years ago I saw the published results of a public-opinion poll on this subject.* Less than one per cent of our people professed themselves to be atheists. But we may take it for granted that not all the ninety-nine faithful sheep were strong professing theists. Many are partial atheists: agnostics, pantheists, practical atheists, and a variety of skeptics and indifferentists.

The number of agnostics is legion. They do not deny the existence of God—in fact, they consider Him fairly probable, since the human mind seems to postulate His existence. But they find no way of proving it. And even if they knew He existed they could, they claim, never know anything about Him.

Pantheists come mostly in two contrasting varieties. They have this in common: they more or less identify God with the world. One group is materialistic; its people hold that matter is the only reality, that life is the sublime product of mechanics and chemistry, that thought is an organic process, and that moral values have no basis outside man and his society. For them God is a dynamic complex of matter and energy, working its way to intelligent goals.

Other pantheists are idealists. The material universe is only an idea, and God is the cosmic idea, the all-embracing mind, in which our little minds participate. Even though they have our word "theist" in their name, I think we will have to exclude both species of pantheists from our restricted group.

Most numerous of all are the practical atheists. They ignore God's existence, give the question no concern, and order their lives exactly as if there were no supreme Being. If you pin them down they admit Him, but promptly forget again. They have a vague belief in God, but fail to integrate it into their lives. It has no practical force in their attitudes or actions.

By excluding all these partial atheists we probably weaken

* *Catholic Digest*, Nov. 1952, p. 1.

4

the impact of our argument that "men in all places and all times" believed in some superior power, but we do retain an impressive company of real, solid theists. Moreover, in most of those we have eliminated we still discern evidence of man's instinctive or intuitive need for some way to account for himself and the world.

I must repeat that our proof of the existence of God is not based on this instinctive need. We do not create or elect Him; neither does He pop into existence because we need Him. Our need might be only a phase of our evolution; something to be eliminated by education and therapy. Still, it is a persuasive factor that all men everywhere have felt this common need.

You are familiar, of course, with the five traditional proofs of the existence of God which are set forth by St. Thomas Aquinas in his *Summa Theologica*. We hold with him that it is possible to prove convincingly that there is a God, using logical proofs based on the observable facts of creation. The proofs are not overwhelming to everyone; we do not see God immediately. Even in our hardy core of theists there are many who are skeptical of our proofs from reason.

Some few, who accept primitive revelation, think that we know about God only because of human tradition, which was originally activiated by this first revelation.

Some accept God because they find his image impressed in the human heart. Man's deep-rooted need and notion of God is their only proof of His existence. If you don't find Him in your heart you will never find Him outside. He is not a phenomenon to be observed. These people accept God by instinct rather than by reason. They reach Him with their will rather than with their mind.

Immanuel Kant found proof of God's existence in the moral order. Our conscience tells us that there is a supreme law-giver. Cardinal Newman liked the persuasive force of this reasoning. Our argument with Kant comes from his rejection of our logical proofs, which we find not only persuasive but convincing. We do not need to disregard instinctive needs, intuitive perceptions, common consent, or even the influence of parents, society, and history. They may all persuade and dispose us. Conviction comes from reason first, and then is fortified by faith.

If we are to know God from reason we must start by accepting two self-evident truths: (1) that our reason and senses are generally trustworthy; and (2) that all effects have causes. These are first principles, and there is no logical proof for them. They shine by their own light. If you deny them I waste my time presenting arguments based on them. We cannot talk about mathematics if you reject my claim that one plus one equals two. We will be lost in geometry if we do not agree that the whole of a thing is equal to the sum of its parts.

Those who question causality never do it on the natural or scientific plane. All science is based on it. Deny causality, and all research loses its purpose. Never before on his path of progress has man relied so thoroughly on the principle of causality, even though he may prefer to call it a compilation of statistical laws.

Men deny causality because they do not trust reason. Everything we observe seems to have a cause, and we accept causality as a working principle as long as we can check it by experiment or mathematical formula. But the mind can never be sure of things beyond itself; it can never reach out to the Absolute. We have no way of knowing that causes are necessary beyond the area of our observation.

Traditional proofs for the existence of God are simple enough. There is no way of doubting them once you have accepted the first principles on which they are based. Once you are convinced that reality exists, that you can know it, and that you can trust your own mind in its reasoning processes, then our lines of argument lead you to God.

Each method of proof starts from a different aspect of existing reality, and calls attention to the fact that each phase needs to be accounted for, and does not account for itself.

The first argument is from motion. Whatever moves is moved by something else. Things change, begin to be, cease to exist, live and die, grow and decline. We can find natural causes for most of these mutations, and suspect unknown natural causes for the rest. The object at rest cannot give itself motion, but one thing moves another, alters another, gives life to another. And you cannot go on endlessly with movers which are themselves moved by something else. You must come ultimately to the unmoved source of all motion, to the unchanging cause of all change. This is God.

To our primitive friends and even to their modern brethren, the impressive force of this argument comes from nature's startling events: the eclipse, earthquake, storms, floods, fires, volcanoes. Routine changes we take for granted. Who sees God in the sunrise? But we may well find Him in outer space.

This argument from motion has its full philosophical force only for the person accustomed to the Thomistic idea of potentiality and actuality. A potential thing cannot give itself actuality. It must receive it from something already actual. And this brings us ultimately to the Being which is all actuality, without any potentiality—any possibility of change.

The second argument is from causality. In all our experience nothing happens without a cause. Nothing causes itself. The cause it always apart from the effect, existing prior to it. We come ultimately to a first cause, which owes its effective power to no other: God.

The argument preferred by the metaphysician is the third one: from contingency, or dependence. Things exist which do not have to exist. We can easily imagine their not existing. Nothing in our known world has a firm, unalterable hold on existence. Nothing we see is necessary by its nature. Each thing depends on other things; nothing owes existence to itself. It might not be; maybe at one time it wasn't; and maybe tomorrow it won't be.

Dependent things can never add up to self-existence. Neither size nor durability makes them less dependent. Dependent things lead us by their nature to something not dependent—to some Being which exists by its very nature —which must be because it simply is, without beginning or end.

This argument is a fruitful source of religious meditation. It gives us understanding of our relationship to God: total dependence. Our very existence comes from Him and is

7

constantly maintained by Him. We live in His hand.

Some persons have thought that it should be possible to arrive at a direct intellectual knowledge of God by a persistent process of abstraction. We might shuck off all manner and circumstance of being until we saw Being alone, stark and clear. That would be God. It is reason's route to mysticism. And it is vain, because God can never be known to us directly in a natural way. But its methods are vitally useful. God is Being, pure and simple; and we can learn much about Him by our study of being—abstracted from our experience of existing things. The metaphysician is at the heart of reality. His notions come as near to God as man can get.

The fourth argument is from the degrees of perfection which are found in created things: the good, the true, and the beautiful, life and the nobility of being. As we observe them in created things they are all relative, in varying degrees. The relative demands the Absolute. Limited perfection is received perfection. Beauty cannot account for itself unless it is perfect. Truth in itself cannot be partial. Life which comes and goes cannot account for all life. Things of limited goodness are not the source of all goodness.

This argument is similar to the preceding one, from Being. It is quite different from an idealistic sort of argument which appealed in various ways to St. Augustine, St. Anselm, and Descartes: that because we have a concept of beauty there must be real Beauty to account for that concept; that our idea of goodness must find its prototype in perfect Goodness; and that since existence is a perfection, and God must be perfect, God must exist.

The proof which makes the greatest impact on most of us is the fifth one of St. Thomas: the proof from the order, design, and purpose of the universe. All nature is obedient to law.

Material things, without a grain of sense in themselves, still have a sense of direction and purpose. They are so elaborately and perfectly constructed and behave with such intricate precision that they achieve goals which only a great mind could plan for them. The simple example used by St. Thomas is that an arrow reaches its target because aimed by

8

the bowman. It might hit it once by chance, but if it flies true on every shot it is being handled by an expert.

Chance might fit a rock to a hole; it will seldom shape a key to a lock. Where there is complicated design, there must be a designer. Material things cannot do their own planning. Where there is a vast machine in which a million parts mesh to achieve a purpose, there must have been some mental blueprints and a skilled artisan to machine the pieces. When things are made for a reason, it must be Reason which made them. The purposeful planner, the great designer, we call God.

We might add a thousand examples to the simple Thomistic arrow: the marvelous instincts of bees and ants, the purposeful perfection of man's eye or ear, the cosmic order of a billion stars, or the phylogenic growth of life on the earth.

The example which intrigues me most is the development of the human embryo. Powerful instincts push man and woman into creative union. Two little groups of cells come together; they never saw each other before and have no brains for mutual planning. They have no skill or experience at their job; they work in the dark without hands or tools. They seem to unite, grow, and divide in profuse abandon; and in nine months they produce the most beautiful, intricate, purposeful, and specialized structure in the world, one which has human life in it: a person who will think and love.

Did chance bring it all about? Like the skilled bowman's arrow, similar little cells will do the same thing a million times over and will seldom make a mistake.

Who put the chromosomes in the sperm and ovum? Who fitted electrons into an atom? Who designed the periodic table, planned the transformations of matter and energy, or gave evolutionary purpose to the mutations of living things? Keep on asking the questions! There are a million of them, and the answer is always the same: God.

We like people to agree with us, Brooks. And it is easy to follow the crowd to God. But I can't help it if men in some times and some places were badly confused. I don't accept God because they all believed in Him, but because I see His creation all about me—and in me.

9

2

CREATION AND EVOLUTION

THE QUESTION

My question is: As I understand it, all the great minds of the day accept the theory of evolution. Does your Church accept it? And if so, how does she explain it? Thank you.

Laurie Fromm

THE ANSWER

May I begin my answer, Laurie, with a personal note? Way back when the roar of the Twenties was growing in volume, I had the privilege of studying biology under one of those rare professors who can make their subject live in the interest and imagination of their students. We called him Father Hauber, although he owned the title of Doctor and later became Monsignor. Since then the good Lord has taken him, leaving his high repute with fellow scientists, strong evidence of his priestly sanctity, and affectionate admiration with all who knew him.

We studied at Davenport, Iowa, and nearby at Linwood was a limestone quarry. Father Hauber used to take us there, explaining beforehand that the stone in this quarry had been deposited by slow sedimentation during some sixty million years of the Devonian period—one of the many stages of development of the earth's surface.

There were living things on earth during the Devonian period; and when they died their bodies often became embedded in the rock which was forming at the same time. In our quarry it was easy to find fossils by the hundreds; most of them I fail to remember, but there were strange creatures called brachiopods, and basketfuls of trilobites. There should have been fish fossils there, too, but I am not sure that we found any. We were told that land plants made their appearance in this same era.

Back in the classroom Father Hauber explained that if we should visit some of the lead mines at Dubuque we might find an earlier stratum of rock, with fossils of simpler forms of life. And still farther north there would be another. I have just looked up the names of these earlier periods, and find that they were called Ordovician and Cambrian. Each of them lasted some eighty million years. In the rocks of those ages we might still find trilobites, but certainly no fish— probably mostly algae and seashells. But even these were not the earliest forms of life on earth, merely the oldest ones which have left many fossils for us. It seems that the rocks of pre-Cambrian ages were so fused by heat and pressure that they crushed all life forms caught in them.

Now if we were to go south from Davenport into the coal mines of Iowa and Illinois, we might find remains of amphibians, reptiles, and some primitive land animals; but there would be no mammals or birds. These didn't appear on earth for another fifty million years after our coal was deposited in its seams. However, if we were lucky in searching the surface gravel of midwestern America, we might find bones of a mastodon or a camel, or of other ancient mammals—the last inhabitants of the earth before the appearance of man.

Our study of the history of life in the rocks of the earth was only one small phase of our biology course. We dissected earthworms, frogs, and other simple creatures, and when these studies were augmented by slides and pictures we were much impressed with the basic similarities of organic and skeletal structures in all animals, great and small. We learned that living things could be readily classified into branching systems, according to phylum, class, order, family, genus, and species—giving new meaning to the structural similarities we had observed.

We studied embryonic development, and saw how simple, microscopic organisms go through stages of growth reminiscent of the life forms found in our successive strata of the earth. And one pompous phrase has always stuck in my mind: embryology recapitulates phylology. The idea is that if you watch a tiny group of egg cells grow into a baby animal you will see along the way stages which remind you vividly of ancient forms of life or of simpler creatures still with us. An egg in the process of becoming a bird looks first like a protozoan, then like a fish, and finally it resembles a reptile.

We also learned in a general way about the distribution of various types of living things in different parts of the world. Almost a century earlier Charles Darwin had made a trip around the world on the *Beagle,* and his studies of plants and animals in many countries—their similarities and differences —had stimulated his thinking toward *The Origin of Species.*

Since our days in college I have seen remarkable genetic changes take place in the cornfields of Iowa. And I have read of even more notable mutations in plant and animal life as a result of radiation.

When the evidence from all these different sources is put together, the theory of biological evolution seems both sound and intriguing. It may not explain all the data observed, but it is by far the best working hypothesis available—and most scientists simply accept it as fact.

We usually think of biology when the word "evolution" is mentioned. But the same general principle of creative growth seems to apply to our entire universe.

The first theoretical stage of cosmic evolution might be called physiochemical. Some of it may have taken place before the stars began. Maybe it started with an enormous cloud of subatomic particles; maybe with a ponderous mass of concentrated atomic material. It is a challenge to speculation that we have been able to change matter to energy, showing that they are made of the same basic stuff; and have discovered that all atoms from hydrogen to uranium are made of the same building blocks: protons, electrons, neutrons, and the like.

Our scientists have used these subatomic forces and materials to create new elements beyond uranium. So it is not hard to imagine that the old ones might have grown from

12

simplicity to complexity by some similar fantastic processes.

Next, or maybe at the same time, came the development of our stellar universe, and here our evidences of expansion and change are abundant. Our spectroscopes show us that nebulae are going away from our galaxy at tremendous speeds, proportionate to their distance from us. And we are able to study stars in various stages of growth and decline: for example, supergiants, those enormous spendthrifts of the sky, which use up their hydrogen supply at such a fantastic rate that a short hundred million years will do them in, and they will be reduced to mere giants or dwarfs.

Since I started my answer on a personal note, I might mention that I was a student at the University of Louvain in 1927, when one of the priest-professors there, Canon Lemaitre, gained the attention of the world by his theory of an exploding universe. I never really understood what he was talking about, but I mention it as added evidence that a Catholic education need not impart a prejudice against evolution, in any of its phases.

Next comes geological evolution. Did some star pass near the sun three thousand million years ago and pull off a blistering blob of magma, which went into elliptical orbit and gradually cooled off—in a few hundred million years—so that a solid crust could start forming on it? It seems possible.

The most baffling problem to the evolutionist is that of the origin of life. The geologist can give no help; his records have been destroyed. If they were intact they might take us back a thousand million years. Recently our laboratories have given us some helpful evidence; if we can't dig up the story of life's origins, maybe we can duplicate them.

Organic compounds have been synthesized from inorganic ones, the basic component of protoplasm—known as DNA —has been put together, and rudimentary forms of synthetic life have been made to demonstrate vital processes. There is still a long—and maybe impossible—way to go before the giant molecules of a cell can be assembled in a test tube, and before manufactured life will be able to reproduce itself.

In this area there is no basic conflict with Catholic thought. Our ancient and medieval ancestors—the Fathers and Doctors of the Church—rather took for granted that living things sprang up right before their eyes: from the sea or from decaying organic matter. Later, science ridiculed such naïve notions, and developed a contrary principle that "every living thing comes from an egg." Now we are not so sure. But it is still hard to imagine all the ideal conditions, fortuitous circumstances, and catalytic factors which might have developed first life from nonlife.

In our elementary biology course we did not learn much about man, but it was clearly implied that his body need not be an exception to the general process by which earlier and simpler forms of life developed into later and more complicated ones. Anthropologists simply took it for granted. We don't like the notion of apes in our family tree, but we cannot deny that even the most beautiful human body has the same basic physical structure as a chimpanzee.

In our college days it seems that historical evidence to back up the theory of human evolution was not abundant. There were hints of Java men and Peking men, of Neanderthal and Cro-Magnon types. But still everyone seemed to be looking for the "missing link." Since then diligent diggers have found our family skeletons in various cavernous closets —and all new discoveries seem to fit nicely into previous theories.

While we were studying biology, the Scopes "monkey trial" in Tennessee hit the headlines of our newspapers. Our sympathies were frankly with the monkey; it didn't seem fair to blame him for the monkeyshines of two of the nation's most famous lawyers or for the mass hysteria created by the threat of a "bar simian" on the family escutcheon.

You know about the Scopes travesty from *Inherit the Wind,* but in the days of the trial the issue was not as utterly false as it may seem to us now. For fifty years the slogan of the atheist had been: 'Man is descended from the ape. Hurrah! We don't need God any more! Chance has replaced the Creator!" The beautiful scientific theory of evolution acquired bad repute in religious minds because of the company it kept in its adolescent years. It has since been baptized and tamed, it serves science faithfully, and it gives magnificent glory to God if it be rightly understood.

The first problem in human evolution is that anyone who believes in the spirituality and immortality of the soul cannot postulate its natural development from lower animal life. However, this problem can serve an important purpose: it should remind us that our evolution is the constant work of a Creator who is apart from the world, who gave existence to everything in the world, who drew up the blueprints for every step of creative change, and who keeps his sustaining and guiding hand on the smallest amoeba and the farthest star.

The religious problem of the average scientist is unconscious. He is immersed every day in the material aspects of the world: its natural laws. He seldom has reason to think of a creative power beyond his matter and energy. So by habit he drifts into an attitude of monism, which holds that the created world is all there is, that it is eternal and unlimited, and that it has inherent in itself any "divine" powers which may be needed to explain its existence and activities.

Notions like these are evidently contrary to Catholic doctrine, but they are not a necessary part of evolution. They may result from a conscious effort to push a personal God from the picture or from the unthinking daily attitudes of a man who saves his faith for Sundays.

To the man who believes in God, the theory of evolution gives most impressive evidence of divine power, wisdom, and constant presence. Surely it requires better planning to develop a vast and complicated world from simple beginnings than to form it all ready-made in the divine workshop. And a growing, changing, purposeful world requires a more active, lively Providence than a static prefabricated world.

We all know that creation is a continuing process; things made from nothing do not stay in existence without the Creator. But still, if God had made everything in finished state right in the first six days, the rest of divine history would be a perpetual Sabbath. He could just sit back and watch His machine work, merely holding on to the string of its existence. In an evolutionary world He must be on the job every moment to perfect His creative work.

15

Once we get this idea of God's personal power in evolution, the special creation of man's soul offers no great problem. Just because He chose to perform most steps in the process in accord with natural laws, using secondary causes, is no reason He must perform every step that way. He is free to exert His power directly when He wishes.

It is our firm Catholic belief that God created your soul and mine, and that of every human person, by a direct personal act. We are made in His image, and this quality cannot be transmitted by genetic process. We do not inherit our spiritual souls from our human ancestors; so Adam presents no special problem. Certainly Adam could not inherit his immortal soul from some subhuman ancestor he might have had. God intervened in a special manner for Adam and Eve, just as He did for you and me.

You ask whether the Church accepts the theory of evolution. Certainly Catholic theologians did not jump on Darwin's bandwagon right from the start, and if they had they would have been pushed off by Spencer, Huxley, Haeckel, and others. But I have mentioned a couple of priest-scientists who were at ease with evolution. And I remember another one: Canon de Dorlodot, a venerable old man whom we used to see on the streets of Louvain. He was a great admirer of Darwin, and I have just finished glancing through a little book which he wrote forty years ago to show that a theory of evolution much more thorough than Darwinism would not be contrary to Catholic doctrine.

He claimed that such theories were rather common among early Fathers of the Church, even up to the Middle Ages. He cites particularly St. Gregory of Nyssa, who writes of nature as an artist, the cause of the world's development; and St. Augustine, who believed that in His original creative act Almighty God had implanted in nature "seminal forces"— the seeds which would be effective in future development.

There is another big problem, however, and I don't have much space in which to discuss it. What about the seeming conflict between the theory of evolution and the inspired story of creation told in the first three chapters of Genesis? Frantic fear of this conflict created the false issue of the

16

Scopes "monkey trial." Does not the inerrant Word of God tell us plainly that the whole world and every living thing in it was created in six short days, and that man's body was molded out of dust by the artistic hands of the Creator Himself?

I would suggest that you get out your Bible and read those three chapters, but keep a few essential points of literary interpretation in mind while reading them.

1. The author of Genesis did not see creation take place. Neither did any other man. There is no evidence that God revealed the details to him.

2. The author's purpose was to teach religious truth, not science. The simplicity of his cosmic concepts is evident: his world was a large plate floating on a vast expanse of waters; it was covered by an inverted bowl, blue and beautiful, in which the sun, moon, and stars were placed; this bowl kept the waters above it from swamping the earth, but it had floodgates which could be opened to let the rain come down. Need I go on? Remember that he was writing for people who had the same ideas; he used language they would understand.

3. The author of Genesis neither argues for evolution nor against it. The idea never occured to him; he had never heard of it.

4. More than fifteen centuries ago St. Augustine warned us against naïve notions in interpreting the Scriptures. We must know an author's intent, style, figures of speech, and form of writing before we can understand his message.

5. Genesis gives two completely different accounts of creation: the one of seven days, and the other of God the sculptor. Both represent stories which were traditional and well known to the people for whom they were written. The inspired writer used these folk tales to teach religious truths.

6. The seven days are seven poetic stanzas, which serve as an aid to memory, and point out to us the important lesson of the Sabbath rest.

7. The story of God the sculptor, anesthetist, and surgeon is evidently figurative: God comes down to earth, molds clay, blows breath up the argil nose, stages a parade of animals,

17

carves a rib, walks in the garden, and talks casually to man and snake.

What is the real meaning of it all, then? Most of its teachings seem matter-of-fact to us. But they were unique and much needed in the world of their day.

1. There is only one God; He is deeply concerned with the world and takes a personal hand in its affairs.

2. God is not part of the world. He made it—all of it—right from the beginning.

3. His creative power is the cause of every single thing: the dry land and the seas, the plants and the trees, the wild beasts and cattle and creeping things as well as the stars in the firmament.

4. Everything God made is good.

5. Man is a special work of God. The Creator planned man carefully, molded him with loving hands, and gave him life by a special act.

6. Man is the most important creature on earth. In the first story, man's creation comes last: a culmination of all the other work. In the second story, man comes first.

7. Man is made in God's image, and his special nature makes him master of the birds and beasts, and of the whole world.

8. Man's natural mortality may be implied by the fact that he is made from dust.

9. Woman is made in the same nature as man: flesh of his flesh, made to be his companion, his helper, and even his equal, as none could be found among the animals.

10. The relationship of man and woman is right and good: a part of the plan of God.

I shall not go into the Eden story, inviting—yes, tempting —place that it is! That is another matter.

3

ORIGINAL SIN

THE QUESTION

Will you please explain original sin? I have been brought up in Protestant churches, and have been unable to find any Scripture substantiating it, even though I have had it explained to me. In fact, the King James version of the Bible (Isaiah) states that the children are not responsible for their fathers' sins.

James F. Culp

THE ANSWER

The scriptural references are a combination of the second chapter of Genesis from verse 8 on, and all of chapter 3, and various texts of St. Paul, especially Rom. 5:12-21. Genesis describes the sin of Adam and Eve in eating the forbidden fruit, and St. Paul tells us how their original sin affected all of us, their descendants.

I am sure, James, that you are familiar with the story of our first parents, but I would suggest that you read it over again. You will not understand original sin from this story alone, however; you must read it in the light of two doctrinal concepts which come largely from St. Paul: (1) the original state of justice or sanctity in which man was created by God; and (2) the unity and solidarity of all mankind.

The Scriptures tell us that God created man in His image. God was pleased with all the things He had made; He saw that they were very good. But He was particularly pleased with man, who resembled Him spiritually, who was intelligent and free, capable of knowing and loving. So God made great plans for man, but these plans did not become entirely clear to man until many centuries later, when Jesus came to earth to reveal them and to restore their lost effectiveness.

Right in the beginning God fell in love with the man whom He had created; He wanted to adopt him as His own son. But He could not adopt a creature of an entirely different nature, even though that creature did bear Him much resemblance. So He decided to lift man to a higher level of life, to share with Him a bit of His own divine life. In that way man would have a tiny part in the divine nature, and be so equipped with divine characteristics that God could make him a real son, take him into His own home, and there share with him His life and pleasures. These were supernatural gifts—above man's nature—but given to him at the moment of creation.

Heaven is God's home, and it was there that He invited man to live forever as His adopted son. But man by his own nature was not equipped to live in heaven. He was created for earth: to breathe air and walk on ground, to see, hear, taste, and touch. He was designed to know and love things in a human way, and to find in this world a human happiness.

His spiritual soul was created, by its very nature, to live forever; but it was not able to live in heaven. God cannot be known directly in any human way. He is so far beyond the range of all created things that He is the only being capable of knowing Himself. And we would have no joy in heaven if we could not know God, whose goodness makes the happiness of heaven.

To fit Adam to live in heaven, God gave him a supernatural life here on earth; He grafted it onto his natural human life. We call it "sanctifying grace." It is a miniscule sharing of God's own life in such way that it transforms man into a creature of heaven even while he remains in this world. It gives us the capacity, now largely dormant, of knowing and loving God in such an intimate way that we can be happy in heaven.

To accomplish this great change in man God came down from His heaven in a personal loving way and united Himself to Adam here on earth. He called Adam to live in close intimacy with Him in Eden, the earthly paradise, as practice for living in much closer union in heaven, the eternal paradise. He came to share His life and love with Adam on earth, that man might share that same life and love forever.

This elevation of Adam to a life of union with God and a participation in God's own life is called "the state of original justice." It means that the first man, already complete in his human nature, received from God many special gifts to which he had no right or claim. The first and greatest of these gifts we have been trying to describe. It is sanctifying grace. It implies God's intimate personal union with man in love, and man's sharing of God's life, with the faculties for eternal living in heaven.

The second gift was a conditional promise of immortality. Man would not have to die if he would remain faithful to God. Man by his nature was designed to disintegrate like all physical things. His soul was naturally immortal because it was spiritual, but his body would wear out in time. Only by special intervention of God could man be made immortal— and actually he never was, because the first man failed to fulfill the condition necessary for this unique gift.

God's third gift to Adam is called "integrity." It kept our first parent's nature in perfect balance. His passions were strong and a source of pleasure to him, but they were easily and sensibly controlled by his intellect and by the supple force of his will. He was all man, but he had no complexes, compulsions, or sense of guilt or shame.

These three great gifts came freely and generously from God. Man had no right to them by his nature. Along with other advantages which sprouted from them, they resulted from Adam's union with God in love. Eden was the symbol of that union. It was a place of pleasure and privilege, of happiness and delights. It had four rivers to supply it with water which gave assurance of fertility and abundance to the people of biblical lands. It had wealth and beauty: gold and precious stones. And it had trees which were pleasant to the sight and good for food.

Eden is a symbol of the spiritual richness and happiness of Adam's life while he remained in union with God. In it was

21

a symbol of man's special gift of immortality: the tree of life. This tree grew only in the garden; man had to remain faithful to God's love or he would not be able to eat of the fruit of this tree.

But Eden had another tree, even more mysterious: the tree of knowledge of good and evil. And the fruit of this tree God had forbidden to Adam and Eve; if they should eat of it they would die. It stood prominently in the center of the garden, and it had a natural attractiveness for them.

Just what kind of fruit did it bear? It seems to symbolize man's freedom. Great as his gifts were God would not force them on man. Adam and Eve must make their own free choice: between Eden and the wide world of separation from God, between God's way to greatness and happiness and some other way they might work out themselves.

To eat the fruit of the tree of the knowledge of good and evil was to learn about good and evil by sampling them. In Eden man already had good in abundance; of evil he would have personal knowledge only if he chose it freely—and that choice would mean the rejection of Eden.

The serpent, of course, represents Satan, evil in person. In his temptation of Eve he was both clever and cynical. He quotes God as saying, "You shall not eat of any tree of the garden." And the woman immediately gives argument: only of the tree in the middle of the garden may they not eat, lest they die.

Then the serpent gave her more exaggeration: "Your eyes will be opened and you will be like God, knowing good and evil." And then the woman saw how pleasing the tree was, and she began to desire the knowledge it would give. "She took of its fruit and ate it, and also gave some to her husband and he ate."

Satan had been through this decision business himself; he had led a group of his fellow angels into rebellion, and now he wanted man to join his unhappy band. When God created the angels He invited them to a life of union and happiness with Him. The angels wanted to be like God, all right, but some of them, led by Satan, had their own ideas of how to go about it. Instead of remaining subject to God as creatures

22

should be, and acquiring resemblance to Him by love and union, they rose up to imitate God in His power and glory. They ended in hell for it.

Now man had the same choice to make. God wanted man to resemble Him, but He had His own way of producing this resemblance in man's soul: by love and union and grace and goodness. Satan suggested another way, quicker and more exciting: imitate God in His divine knowledge and power. Man fell for the ruse. He fell farther than he expected to.

Unless we take the Scriptures more literally than we need to, they do not tell us the exact nature of man's sin. It was basically a matter of disobedience, of course, as symbolized by eating the forbidden fruit. It could hardly have been a sin of passion, because of that gift of integrity which put man's emotional life under easy control of his mind and will. It must have been a type of pride, similar to Satan's own sin: an effort of man to reach beyond himself, a refusal to remain subject to God in love and obedience.

Whatever the precise nature of Adam's sin, it was a real, personal sin. The Genesis story tells us of a factual happening, even though it tells it in figures and symbols. This sin of Adam deserved personal punishment, and it did not long await the results.

The first sinner was expelled from the garden. Eden is union with God; sin is separation from God. When Adam rejected God's law he severed the bonds of love which had united him with God. When we sin we do the same, and like Adam we lose at the same time God's grace and all the special gifts of God's love which come with His grace.

Adam's first loss was Eden: his elevation to a sharing of life with God on earth, his preparation for continued sharing of that life in heaven. And it was only in Eden that the tree of life could be found; so now it became necessary for Adam to die. And it was only in Eden that his emotional life was calmly under rational control. Once he had committed sin he found himself in the turmoil and conflict that we all know so well.

But why should all this affect us? After all, it was Adam's

23

own personal sin. Why blame us? And if we are not to blame we should not be punished.

We should first recall that God's special gifts to Adam were entirely gratuitous. The human race had no right to them; no one of us has any just claim to them. So God's decision not to give them to us cannot strictly be called a punishment.

Neither has God changed His mind. In the original grant man's retention of these gifts was conditional on his love and faithfulness, and the condition was never fulfilled.

Yet, in our ordinary understanding of words the human race does seem to be punished. It is worse off. It suffers. It limps and wavers. Certainly it is deprived of something it once had, something it might have retained.

To understand this, we should examine our second basic notion: the oneness of the human family. We learn it best from St. Paul, not from any one text but from the whole tenor of his Epistles: There is a certain moral and spiritual and even physical solidarity in mankind, between all the individuals, races, and generations of men. We are one sprawling, proliferating tree, with branches, shoots, sprigs, and trailing twigs growing world-wide from the same gnarled and twisted trunk, which is centuries old.

St. Paul makes this doubly emphatic as regards Christians: we are one body in Christ. But it is also true of humanity in general. Adam's sin tainted the sap of the human tree. "Therefore as through one man sin entered into the world and through sin death, and thus death has passed unto all men because all have sinned. . . . even . . . those who did not sin after the likeness of the transgression of Adam. . . ." The results of sin are in us racially, even though we might commit no personal sin.

At the time of their sin Adam and Eve were the whole human race. When they rebelled all mankind was refusing to obey. Sin entered into the vital texture of humanity, which was entirely contained in them at the time; and we are directly descended from them, receiving from them the only nature they had to give us, a blemished one.

Original sin is a racial—that is to say, a human—fault. There is nothing personal in it as far as we are concerned;

24

so we will not be punished personally, but we must participate in the punishment of the human race in this sense: that we cannot inherit what the human race has lost.

It had been the plan of God that all His great, free gifts to man, like sanctity, immortality, and integrity, should be transmitted to all the descendants of Adam in the process of generation. Adam could not transmit what he had lost. We, his children, cannot inherit the wealth our father squandered. If we had come from different lineage we might be born into the world with sanctifying grace, but as members of Adam's sinful race we are born without it. We are still destined to heaven by God's explicit invitation, but the sin of mankind has deprived us of the means of getting there.

Because human nature became infected with sin its immunity to death was lost. So we who get our human nature from that infected source must face natural disintegration. And since the human race, to which we belong, lost its gift of integrity right in its very origin, we naturally find our desires and impulses quite out of sensible control.

That is what we mean by original sin. And surely much of the conflict and fear and suffering and vacillation which characterize all of us can be traced to that sin. But there is a happy side to it also. As a result of sin we have a Redeemer. If Adam had not sinned God would not have become man. The human race rejected its Creator's love and gifts, but God did not abandon it. Even while putting Adam out of the garden He gave him an obscure promise of the Redeemer who would come to crush the head of the serpent. And that promise was renewed with increasing clarity throughout the history of God's Chosen People, who were put in a rugged and unprotected sort of Eden. There they would live in wavering closeness to God, for the express purpose of preparing the way for the Savior.

You may feel inclined to resent the solidarity of the human race which makes us all participate in Adam's fault and punishment. But if so you can rejoice in that same solidarity which gives us all a part with Jesus Christ in the work and benefits of the Redemption.

It is true that God's new plan for our sanctification and

salvation has many more personal features than the original plan. Each one of us receives grace directly in Baptism. Each one loses it by his own sin. Each has it restored by personal repentance. But still it is because of the closeness of our union with Jesus Christ, because of our oneness with Him in race and in love, that His graces flow into our souls. Because each of us is so closely united with Him, we are intimately joined to each other. We can help each other. We depend on each other, not only for example and teachings, but for an effective communication of God's graces through our prayers and ministry, sacrifices and penances, joys and sufferings. These are effective because our personal acts participate in the redemptive acts of Jesus.

We may have lost much by belonging to Adam's race, but we gained more when God became part of our race, and gave us part with Him.

4

THE PROBLEM OF EVIL

THE QUESTION

What does the Catholic say to a statement like this: "I did not ask to be here"? (meaning, of course, "in this human condition")?

I have stood behind a bar for more than twenty-five years, and I have a fair record in trying to help persons in despair. I am always weak on this one.

George F. Ruth

THE ANSWER

George, my friend, you and I have an affinity of vocation. We get similar questions thrown at us in different guise. Our methods of counseling may differ; we often use the same words, but in diverse context. My profession is usually reverent of sacred names; yours often inclines to the scabrous, without evil intent. And (I can't resist a puny pun's allure) we both deal with things of the spirit: my help is spiritual; yours is spirituous.

If we are to avoid frustrations in our professions we must both realize that we will not be able to solve all the problems presented us. Your answers are aided by soothing libations; my counsel is often reinforced by prayer and the sacraments. But we must both report failures. We may serve as God's agents, giving strong licks for His cause; but we may not play the role of God, who alone can solve everything. And even He often delays solutions.

Your customer's question echoes the query of all thinking

27

men through the centuries. It is: How can you account for all the evil in the world, all the pain we must endure, all the sadness we must suffer, all the fear we must face? No man has found all the answers, because the problem involves mysteries which only God can fully understand. For instance: Why did He decide to create this particular world? In His wisdom and power He could surely have created any one of a thousand other worlds. When we meet Him in heaven He may tell us the answer to that. Meanwhile, we should be content to trust His judgment.

Our friend "did not ask to be here." This querulous plaint makes me suspect that he may be a member of the beat generation, basking in self-pity, perversely enjoying his plight because it gives him reason to whine. He is beaten before he begins to fight, discouraged at the very thought of effort.

But maybe I misjudge him; he may be really licked by life. You see both kinds daily; so you can distinguish the whimpering jellyfish from the man who is beaten and bruised. Life's evils are so real and painful that our words of comfort often sound false and futile. Even the brew you serve can ease the anguish for only a moment, and it may well add a headache and remorse to the other pains.

However, your entire question really suggests to me that your customer is a budding philosopher, with one foot on the rail and one hand free for gestures.

If that is the case, then I would begin by throwing him a challenge: "Listen, buddy, are you ready to swim in deep water? How does your aqualung fit and function? You have just broached the deepest and oldest and most puzzling question to defy mankind since the dawn of thinking. It is no good just wetting your toes in a sea so vast. You cannot solve the problem of the tide by watching trifling eddies in some shallow personal inlet.

"If you would broach the problem of evil, then be prepared to contemplate earthquake, typhoon, and tempest; train wrecks, plane crashes, and slaughter on the highways; famine, starvation, and destitution; deformities, deficiencies, and abnormalities; death, desperation, and despair; injustice, injury, persecution, discrimination, abuse, torture, murder.

"It is the beginning of a litany; and if you are ready for serious discussion your own experience and imagination should add a hundred more choice evils to the list, and then compound them all with fear, anxiety, remorse, and the threat of atomic extinction."

Now, George, if your customer is still there he will probably need another drink. And then if he wants to continue the discussion, you should begin by asking him whether or not he believes in God. For the atheist and the agnostic there is no problem of evil, only the bald fact of it. For them, evil is just as real and raw as it is for you and me. But for the atheist it needs no explanation and for the agnostic none can be found. So their only question is what to do about it: how to eliminate some of it, endure part of it, and try to escape from the rest of it.

For the atheist, evil can have no purpose; and the agnostic can never know the purpose it does have. So they can only hate it, and fear it or fight it. Some may try to harden themselves to it by stoicism or nirvana. Others may seek to eliminate it by scientific advancement and social improvement. Still others may simply fold up in the face of it.

Some have unfortunately chosen the superman approach. A German philosopher of the nineteenth century, named Friedrich Nietzsche, thought that man's basic drive was his craving for power, and that only by fostering this drive would he triumph over the evils of life. He held that Christianity preached a morality for slaves, teaching servile virtues like obedience, humility, and chastity. What we need, said he, is a morality of the master. Only the strong deserve to live. Man must be ruthless, clever, conniving, pitiless, and practical if he is to dominate the evils which oppose him. If he be strong enough he can eliminate the men who are against him and control the cosmic forces which threaten him.

Two world wars, concentration camps, genocide, and uncountable present evils have resulted from this concept of the superman and the master race.

Some men of cold logic have followed the teachings of an ancient Greek philosopher, Hegesias. To him, life had no value or purpose; pleasure was the only good. And when things come to such a pass that pleasure cannot be had, or that life's pain outweighs it, then the only way out of the mess is suicide.

Schopenhauer is the philosophical father of all pessimists. To him, evil was the fundamental principle of human life. Suicide was a selfish solution. It only eliminated the individual. It did not help the human race, which still languished in its muddle. The only ultimate solution was the elimination of mankind. General refusal to generate new life would eventually take care of the situation.

Schopenhauer died a century ago. If he were living today we might console him with a quicker and more thorough method we have devised: a string of H-bombs with heavy fallout. With these we might also satisfy Swinburne, who complained that there would be no end of human misery until "this old earth will be a slag and cinder, revolving around the sun without its crew of fools."

Poets generally like to dwell on life's sufferings; it seems to make them profound and perceptive. The Pollyanna poet is a superficial rhymester; only tragedy and trouble can produce a Byron or a Heine. Soulful imitators often create their own tragedy, even as Byron, the master, did. They starve themselves in left-bank garrets, sit tragically in sidewalk cafes, or whine at your bar. And then, in odd moments, hopped up by a chemical muse, they pour forth their pain and hopelessness in unpunctuated verbiage, at once vivid and vicious.

To men who believe in God there is still a problem of evil. But it is simpler because they can often see a purpose in it. Their big difficulty is to reconcile it with God's wisdom and power and goodness. Why should a wise God make a world so defective? Why should a just and omnipotent God permit the good to suffer and the wicked to prosper? And how can a good God punish those whom He loves?

The problem is so real and difficult that some early and naïve thinkers hit upon an easy solution: there are two gods, one bad and one good. The good god makes the light and the beauty. The bad god makes darkness, sin, and suffering. And the two creations are in constant conflict. If you are an optimist you may expect the good god to win eventually, but it is sure to be a long fight.

As man grew up in his thinking and began to delve deeper into the mysteries of being, he saw that two gods were impossible. Neither would be infinite, because what one would have the other would lack. Each would limit the other; so each would be a limited being, explaining nothing, but needing to be explained itself.

Now I see that we must stop tracing all the varied solutions which thinking man has sought to this problem. Otherwise our customer may have drunk too deeply to appreciate the Christian answer when we outline it for him. Remember that the problem is complex; so we should not expect to find the answer simple.

We should start out by eliminating from consideration those things which are not really evil. Many things which are called evil are only the necessary limitations of created things. Only God is perfect; anything created must lack perfection, and its imperfection might be called evil. Darkness is but the lack of light, sickness the lack of health, weakness a limitation of strength. Such evil exists only in comparison with greater good.

One great Christian scientist and philosopher, Gottfried von Leibnitz, thought that our old cosmos is the best of all possible worlds, that God's wisdom and goodness required Him to make the best choice of all possible creations. But even Baron Leibnitz had to admit that his best world had its defects. Most Christians hold that God's choice was less limited: that He might have done better, or worse, or at least differently. But what He created had to have defects when compared to the perfection of divinity.

Much of the evil we see results from our point of view. To an ant, a pebble may seem like a mountain. To the child, school is evil and discipline a pain; when he is older he will be grateful for both. One man's failure is his neighbor's profit. And the world looks different from an airplane at thirty thousand feet. Sometimes when we get away from our troubles and look at them objectively they don't seem so bad at all. They may even be good for us.

Much that seems to be evil in the world is simply the natural spasm of living. Life is precious, but it is expensive. It takes origin from life, with pain in the process, and it lives and grows by destroying life. Without the mother's pain the child will not be born. Unless the seed die the tree will not sprout. Without little fish to devour, the big fish would not live to become our food in his turn.

Ruthless is the life of the jungle and the desert; each living thing is a hunter in search of its prey. Yet every instinct of the prey is attuned to self-preservation, and much of life's thrill seems to be in its challenge. It would be dull without its danger, empty without its effort, monotonous without occasional pain to make us appreciate its pleasures.

Much of life's evil is created by our own thinking and feeling. I am not an idealist who thinks that things are only ideas, without objective reality. I am not a Christian Scientist who holds that pain and disease are only errors of the mortal mind. I am not even a mental-health addict of the positive-thinking school who claims that a broad smile and a happy attitude will drive all evils away. I am simply stating a blunt truth: that many of our troubles are in our minds and emotions, primarily. We brood on fancied insults and magnify them; we nurse grudges until they become mordant and gnaw at our own viscera; we fight battles in our imagination and win them without joy; we worry and doubt and debate; we fear and fret in torments of anxiety; and we let discouragements grow while dark moods blacken.

But even when we eliminate all the seeming evils of being and living and thinking, we must frankly admit that this life retains a plethora of woes which are very real and wrong, and must be faced. Here it is that we must apply the Christian answer. All the actual evils of the world result from sin; from original sin in the beginning, and from sins like yours and mine, multiplied by millions. God is responsible for these evils only because He permits man to be free. He does it because freedom is worth the price. Precious things are expensive. Freedom permits man to love God by his own choice, but it also allows him to hate. Evil is the price we pay for the ability to make goodness our own.

The third chapter of Genesis tells us explicitly that distress and pain and toil and sweat result from the sin of Adam. And St. Paul tells us that even death is caused by original sin: ". . . as through one man sin entered into the world and through sin death, . . ."

It does not require profound study to see that many of the social evils and personal sufferings around us result directly from sin; from injustice, selfishness, greed, cruelties, lust, dishonesty, brutality, and our general lack of charity and consideration even for those we love. If you will question your customer at the bar, George, you may well find that his own depression has been brought on by the treachery of some man, the deceit of some woman, or the general unfairness of our social system.

The consolation of the Christian concept is that it finds a purpose in evil. Pain is not pointless, suffering need not be wasted, and temporal defeat can end in eternal victory. Evil is often a punishment for sin, just and deserved. But when the good suffer they take courage from Christ who turned His agony into profit for all of us. Our anguish, too, when joined to His, can be an expiation of sin and a pledge of heavenly reward.

The Christian frankly looks beyond the stars for ultimate consolation. It is better to have an opiate of hopeful truth than to grovel in despair. This world seldom offers its own reward. Often good men do suffer while wicked ones prosper. But for good men, pain and suffering are not really evil; they are a difficult striving to great happiness. No strong character is developed without the tempering fire of sorrow; and no great reward is obtained without the pain of effort and sacrifice.

In summary we may say that evil exists for a greater good, either in this life or the next. Being is better than not being even though created existence must of necessity be imperfect. Life is better than no life even though it must destroy living things to exist. And freedom is better than compulsion even though it be a wobbly freedom which is able to choose evil.

5

WORLD RELIGIONS

THE QUESTION

For some years I have had a certain interest in the Catholic religion. My wife is a Catholic, and our daughter goes to a Catholic school. Also, there is a Catholic employee in our office with whom I occasionally discuss this subject. I was raised a Protestant, but actually am a member of no sect.

There is considerable confusion in my mind about the claims of the many different religions. For instance, there are the many ancient religions of India (Brahmanism and Buddhism), of Persia, China, Egypt, and Greece, and the multitude of modern non-Catholic religions.

No doubt, there are some good points in many of these different sects. With what universal standards should each religion be compared to determine its qualifications? What has the Catholic Church to offer that the other religions don't have?

Lowell F. Parks

THE ANSWER

Listen, Lowell, if you want that question answered thoroughly you will have to give me a few years for study and preparation; and then you must be ready to read a big thick book. I can't put the answer in a capsule.

I presume that you believe in God, and that you see the necessity for some religion to inspire and guide us in this life and to prepare us for eternity; thus we narrow the field.

34

You are not an atheist, agnostic, or an indifferentist. Your problem is to find out which of the world's religions is the true one.

You are right in supposing that each religion has some good points; otherwise men would not accept it. Our standards for comparing religions can hardly be as firm and clear as physical tests might be. I will have to suppose a certain agreement from you on the criteria I will propose.

To begin, I presume that we can eliminate from consideration various ancient religions which have long since passed from the world's scene, and the lingering forms of animism or superstition which might be found among some primitive people. So I propose to narrow our comparison to eleven forms of religion which show signs of life in the world today: Christianity, Judaism, Islam, Buddhism, Hinduism, Confucianism, Shinto, Taoism, Sikhism, Jainism, and Zoroastrianism.

It has been claimed that some of these are not really religions, since they are not primarily concerned with worship of God and salvation of man, but are rather systems of philosophy and morality. This is particularly true of Buddhism and Confucianism, especially in their original forms.

Size has importance to us; our convictions seem often to be formed by popularity polls. Christianity is more than twice the size of any other religious group. We can honestly count more than eight hundred million Christians, if we take them all together. Islam would be next largest, with half that number. Hinduism and Confucianism have about three hundred million each. On the basis of numbers alone we could practically eliminate Zoroastrianism, with about one hundred and fifty thousand, and Jainism, which has about one and a half million members.

Antiquity has more than casual bearing as a criterion of the true religion. Historically Christianity has its living roots in Judaism; so in determining the age of Christianity we rightly consider the total Judeo-Christian tradition. If we are conservative, and date it from Moses, we would have to yield in age to Hinduism; but if we go back to Abraham

35

the Judeo-Christian history is just about equal with the ancient religious tradition of India, and thus older than any other living religion.

The truth of a religion is reflected in its own concept of its scope and purpose. Only three groups seem to have any notion of universality, any realization that the true religion should bring truth and salvation to all men. Islam is strongly expansive, but it seeks to grow by accretion rather than dispersion, to acquire adherents rather than converts.

Buddhism is the only other religion except Christianity which has any particular concern for those outside its own nation, race, or tradition. And Christianity is unique in the practical missionary effort by which it constantly strives to bring itself to the whole world; it seeks the sanctification and salvation of all mankind.

The most critical criterion of all is a religion's concept of God. Hinduism, Confucianism, and Shinto were hardly theistic in their origins. They grew up from a sort of nature worship. Confucianism today worships many spirits: those of nature and those of deceased ancestors. Hinduism has its Brahma as a subject for meditation rather than for worship. Zoroastrianism is peculiar: it has only one god, Ahura Mazda, but his power is offset by demons who created the evil of the world.

For all practical purposes all the other religions of the world are polytheistic except Islam, Judaism, and Christianity. For Islam there is no god but Allah, and he is rather remote and arbitrary. Judaism has a God of justice, but also traditionally one of vengeance. Only Christianity has a God of goodness, justice, love, mercy, and forgiveness, who seeks with divine solicitude the redemption and eternal happiness of all men.

The next most important criterion is a religion's notion of man. Only Christianity stresses the individual's dignity as a child of God. As such, he is destined to eternal happiness with the Father, endowed by the Creator with unalienable rights, posessed of great intrinsic value: free, intelligent, and immortal.

Our concept of man is only partial when we consider him

36

alone. He is part of a group. So a religion's notion of society is a definite standard of its truthfulness. In this aspect Hinduism, with its castes, ranks lowest. Islam, with its degradation of women, can hardly qualify. Taoism, which seeks a return to uncivilized simplicity, must be counted out. Confucianism lacks any program for social betterment; it seems content with a lower status for certain elements, especially women.

Christianity doesn't always practice what it preaches, but it does insist strongly on the equality of all men, their brotherhood in Jesus Christ, and the justice and love which should govern their mutual relations. It proclaims the peace, order, equity, and security which should reign in society.

The true religion must be aware of reality, and one of the great facts of life is the existence of evil: suffering, ignorance, sorrow, injustice, crime, selfishness, ugliness, and sin. Hinduism denies all evil; Islam largely ignores it; Buddhism says that all existence is evil, so we must withdraw from life to escape it. Jainism and Zoroastrianism hold that half of all being is evil. Confucianism thinks that man is inherently good; so there really isn't much evil at all.

Christianity alone faces up to the widespread fact of evil. It offers a satisfying explanation of it, and has a specific program for coping with it. Christianity eliminates some evil, adapts to the rest of it, and puts all of it to profitable spiritual use.

Much light will be thrown on the world's religions if we compare their founders: their character, personality, claims, teachings, example, achievements. In this area Christianity transcends all others completely; just try comparing Jesus with Mohammed, or with Buddha, Confucius, or even Moses! Compare His simple and sublime teachings, unspotted life, outstanding miracles; His kindness, forgiveness, love, and generosity; His unpretentious claims to divinity and His proofs of these claims; His patience, strength, and courage in suffering and death; and finally His resurrection from the dead.

Many religions have some tradition of a divine founder, but with all except Christianity the stories of a supernatural origin grew up centuries later. It is only in some late writings that Buddha is presented as a heavenly creature who became the child of his queen mother through a prophetic dream. Not until 1,000 years after his death was Lao-tze described as being born in full maturity, with white hair, after having spent 72 years in his mother's womb. Most of these stories are fantastic.

Jesus alone is presented by authentic documents of His own age as coming directly from God, to represent God to us; as living in constant intimacy with the Father; as being God Himself come in human form to make the divinity known to us, to show us how to attain union with God, and to make that union possible. Jesus alone has the moral character to represent God before man, as fully as human nature can picture Him.

All religions have sacred writings, which are held to give unique divine truths, not otherwise available to man. The Hindus have the Vedas, Confucianism its Classics, Islam the Koran. The Vedas and the Koran are held to be really inspired, in a manner similar to our Scriptures. The best practical test of the value of these claims is to compare the intrinsic value of these various writings: the knowledge they give of God, man, and goodness; the inspiration they give to love and sanctity. The Bible forms the great national literature of a people, accepted as literature of the world. It is God's Word to his people directly, usually in words they could easily understand; it has nothing of the esoteric, cryptic, or cabalistic about it.

All the living religions of the world make claim to divine revelation, to saving truths which come from God, and are not man-made or discovered by man's ingenuity. If you examine them you will find gleams of truth in all, one ray in this one, another in that. But you will find all these specific truths in Christianity, and you will find much more besides. We lack nothing of sound value that any other religion has, and we have much that none of them has: for instance, that God is a person, infinitely perfect; that He is a Father to all of us; that Jesus Christ is God incarnate; that we should serve God in love and obedience; that He sanctifies us by His personal presence in us; that we should love our fellow

38

man as our brother, even though he be an enemy to us; that heaven is an intimate personal union with God, which will bring us complete and enduring happiness; that God Himself has redeemed us and shares His divine life with us.

We might go on and on. All religions report some miracles. Buddha crossed the Ganges instantly without a boat. Mohammed disclaimed the power of working miracles; yet some are attributed to him. Only in Christianity are the miracles well documented, specific, and reasonable.

All religions have rules of morality; nearly all give evidence of the Golden Rule in one form or another. But Jesus Christ alone applied the principles of justice and love consistently and with sacrifice, even toward His enemies, and even to the point of death. He alone taught by word and example that we base our morality on the sanctity of God: that we should be perfect even as our heavenly Father is perfect. He alone provided the divine help which could make such sanctity possible in man.

All religions have some notion of a future life: the spirit of man will somehow continue to live beyond the grave. For some this immortality is an affliction, inescapable but undesirable. This is particularly true of Hinduism and Buddhism, which consider the present life to have little value, with the prospect that the future may be worse. Their only hope is that in time individual existence may be destroyed. They believe in the transmigration of souls, that man after this life will be reincarnated in some other earthly body, and that the nature and desirability of that body will depend on our conduct in this life.

For Confucianism the future is ghostly at best, with no hope of heaven and no fear of hell. Our lot in the afterlife depends in no way on our human acts here on earth. Islam has a rigid system of rewards and punishments, with a paradise of sensual pleasure for the faithful, and a hell of eternal agony for unbelievers. Only Christianity has a clear and definite teaching of a just and merciful judgment, of the perpetual happiness of union with God, and of the sufferings of separation from Him, which results from our own choice.

Study these various religions as much as you want and

from any angle you choose. You will find invariably that Christianity shares anything good you find in any of them, and that it has much more besides: values and insights, helps and motives, goals and consolations, which are not found in any of them.

This is not the usual way of demonstrating the truths of Christianity, but this is what you asked for. After you have finished your comparisons, I suggest that you put the other religions out of your mind for a while, and concentrate on the intrinsic evidence which comes from the truths of Christianity. Consider the historical evidence for the claims of Jesus Christ and the credibility of the Gospels. Ponder the practical success of Christianity in transforming the lives of men and the shape of society.

But that is another story, and I still have another step of proof to indicate before I am near the answer to your question. Even when you have accepted Christianity as the true religion, you will still be in the midst of confusion. There are about two hundred Christian sects, all making some claim to authenticity. Can they all be the Church of Christ? Can both sides of a contradiction be truth? Can confusing factions be the one flock for which the Good Shepherd prayed?

It would be well worth your while to go through a list of comparisons similar to those we have just used. In size, scope, and antiquity the Catholic Church would clearly stand out. In the perfection of her notion of God and man she would certainly equal all sects and excel most of them. In her clear concept of a divine Founder and Savior, she would stand firmly above many who have compromised their notion of the divinity of Christ.

Her notions or redemption and sanctification are explicit. Her concepts of virtue and sin are emphatic. Her teachings on the future life are precise, offering strong motivation to goodness, sound reason to hope.

Yes, Lowell, in all forms of Christianity you will find much that is good, gleams of truth, and motives for sanctity. But you will also find that the Catholic Church lacks nothing of positive truth or sound value which may be found in any of them; and we have much that none of them has: security in our faith which comes from a divine teaching authority, union with Christ in the sanctifying worship of the Mass, effective grace from the sacraments, and a vitalizing membership in the mystical Body of Christ.

6

JUDAISM AND CHRISTIANITY

THE QUESTION

My question would take pages if I were to ask it properly, but I'll try boiling it down to a few lines.

I am of the Jewish faith, and I have always felt that mine was the true religion. I have many reasons for feeling this way, among them being the fact that God made us his Chosen People and that He gave us the Ten Commandments. I feel, too, that Catholicism basically is built upon many Jewish moral principles, differing only in our concepts of Jesus.

Perhaps my question shows ignorance, of which I have a tremendous amount. But I often wonder why, in view of what I have just mentioned, Catholics refer to Catholicism rather than Judaism as the true Church or religion.

Louis Penesick, POD. D.

THE ANSWER

We say, Dr. Penesick, that Catholicism, rather than Judaism, is the true religion because we are using the present tense rather than the past. On that Pentecost Sunday when the Holy Spirit came upon the Apostles there were in Jerusalem a variety of Jews, "devout men from every nation under heaven."

If they had looked toward the Temple, they might have said, "There stands the symbol of the true religion of God; it has brought the Lord's message to us and preserved the true faith, in the midst of idolatry, for at least fifteen centuries." And then if they had turned to listen to the Apostles

42

speaking of Jesus in their various languages, they might have said with equal accuracy, "Those are the men who preach the true religion of God; they and their successors will bring the Lord's message to us and preserve the true faith in the midst of heresy and materialism for all time to come."

That was the moment when the old truth was blending with truth newly learned, to form that total verity which is God's complete revelation to us. At that time there was little need for concern about tenses. Judaism did not suddenly cease to be true; it was simply being absorbed into a greater truth. But once it had refused to be absorbed it became only partial truth, which is never entirely true, and so is partly false. And from that time on we must watch our tenses if we would speak precisely.

In other words, Doctor, I am in complete agreement with much of your letter, except for a few changes in verb forms. Your Jewish faith was the true religion. God made you His Chosen People; He gave you the Ten Commandments and constant signs of His personal love and care for you. And Catholicism is indeed built on Jewish principles, not only in morality, but in every basic phase of man's relationship with God.

The difference between us you indicate rightly, but I would state it with added force. Jesus makes all the difference: between continuing truth and growing falsehood, between past and future, between the expectation and the fulfillment. His life on earth was the focal point of the world's history; backward He looked at the truths of Judaism; forward He looked at His own truths of Catholicism; in the past, man was hopeful of Jesus' coming; in the future, man would rejoice in His presence.

Pope Pius XI gave the key to correct Catholic thinking on Judaism when he said, "Through Christ and in Christ we are all of the spiritual lineage of Abraham. Spiritually we are all Semites."

In meditating on these words we might keep in mind the following points:

1. There is a basic unity of the past, present, and future of all history. In the natural order of things there may be

43

abrupt transitions and sharp turning points, but the past always blends into the present, showing its causes and explaining its meaning; and the present will become the future, often surprisingly, because man is not entirely predictable, but always with cause and continuity.

2. In His supernatural dealings with man, God seldom upsets the natural order. Rather He elevates it to serve His higher purposes. So it should not surprise us that there is unity in the Old and New Testaments. They are one and true; both are the Word of God, and He does not contradict Himself. His revelations to man were often progressive, to fit man's growing comprehension, but the new facts He told fitted onto the old and were one with them.

In the early days of Christianity, a Gnostic named Marcion came to Rome from the Black Sea area, and set up a church of his own. He differed from true Christians by rejecting the Old Testament. To him the God of the Jews was not the same as the God revealed by Christ; the one was cruel and just; the other was loving and merciful. Marcion taught that the Lord God of Israel was real, but a sort of demiurge, definitely inferior to the God from whom Jesus came.

The Church strongly condemned Marcion and his teachings, and later declared, "If anyone says or believes that one is the God of the Ancient Law and another the God of the Gospels, let him be anathema."

3. For many long centuries Israel was the only guardian of the light of God's truth, which flickered faintly in a world of dark errors.

4. The children of Israel were the people specially loved and chosen by God. They were His own people, and their religion came directly from Him.

5. They prepared the world for its Savior, and were the instrument of salvation for us, by bringing us our Savior. And then they largely rejected the blessings they had brought to others.

6. They are blood relatives of the Son of God. Jesus is a direct descendant of Abraham and David; His Mother was a Jewish maiden.

7. The truth which Jesus taught is a completion and refine-

44

ment of the truths which the children of Israel gave to the world through the centuries. Precious little, if any, of the doctrine of Christ is without plain roots in the Old Testament.

It was furthest from the mind of Christ to declare war on the God of Israel; rather, He proclaimed Him as His own Father. It was His purpose to make Yahweh better known and loved, and to extend His reign to the whole world. For Christians, He remained the God of Justice, even while giving proof of His love; and for Israel He had always been a God of Love, even while they feared His vengeance. For Israel, He was the God who promised redemption; for Christians, He is the God who became man to bring that redemption. And the Holy Spirit which enlivens the Church today is the same Spirit of God that inspired the prophets.

There is only that one basic difference between us, Dr. Penesick, but it is an all-pervading difference, the most stupendous truth of all time: that God became man and was known on earth as Jesus. We must never minimize that truth, but once we have set it forth starkly and saliently, there is no reason why we should fail to recognize the close spiritual affinity between your faith and ours, and our reasons for mutual charity:

1. Israel represents, historically, the supernatural viewpoint. God's Chosen People lived close to Him, and He communicated with them directly by word and sign. He lived in the midst of them and often made His presence known in miracles of protection and in the lightning strokes of His punishments. He inspired the writers of their Scriptures and gave direct revelations to their prophets. And His plan for them was most supernatural of all: they would provide the link between God and man; through them God would become man; they would provide His race and His homeland, and the setting for the Redemption.

2. Israel represents faith. Its history began with the faith of Abraham; and it fought through the centuries to keep its faith pure from the attacks and infiltrations of surrounding idolatry.

3. Israel represents hope. Long centuries of Messianic

longing sustained it in its trials, and provided a persistent thread of confidence in a world of discouragement, destruction, and exile. The hope and the promise of Israel gave a theme of purpose to pagan centuries in which existence was otherwise aimless.

4. Israel represents love. Its people were intimately loved by Yahweh, who chose, protected, prodded, and punished them, sent them His prophets, and called them His own sons. And the children of Israel loved their God; they feared Him at times with terror and trembling, but they knew His anger was just, and they loved Him in the midst of their fear and never forgot His goodness. He was the God who had brought them out of Egypt's bondage and into the Land of Promise; no other people had a God so close to them; no other had a God so good and strong.

5. Israel represents redemption and salvation. I have already noted this; but I am not being entirely facetious when I mention that the Chosen People of Yahweh had a certain flair for the price of ransom right from the beginning. Abraham bargained with the Lord, and from a first offer of fifty just men, he talked Him into sparing the cities of Sodom and Gomorrha for the sake of ten. And Moses offered himself as ransom for those who had sinned by worship of the golden calf. It was only when Jesus paid the final price that there was no quibbling about the ransom.

6. Israel represents the fumbling faithfulness, the recurrent repentance, and the frequent forgiveness which has continued through Christian history. And Israel was the vehicle for bringing that frequent forgiveness to us.

7. Israel represents the closeness of ties of blood. Jesus will never forget His Semitic Mother, and He will not be pleased if we spurn her people, and His. Spiritually we are all Semites, but racially He is a Jew. The blood of the Jew was in His veins; the blood of the Jew redeemed us.

The modern Jew is a direct descendant of the Israelites who represent all these things. So our kinship to them should be evident.

We, as Catholics, represent the supernatural; and sometimes in the modern world we seem rather lonely at it. Our religion is based on a supernatural revelation; our hope of salvation rests on God's direct and personal intervention to redeem and sanctify us; we are prepared for heaven by the supernatural life of His grace; and we hope for eternal happiness in the vision and love of Him. All these things exceed the natural, even as the miracles which we accept, the sacraments which nourish us, and the Mass with which we worship God.

In a world which lives by the natural, and sometimes even forgets the spiritual part of nature, we should feel a warm affinity for a people who have a tradition of the supernatural.

Our religious lives are firmly based on faith, bolstered by hope, and animated by love. And in sharing these virtues with the children of Israel we are likely to share also the hatreds and persecutions which were constant in their lives. To them as to us, the enmity often comes from those who lack knowledge and belief in the Lord God, who have no hope of salvation from Him, and who love only themselves. But sometimes to both of us it comes from cousins, like the Samaritans, who have departed from part of God's law.

But if we share similar persecutions, we should be vigilant lest we inflict them on each other. It is basic Christian teaching that the human race is one; that God created all men, and loves them each and every one; that Jesus Christ died for all, and wants all to be saved. Our Master has commanded that we love our neighbor, that we love even our enemies.

That man departs far from the teachings of Christ who makes distinction in his love by reason of race, color, nationality, or creed. Charity begins at home, but it does not stop at the threshold; it goes over the tracks and beyond the frontier. But if we love the pagan, the foreigner, and the materialist, we should love even more those who share with us traditional belief in the one, true God and who gave us our Redeemer—even though they will not share their own gift with us.

We know that it has not always been thus. The history of

Judeo-Christian relations has not always been happy. Historically we have sometimes practiced segregation and imposed second-class citizenship. Vestiges still remain. While we deny any part or pact with Hitler, the Nazi persecutions did come from those who pertained to the Christian tradition. Maybe the culmination of shame which followed them has started a trend in the opposite direction.

One hint of hope is found in the Institute of Judeo-Christian Studies at Seton Hall University, which functions under the direction and inspiration of Monsignor John M. Oesterreicher, and publishes each year a volume of studies by Jewish and Christian scholars under the title *The Bridge:* for a "bridge links two shores, spans an abyss, opens a road for communication; it is thus an instrument of peace."

7

PROTESTANTISM

THE QUESTION

I take you up on your offer to answer a question about the faith.

Appearances tell me that Protestantism is a vital, living force in the world, here to stay. As the leading religion of the leading nation on earth, one cannot but suppose God has smiled on it. If God *has* blessed America, He has blessed it to some considerable degree through the Protestant faith. No honest person, I should think, would contest this.

But how does all this square with the claim that Catholicism is "the only true Church," and the implication that through it alone God's grace can be taught?

We're told of Christ's guarantee that the gates of hell shall not prevail against the Catholic Church, and so be it. But how about this "heresy," not only prevailing but thriving?

Would you say it is operating against His will, in defiance of His wishes?

What, if you please, is the explanation you'd give a determined and fishy-eyed questioner?

Ray Harvey

THE ANSWER

Fishy eyes are supposed to be dull and expressionless, Ray, but your question presents a sharp and lively challenge. I will admit that you are determined, because I answered a question similar to this only a few months ago, and tried to explain how it is that we Catholics can say that there is no salvation outside the Church and still hope to see our Protestant neighbors in heaven. But your question uncovers a different aspect of the problem; so I will risk repetition.

I think we can rightly say that God smiles constantly on His world, in spite of the sin and error in it; but the gracious approval in His smile is directed on struggling, erring man: upon the weak and humble people who are often guilty of sin in spite of their belief and trust in Him, and upon the sincere and righteous people who flounder in error in spite of their love and service of Him.

However, when we look at the world so full of evils we are convinced that the Lord must frown too, constantly. But surely the deep shadow of His frown must fall on those rank injustices, immoralities, oppressions, and vicious forms of godlessness which pervade our social, political, and commercial lives, leaving only the dim fringe of it for the minor errors of Protestantism. When He looks at America, His scowl must be centered on those worldly minded millions who give Him no thought or reverence rather than on our errant brethren who own Him as their God, love Him as their father, fear Him as their judge, and accept his Son, Jesus Christ, as their Savior.

I can readily agree with you that God has blessed the United States, in many ways much more than He has blessed any other country of modern times; but we must be wary of the conclusion that prosperity, enlightenment, and general well-being are proof of God's approving smile. We would not jump to the same judgment because an individual happens to be wealthy, wise, and wonderful. We might know him for a devil incarnate.

Even those abundant blessings which may represent God's approving smile upon us do not necessarily come through Protestantism, and certainly not through those exclusive features of Protestantism which distinguish and separate it from Christ's true Church. They may rather come through those positive elements of Catholic doctrine and practice which Protestantism retains. But much more they probably come through those devout and sincere Protestant indi-

50

viduals who have strengthened our society with their natural virtues, and sanctified it with those effusions of divine grace which God makes to inhere in a deep and trusting faith, despite its defects.

You know that I am not about to gloss over Protestant errors or equate heresy with the true Church of Christ. But we must keep things in perspective. Protestantism is far from the world's worst error; it merely happens to be close at hand, where its defects stand out. Protestants believe in God; the world has many millions who ignore Him entirely. Protestants believe in immortality, with reward for the good and punishment for the wicked—a belief which gives orientation to living and sanction to sanctity.

Protestants believe in sin and redemption, doctrines which teach us humility and trust in God, and give us that sound moral strength which results from His grace. Protestants accept Jesus as their Savior, and vast numbers of them still believe that He is verily the Son of God. They know His words, believe in the merciful merits of His death, and have that love of Him which He promised would bring Him and His Father to dwell in the lover's soul. They have the lessons of His life to meditate and His virtues to imitate.

Most Protestants have kept as their own some of Christ's precious gifts to His Church: not only the basic truths we have mentioned, but also some instruments of sanctification, especially Baptism, which produces in their children the same salutary effects it does in ours. We do not resent their keeping these treasures; it makes the Church no whit poorer and the world immensely richer.

We wish they had taken more: the Eucharist, of which they retain an imitation; and Penance, for which they profess no need. And we wish they appreciated more thoroughly some of the things they do have, like the sacrament of Matrimony, which they do not recognize as a means of grace.

Protestants have generally a sound morality, rigorous on some points, with special stress on the practical social virtues; their concepts and convictions have largely formed our national code of morality and our accepted customs of behavior. They have a traditional love of freedom, a sound sense of man's rights, and a sentimental searching for tolerance. These may cause them to discredit Christ's earthly authority and lead to indifference of doctrine, but generally they contribute to the justice and charity of social living.

The world is full of various systems of thought and action which reject the supernatural entirely, see life's only goals in material pleasures and gain, recognize in man no inherent rights, and make convenience their only moral code. Compared to them, Protestantism is a culmination of truth and sanctity.

All this restrained encomium does not detract from our firm acceptance of the doctrine that Jesus Christ established only one Church and that no other church can be that one as long as it differs and divides itself from it. The Church of Christ is His own mystical Body, an organic spiritual unity, extending itself throughout the world and the centuries, and encompassing into its sanctifying folds all the good and the bad of us who lend ourselves to its unity.

We remain organic parts of the mystical Body until we cut ourselves off by rejecting essential features of its unity: the faith which is its basic fiber, or the earthly authority established by Jesus Christ, which is the active instrument for maintaining that unity. Protestants have rejected both, the first in essential part, the second in entirety. So they have cut themselves off from the organic unity by which Christ extends Himself to His members. Having rejected the principle and instrument of unity, they have naturally become multiple.

And yet, separated as they are from the sanctifying Body of Christ, they still retain a certain subjective unity because of their good faith and sincerity. We call it a membership in the Church by desire; implicit desire, of course, because they would scorn any explicit connection with it. But suppose that they were baptized as infants; their Baptism incorporated them into Christ and sanctified them. Only their own wilful divisive action can rupture that union.

As they grow up they become heretics by every external evidence and for every practical objective purpose. But subjectively they remain in honest error, still united to Christ in heart and desire. These bonds of union are strong and effective enough to permit the graces of Christ to flow through His Church to them, even though they are outside it.

So now you see why I said that God may well have blessed America because of its good Protestants, rather than because of Protestantism. These Protestants are pleasing to Him in their good faith and righteousness, and in the graces they have received through His Church.

In His mercy He is willing to overlook the fact that they have set up churches in competition with His own. He is less concerned with the errors of their institutions than with the sincerity of their hearts. Love is as important as faith. True love cannot exist without faith, but it can inhere truly and ardently in a defective faith which is deep and honest.

I agree that Protestantism is a vital, living force in the world, and especially in the United States. It seems here to stay—a very long time. But it does not share with Christ's own Church His promise that He will remain with it all days even to the consummation of the world. There are probably two things which keep it living and strong: (1) the inherent vitality of its native heritage; and (2) its natural flexibility in accommodating itself to changing customs.

We have already spoken of the former: the many basic elements of Catholicism which the Reformation retained. And the latter is evident from a brief glance at the course of twentieth-century Protestantism. As growing enlightenment has weakened its fundamentalism, it has rethought its stand and extended its appeal. As popular customs and attitudes have changed in the face of weakening faith and economic and social demands, it has accommodated its marital and sexual morality to the trends of the times.

Such adaptability may gradually thin out its spirituality and make it indistinguishable from the secularism to which it accommodates itself. But, meanwhile, it prolongs its life and extends its popularity. When Protestantism dies the event will be unnoted; it will expire by gradual absorption.

We may rightly pray that this absorption process may be

slow, and that Protestantism will continue to prevail and thrive until the integral truth can replace it. Imagine the exposed and isolated position of Catholicism if Protestantism were suddenly to disappear from America and leave its vast millions to become outright pagans or secularists.

You will hardly expect me to exclaim, "God bless Protestantism!" But I can pray fervently that God bless abundantly His millions of good and fervent Protestants and permit them to retain the faith and love they have.

If Protestants cannot become members of Christ's mystical Body, then let them retain their various semblances of it and their vital connection with it through their good faith and intentions.

Granted that Protestantism is a vital, living force; granted that God has blessed America through the positive elements in it, and through the sincere goodness of its members—yet there is no trouble squaring all this with our doctrine that the Catholic Church is the only true Church. Here are the points implied in that doctrine:

1. No man is sanctified or saved except by the grace of God.

2. That grace was obtained for us by our Lord, Jesus Christ, especially by the merits of His death on the cross.

3. Jesus distributes His graces to us in the way He judges best. He requires some sort of union with Himself, which is grounded in faith, strengthened by hope, and enlivened by love.

4. To facilitate that union He has extended himself spiritually throughout the world, encompassing those who believe in Him in such manner that they become a part of Him—like cells of His earth-wide body. This extension of Himself is His Church. It is more than an external organization; it lives and functions spiritually, like an organism.

5. Jesus decided to sanctify and save us in accordance with our human nature, keeping in mind our body as well as our soul. He knew that our normal way of learning was through sight, touch, and hearing; that we are most impressed, moved, and influenced by those things which affect our senses; that we are social creatures, dependent one on

the other, learning and teaching, helping and influencing each other.

As He came to teach, so He sent others to teach in His name. As He came to sanctify, so He gave others powers and instruments of sanctifying. To be more exact, it is He who sanctifies through their ministry; they bring souls into effective union with Him.

6. Since the Church which Jesus established is His own mystical Body, it must have that unity essential to a living body. He gave it authority to teach in His name and required that all accept its teachings; He would not have it teaching a hundred diversities of doctrines all in His name. He promised to remain with it all days: He does not split Himself among a hundred contradicting groups.

As a matter of historical fact, Jesus established only one Church. By its nature it may grow and proliferate, but never cast off distinct and separate organisms which share its life. Since Jesus established it as His own means of salvation, and established no other, it must be the only means. Who else but He, the author of sanctity, can authorize means of sharing His sanctity?

Along with these truths we remain aware that God in His love and goodness desires the salvation of all men; that God in His justice will damn no man unless he personally deserves and demands it. So we believe that He must find some way of sharing His graces and blessings with men of honesty, sincerity, and good will.

Since He has established no other means of salvation but His Church, this sharing must be through the Church. So these men of good will must have some connection with His Church. We believe that their good faith provides such connection, that their desire of salvation becomes a channel of grace, by way of the Church, and that their love of God becomes a bond of union with Him, but not despite the Church.

So on the basis of that, and at the risk of offense, we may say that God blesses Protestantism because of its connection with His Church, and that He would bless it more if its connection were closer; and that He blesses Protestants because their errors are honest. If they knew better it would be too bad—unless they also conformed.

And now I shall risk being more offensive as I try to answer your next question: how do I account for all the prevailing and thriving of this "heresy"? Read Matthew 13:29-30. Shall the weeds be uprooted? "No, . . . lest in gathering the weeds you root up the wheat along with them. Let both grow together until the harvest; . . ." If Protestantism were suddenly eradicated in the United States it might leave only the infectious fallow of atheism.

And now for your final question! Will a determined and fishy-eyed questioner accept a yes-and-no answer? Does Protestantism operate against God's will? Yes, insofar as it is divergent from the true Church of Christ, disruptive of the organic unity of Christ's mystical Body, and contradictory to His express wishes that they all be one. No, insofar as it represents the honest belief of sincere men who use it to worship God in accordance with their own sincere conscience, and are much better than they would be without the salvaged truths and purloined sacraments which it gives them.

8

JACOBITES

THE QUESTION

I am a Syrian Jacobite priest in India, now studying Catholic doctrine, and I have cleared many misunderstandings.

An oath I took before my bishop on the day of my ordination stands in my way to reunion with the Roman Catholic Church. I have promised him that I will abide by his authority in the Jacobite Church all the days of my life.

Am I not violating an oath which I have taken by joining the Roman Church?

Father K. C. Markos

THE ANSWER

You know, Father, I am much more interested in you than in your question. Since I received your letter I have been reading quite a bit about the Jacobites, and it all ties in beautifully with some of my other interests.

Preparations are now being made for the twenty-first general council of the Church, which will probably be called the Second Council of the Vatican. So I have been reviewing the history of the twenty general councils already held, and I find the origins of your Church deeply rooted in three of them. The scene was set at Ephesus in 431; the main battle was fought at Chalcedon in 451; and your separation from us was confirmed at Constantinople in 553.

In the last few years the ecumenical spirit has tinged the zeal and hopes of many Christians. The violent conflicts of the fifth century, which caused you to be separated from us, furnish us a glaring and salutary example of the methods and attitudes which should be excluded from the proposed dialogues between us, and, indeed, from all our relations with those of other faiths.

It is easy to look dispassionately on historical conflicts which have been calmed by fifteen centuries of time; but it does seem to me that our separation was both sad and needless. There were points of doctrinal difference, certainly, but it seems that charity, patience, accurate thought, and quiet discussion might easily have composed them, because most of the argument was about formulas, a problem of semantics. Instead of a theological dialogue we had dynamic shouting, regional pride, civic rivalries, personal vendettas, and imperial interventions.

But I think, Father, that I should really start out by telling our readers who you are. It may surprise you, but many people in America have hardly heard of your religion. When I mentioned Jacobites to some of my friends they identified them as supporters of the forlorn claims of the Stuart kings to the throne of England. Even some of my Syrian friends, well acquainted with Maronites, Melkites, and Orthodox, were unable to identify the Jacobites.

It would be much better if you could write this part of my answer. I know you only from books. There are about fifty thousand Jacobites in the United States, and they have twenty-three churches, but I have never visited one of these churches or seen their liturgy, even though they use the same rite as Syrian Catholics. As you probably know, there are about six thousand Catholics of Syrian (Antioch) rite in America, but they have no church of their own in this country.

The Syrian Catholics have a Patriarch of Antioch who lives at Beirut. The Jacobites have a Patriarch of Antioch also; he lives at Homs, in Syria, between Lebanon and Turkey. Some of the Jacobites in India separated themselves from the patriarch about fifty years ago, and acquired their own metropolitan, or archbishop. Possibly you belong to this independent group, Father; you do not tell me in your letter. Catholics know this group best, because during the last thirty years at least three of its bishops—beginning with Mar

Ivanios and Mar Theophilos in 1930—have joined the Catholic Church, with some seventy-five thousand of their people.

It is probable that many of the customs of India are different from those of the Near East, but my books tell me that the Jacobites are very rigorous in their fasting, that they use leavened bread in their liturgy, using leaven that has been handed down for generations, and baking the bread specially for each service. As is generally done in the Eastern rites, babies are confirmed right after Baptism—and then, in many places at least, the Jacobites immediately give them Holy Communion. It seems that Confession, though recommended, is not much used.

My books also tell me that Jacobite pastors are supposed to be married men, and if a pastor's wife dies he is expected to give up his parish and enter a monastery. He cannot marry again. It seems, too, that the priests wear beards and shave their heads.

I hope I have not tried your patience too far, Father; maybe you will write and tell me how your practices in India differ from these things I find in books.* Anyway, one of the

* Father Markos has replied. He is pastor (he calls it vicar) of two small parishes; and on a meager salary has raised a family of six children, one now in college, one in high school, and four married. He belongs to the "Patriarch party" of the divided Jacobite Malabar Church, which has declined badly in recent years as a result of the factions and litigations between this party and the independents—called the "Catholicos party," since their supreme head has the title "Catholicos."

Many members of the "Patriarch party" have become Catholics, joining the Syro-Malankara rite of Mar Ivanios. They are prevented from reunion with the "Catholicos party" because they doubt the validity of the Holy Orders in this independent group.

Father Markos insists that the Malabar Jacobites are not Monophysites; there is still argument about the "one" or "two" natures in Jesus Christ, but it is a matter of words. They recite the same creed as the Catholics of the Syro-Malankara rite.

Purgatory, Indulgences, the Immaculate Conception, Transubstantiation, the veneration of Images of Saints, and the Supremacy of the Pope are not in the code of their faith, literally. However, the Syro-Malankara Catholics do not have Images either; and Father Markos sees no difficulty about Purgatory or the Immaculate Conception. But he needs further study on Transubstantiation, Indulgences, and the Supremacy of the Pope. However, he insists that the main differences between the Jacobites and the Catholics are not doctrinal.

The supreme head of their church, the Patriarch of Antioch, now lives facts which interests me most about you is that you and your people are descendants of the "Thomas Christians," that hardy group along the Malabar coast who fondly trace their faith back to St. Thomas the Apostle—and with some reasonable claim.

The Jacobites' existence as a separate church should probably be traced to the Council of Chalcedon, which was held right across the Bosporus from Constantinople, in the year 451. This Council was called to settle a bitter controversy about the exact nature of Jesus Christ: whether there was only one nature or two distinct natures in God Incarnate. The bishops at the Council agreed upon a formula for precise expression of the Catholic doctrine, but as soon as the Council was over they renewed their dispute, arguing about the real meaning of the formula they had chosen.

Antioch and Alexandria, the two most venerable apostolic sees of the East, were the centers of Monophysite influence, holding, in simplified words, that the human nature of Christ was not really distinct from his divine nature. As a result most Christians of Syria and Egypt separated themselves from the Orthodox, who insisted that after the Incarnation the Son of God had two definite natures. Descended from these early Monophysites are most Coptic and Ethiopian Christians, the Armenians, and the Syrian Jacobites.

Most Jacobites have been Monophysites in name only. I suspect that you and I would find little real difference, Father, in our beliefs about the person and nature of Jesus Christ. When Mar Ivanios came into the Church in 1930 the Pope permitted him to retain in the liturgy a controversial phrase which in earlier centuries had been considered an emblem of

---

in Damascus; and he claims succession from St. Peter, who was first bishop of Antioch. The Jacobites accept the first three ecumenical councils: Nicaea, I Constantinople, and Ephesus.

Confession is not neglected; instead it is compulsory, at least once a year; and most people go more often. Those who fail to confess may not receive Holy Communion on Passover Day—during Passion Week—when all Jacobites, including the little children, are accustomed to receive.

The rule that parish priests should be married men is no longer strictly followed.

Priests are expected to grow beards, but do not shave their heads.

60

Monophysite heresy. Words are only as important as the meaning we give to them.

Since the seventeenth century many of your people have become Catholics, but many others have lost their Christian faith after centuries of Muslim influence and oppression. During the First World War they were massacred in great numbers by the Turks. Today your Malabar group has more Jacobites than any other area of the world—probably more than all the rest of the world. And we are happy to see that in the last thirty years many of you, who credit your Christian faith to St. Thomas and your liturgy to St. James, are rejoining the leader of the Apostles, St. Peter, the Rock on which the Church of Christ was built.

Now after all that, it is high time I got to your question. To assess your obligation under that oath you took, let us review briefly: (1) what an oath is; (2) how it should be taken; (3) what kind of obligation results from it; and (4) the duty we have of carrying out a promissory oath.

1. When we take an oath we call on God to give testimony to the truth of our statement or to guarantee that we will fulfill our promise.

It is a kind of prayer by which we implore God to demonstrate the truth of what we are saying.

An oath is an act of religion; it is a profession of belief in God. When properly taken it shows our reverence for His holy name, our fear of His justice, our awareness that He knows all things, our trust in His truthfulness, and our reliance on His fidelity. If God backs up our statement there can be no doubt or argument.

Our oath convinces others because they reason this way. If this man were lying he would never dare call on God, who knows all truth and detests falsity. God could easily show him up as a perjurer, or strike him dead on the spot, and surely there will be just punishment for anyone who has the audacity to insult divine truthfulness.

The value of our oath is based on the strength of our faith. The oath of an atheist adds nothing to his bald statement. The oath of an agnostic has doubtful value. But in the ages of

61

great and simple faith the courts were able to accept an oath as fairly conclusive proof. Perjury was feared like hell.

2. Since an oath is an act of religion, a solemn and sacred thing, it must only be taken when we are utterly honest and sure that we are right. It must be reserved for serious and important affairs, not be taken lightly or flippantly about trivial matters.

The use of oaths is clearly sanctioned in sacred Scripture: "The Lord, your God, shall you fear; Him shall you serve, and by His name shall you swear."

St. Paul swore oaths often. He took an oath that he was remembering the Romans in his prayers: "The Lord is my witness." He swore to the Corinthians that he had stayed away out of concern for them: "Now I call on God to witness against my soul." And he invoked the Lord's name to bolster his message to the Galatians: "Now in what I am writing to you, behold, before God, I do not lie."

Of course, there always remains the problem of finding the true meaning of the message of Jesus on the Mount: "But I say to you not to swear at all: . . . But let your speech be, 'Yes, yes'; 'No, no.' " This is not the place for exegesis, but our Lord was probably counseling His disciples that they should be so simply good and obviously honest that no one would question their statements—that no oath or emphasis would be needed to command belief or trust in what they said.

Anyway, Jesus Himself took an oath, implicitly, when Caiphas challenged Him in the name of the living God to state whether or not He was the Christ, the Son of God.

The Prophet Jeremias gave us the rules for a proper oath. "And thou shalt swear: As the Lord liveth, in truth, and in judgment and in justice."

In truth: excluding all lies and doubts, and all false promises.

In judgment: with careful thought, in serious matter, showing deep and honest reverence for the God of truth and fidelity.

In justice: we must have a right to reveal the truth we swear to. We may not ask God to back us up in betraying a secret or in defaming someone; nor can we expect Him to bolster our promise to do something wrong.

3. An oath puts a moral obligation on the one who uses it, binding him under the virtue of religion to be truthful in his statement, honest in his promise, and faithful to his pledge. This obligation can be very serious if the matter involved is important. If I perjure myself in court by giving false witness I am guilty of at least two sins: one against veracity, by lying, and another, more serious, against religion, by my snide irreverence toward God. There are probably other sins also against justice, civic duty, and the reverence due to the court's authority.

If I promise something under oath and fail to keep my promise I am guilty of infidelity to my own pledge, and of disrespect for God, whom I had asked to back up my pledge. And here again I may also violate justice and charity, lessen public trust, and give bad example.

One point we should keep clearly in mind. An oath does not change the nature of the statement or promise to which it is attached. It cannot make the false true, or the bad good. It cannot oblige us to do something wrong, just because we swore we would do it.

4. Your oath, Father, was a promissory one. You called on God to witness your sincerity in pledging your fidelity, and you solemnly asked Him to guarantee your fulfillment of that pledge throughout the years.

You swore in truth: in accordance with your firm convictions and honest intentions.

You swore in judgment: with mature deliberation and reverent solemnity.

At the time you took your oath you were sure that you were swearing in justice. You were convinced that you would be pleasing God by remaining faithful to the authorities of your Church every day of your life. Now your conviction is changing. You see that Jesus established His Church on Peter, the Rock, and that you cannot really be in the house of the Lord if you are on another foundation. You see that Peter's successor, Pope St. Leo, was guided by the Holy Spirit at Chalcedon, and that your Church has been in substantial agreement with his declarations for centuries. And you see that the history of Christ's Church did not stop at Chalcedon; that there have been sixteen general councils since, and that you would like to have vital part in the next one.

You are a priest of Jesus Christ; you have Baptism, the Eucharist, and the power to forgive sin. You have all that the Savior gave us for our sanctification, except a living union with His life-giving Body on earth.

As soon as your reason and your faith convince you that the Church of Peter is the Church of Christ, then your oath loses all power to bind you. It was made in good faith, but in error. It cannot change the nature of the basic obligation to which it is attached. You cannot please God by going contrary to your convictions—by staying out of the true Church when you know you should be in it. An oath does not oblige us to stubborn persistence in honest errors we have made. It does oblige us to faithfulness in the good we have promised in God's name.

9

THE BIBLE

THE QUESTION

Like many persons, I was baptized a Catholic as an infant, but was never reared in that faith.

I am serious about a Catholic boy who is very strong in his religion, and his faith has made me want to join the Church, though I dropped the Protestant church two years ago, when I also dropped Christianity.

What keeps me from accepting and following Christ is the inability of anyone I have talked with to prove to me the historical validity of the Scriptures. It has always seemed to me that the whole Bible could be a deliberate hoax. Is there evidence that the Bible is actually recorded history? Did the Apostles really record the same incidents without collaborating? Is there proof that masses of people heard a strange young man speak and saw him perform miracles? Did Christ *really* live?

If you will answer these questions for me I shall be grateful; I love God very much and I want to believe the Bible. If I can accept the Bible, I can and will accept the Catholic Church.

Nora E. Ingram

THE ANSWER

Since you love God, Nora, I am sure that you will come to recognize and love His written word, too, if you will permit yourself to become thoroughly familiar with it. The Bible is a unique book. It was written by God; yet it has human authors. It is the best seller of all books of all time; but it is one of the least read of great books. People buy it in costly editions and handle it reverently; then they let it collect dust for months, undisturbed except for its use as a file for family mementos. It is the inspired Word of God; but it inspires many people only to bitter controversy.

Sometimes we Catholics are a bit apologetic about our lack of knowledge of the Bible. We take for granted that Protestants must know it better because it is their exclusive rule of faith, and they were going to Bible classes while we studied the catechism. Actually, Catholics know quite a bit about the Bible, especially about the Psalms and the New Testament, from their liturgical use. But I am afraid that neither we nor most of our Protestant friends know the Bible thoroughly as a book.

I really believe that you will find your best proof of the authenticity of the Bible in a friendly familiarity with the book itself. Without such personal knowledge you may find the evidence I present a sort of academic exercise.

I will not try to go into detail about the historicity of the entire Bible. Your question indicates that if you were thoroughly convinced that the four Gospels were reliable history you would be in good position for an act of faith; so we will concentrate on those, after a brief survey of the Old Testament.

The Bible is a collection of seventy-two books*—a small library. Originally it was a polyglot work: about forty-two of its books were written in Hebrew, two or three in Aramaic, the language which our Lord spoke, and the rest in Greek. The seventy-two books probably had a similar number of authors or collaborators, some of them known and more of them unknown or uncertain. And the composition of their work, in its various stages, may have extended over a period

---

* Most editions of the Bible used by Protestants have only sixty-five books, though they may have the remaining seven—Tobit, Judith, Wisdom of Solomon, Sirach, Baruch, and the two books of Maccabees—together with some fragments of other books in a separate section entitled "Apocrypha of the Old Testament." They are not held of equal value with the rest of the Bible, largely because they were not included in the Hebrew Canon of Holy Scripture.

MR. & MRS. L. O'CONNOR
742 CARLISLE WAY
SUNNYVALE, CALIF. 94087
409

739-6157

10 7

of fifteen centuries. These authors wrote in different styles, with varying degrees of literary ability, and with divergent attitudes and concepts. Often the same book, like Genesis, will show evidence of different styles and sources.

As these books come down to us they have been often translated, and much more often copied by hand. Some errors have naturally been introduced into the text, but usually these have been incidental and have not greatly changed essential meanings. No book has been so thoroughly studied, criticized, revised, and amended by so many generations of scholars, in a constant effort to restore the original text and meaning.

The many authors of these various books, written in diverse places, centuries, languages, and styles, had this in common: all wrote under the inspiration of God and wrote what God wanted written, each in his own peculiar manner. This we call inspiration; but it is a matter of faith rather than historical study. It is not readily apparent from the books themselves. So we will put it aside in considering your question.

For our purpose, as Christians, the precise historicity of the books of the Old Testament does not greatly matter—at least from the apologetic point of view in which you are interested. The Ark of Noe, the plagues of Egypt, and the vagaries of the kings of Israel have little direct bearing on the divinity of Christ. The thing which we do know historically is that around the time of Christ the Jewish people were in possession of this great collection of ancient literature, which they considered very precious and sacred.

For the Christian the Old Testament has primarily the value of a background. It provides the setting into which Christ appears. Without it the drama of the Redemption would be enacted on a bare stage, although it would be none the less authentic and hardly less forceful in its stark realism.

We will devote our attention primarily to the four Gospels: Matthew, Mark, Luke, and John. If they are to convince us of the historical fact of Christ they must be genuine and authentic, written by men who are truthful, reliable, and informed; and they must be well preserved through the centuries, so that they come to us substantially as they were originally written.

Our first question is: Are the Gospels genuine or are they fakes? In examining the authenticity of any ancient book we look for two types of evidence: internal and external. Internal evidence comes from the book itself; if a book pretended to date from near the time of Christ, but actually came from a later period, we might expect the author to unconsciously betray himself by lack of personal familiarity with the period about which he writes or by anachronistic references to later events. External evidence would come from other sources: other contemporary writers who were familiar with these books or who corroborate the facts they present.

During the nineteenth century, particularly, there were various biblical critics, generally called rationalists, who began their studies with the conviction that the Gospels could not be authentic. They advanced a variety of theories to account for the origins of the Gospels and sought with diligence and skill to prove these theories. The Gospels were given a bad time for many years, but they weathered the storm. As a result of studies provoked by the rationalists, the authenticity of the four Gospels is probably better established today than ever before.

The most extreme rationalists claimed that many of the stories of the Gospels were Christian myths written during the second century, some of them even as late as A.D. 200. Most of these claims grew out of preconceived notions of Christianity; for instance, that St. Paul was its real inventor, and that it was only through the teachings of St. Paul that the Christians came belatedly to believe in the divinity of Christ, the sacraments, and the visible Church. So, the rationalists claimed, those portions of the Gospels which present these doctrines must have been added later.

Another theory of the rationalists was that miracles were impossible; so the stories of Christ's many miracles could not be authentic. They also rejected the supernatural, and they despised mysteries. So they tried to explain away those parts of the Gospels which deal with these points.

In modern times sound historical study has prevailed. It is now generally accepted that Matthew, Mark and Luke wrote before A.D. 70, and that St. John's Gospel might have been as early as 80, but certainly not later than A.D. 118.

A study of the Gospels shows clearly that they were written by Jews who were either contemporaries and associates of Christ or men in close touch with contemporaries and associates. The language is that popular Greek, generally called Hellenistic, which was regularly used by the Jews of the first century after Christ, but not much after that. This Greek has many evident signs of Hebrew idiom, which only a Jew would use. The writers display no knowledge of Greek history, philosophy, or literature, but they are thoroughly familiar with Jewish customs and with the Old Tetsament.

No one has been able to trip up the authors of the Gospels on matters of the geography, history, politics, and customs of the land and period about which they write. Their references to these matters are casual and popular, but always accurate. For instance, the government was administered by the Romans, but much power was left to the Sanhedrin, and this resulted in frequent conflicts, which appear in the Gospels. Three types of money were in common use in the country; the Gospels correctly designate Greek money for taxes, Roman coins for commerce, and Jewish money for dues to the Temple. Different languages were in use at that time, especially Hebrew, Aramaic, Greek, and some Latin, and these diversities affected the lives of the people. Historical facts like these are simply taken for granted in the Gospels.

The precise conditions of life which Christ found in Palestine did not long endure after his death. About thirty-five years later a rebellion began against the Romans which resulted in the destruction of Jerusalem and its Temple. After the year 70, a person who had not been personally acquainted with earlier conditions could never have written the vivid details in the Gospels.

This internal evidence of authenticity is firmly bolstered by testimony from other sources. Writers of the early Christian centuries give us many quotations from the Gospels; it is nearly true that if our texts of the Gospels had been lost we could rewrite them today from these quotations.

Both Christian and non-Christian writers of the first two

centuries after Christ give us definite evidence that the Gospels were widely known within one hundred years after the death of the Apostles, that they were generally used by Christians, and were held in great reverence.

The fact that they were so widely spread argues against forgery. Here were writings purporting to come from the Apostles or their immediate successors, circulating while some of them were still alive. If they were false would there have been no protest? But we find no evidence of protest. Then, too, pagans and heretics of those days found all sorts of arguments against the Church, but never do we find them challenging the authenticity of the Gospels. We can be sure that they would not have neglected to do so if they could have found any evidence.

When the Gospels were written, Jewish converts apparently accepted them on a par with the Old Testament. Many of them were either personal or secondhand witnesses to the facts narrated; so they were in good position to detect any falsity.

Christianity made many highly educated converts in those early days. Is it possible that they would have accepted a religion which meant loss of their social standing and possibly of their lives if they had not recognized its basic documents as authentic? None of the early Christians of those first two centuries, when the Gospels were widely known and used, ever left a record of any questioning of their genuineness. Rather, they suffered martyrdom for the religion based on them.

Pope Clement quoted from the Gospels before the end of the first century. Ignatius of Antioch made similar quotations only a few years later. A document called the *Didache,* or *The Teaching of the Twelve Apostles,* written around the year 100, also quotes the Gospels, and there are various other quotations made during the next fifty years.

St. Justin became a Christian in A.D. 130; he testifies that the Gospels were written by the Apostles and their disciples, and were read by the Christians during their Sunday meetings. Papias of Phrygia was a personal disciple of St. John. He tells us about the Gospel according to St. Mark and makes reference to writings of St. Matthew.

About 180, St. Irenaeus, a second-generation disciple of St. John, gives us the following account of the Gospels:

> Matthew wrote a Gospel for the Jews in their own language, while Peter and Paul were preaching and establishing the Church at Rome. After their departure, Mark, also the disciple and interpreter of Peter, handed down to us in writing the information which Peter had given. And Luke, the follower of Paul, wrote out the Gospel which Paul used to preach. Later, John, the disciple of the Lord, who had reclined on his breast, published his Gospel during his sojourn at Ephesus in Asia Minor.

And now you may well say, "All right, granted that the Gospels are genuine, how do we know that they are reliable and credible? Maybe the Apostles invented the stories, or exaggerated them."

The first requisite of a reliable witness is that he must have knowledge. You would not believe a man who didn't know what he was writing about. But as we have seen, the writers of the Gospels had knowledge. They were either eyewitnesses of the events they narrate, or at least, like Mark and Luke, they were disciples of eyewitnesses.

The second requisite of a reliable witness is that he be honest. How do you check on a man's honesty? You look to his personal life and character. The Apostles led holy lives; they were good, simple men; and they gave their lives for the truths they taught.

Third, we should ask how much a man has to gain by the story he tells, or how much he blows the trumpet of his own praise. The Evangelists had nothing to gain in a worldly way; they rather faced the constant threat of death for preaching and writing about Christ. And they tended to show themselves in a bad light: bickering among themselves, or betraying Christ, or denying Him, or at least deserting Him.

Next, we might inquire what chance the witness would have of getting by with a hoax. The Evangelists were writing for contemporaries of the events they narrate, or for men

71

who knew those contemporaries. They would have been quickly caught up by critics who knew the facts, especially by the many enemies of Christianity. But we find no contemporary denial of any of the astounding things they narrate: the miracles of Christ, His Crucifixion and Resurrection. Why didn't someone who was there come forward and challenge their story? The absence of any denial is in itself a strong argument.

Next we might ask for corroboration. The four Gospels are distinct and separate narratives. Of course, they use the same sources, either written or oral, and they depend to some extent on each other, but at times their separate narratives are so distinct that it is hard to reconcile them. If they had been impostors working in collusion they would have avoided these appearances of conflict. Each one tells in his own way the common preaching about Christ. They are separate witnesses to the same story.

Finally, we may judge the veracity of a witness by the story he tells. That does not mean that the extraordinary must always be questioned and commonplace matters always accepted.

Historians usually concentrate on unusual events. It is improbable that the Evangelists could have invented the character of Christ. They would not have found inspiration for Him in the Old Testament aspirations for the Messias.

Most of the contemporaries of Christ expected the Son of David to restore the kingdom of Israel in all its power and glory; He would hardly have been meek and humble; He would not have lived in poverty; and He would certainly not have ended up in suffering and crucifixion. Subsequent searching of earlier prophecies showed that these things were to happen to Christ, but the whole idea was strongly at variance with contemporary thought, even with the earlier thinking of the Apostles themselves. Then, too, the Apostles were simple men, and it would have taken a remarkable combination of profound religious philosopher and imaginative poet to invent a character so sublime as Christ.

The manner of telling a story often has a bearing on its credibility. The Gospels tell the story of Christ in simple, unpretentious fashion. Even the greatest miracles are matter-of-fact. There is no striving to convince, no fear of doubt.

The final question about the reliability of the Gospels is this: granted that they were written truthfully by men who knew what they were writing about, how do we know that we have them today substantially as they were written?

The fact is that our manuscripts of the Gospels are much earlier and more numerous than those of the great classical works. Manuscripts of Horace date only from the seventh or eighth century; those of Cicero, Caesar, and Plato from the ninth. We have many early manuscripts of the Gospels, some as early as the fourth century. They come from various parts of the world and are substantially the same; and they are in agreement with earlier fragments.

It is generally acknowledged that the great reverence in which the four Gospels were held by the early Church would have prevented changes in them, and their wide usage in the early Church would have immediately shown up such changes had they been attempted.

In a general way we can say that the facts narrated in the Gospels are confirmed by secular history and the findings of archaeology. Possibly the negative proof is the most forceful: there is no historical evidence to refute the claims of the Gospels. However, there are various positive references from Jewish and pagan writers, and from a variety of early Christian writings outside the Gospels.

Other parts of the New Testament give their own confirmation of the Gospels. The Epistles of St. Paul are independent of the Gospels. They were being written during the same years as the Gospels of Matthew, Mark, and Luke, from about twenty years after the death of Christ until the year 66. They speak only incidentally of the material of the Gospels, but they were written to Christians who knew the subject matter of the Gospels, at least orally, and they simply take the teachings of the Gospels for granted.

Flavius Josephus was a Jewish priest, born about A.D. 37, who became official court historian of the Emperor Vespasian. He wrote of John the Baptist with much respect and told of the violent death of St. James the Less. In his book *Antiqui-*

ties of the Jews, written about A.D. 93, he has a famous account of Jesus, the divine teacher and wonderworker, who attracted a great following and was crucified by Pilate, but arose on the third day. This passage is found in all manuscripts of Josephus as early as the fourth century, but since the sixteenth century it has often been called into question by critics who think it was a Christian interpolation. Scholars are not in agreement about it today.

Roman writers of the second century, like Pliny the Younger, Tacitus, and Suetonius, have references to Christians and to Christ, or Crestus.

It seems to me, Nora, that you should have no more trouble accepting the Bible's credentials than those of the Catholic boy you are serious about. God bless you.

10

TRADITION

THE QUESTION

Why does the Roman Catholic Church place tradition on the same basis as the Holy Word? Is tradition worthy enough to be placed so?

Kay Truesdell

THE ANSWER

I am glad you asked me this question, Kay, because it is one which theologians consider quite timely. The careful study of it is one of the basic projects of the interfaith dialogue about which we hear so much these days.

Shortly after the Reformation, Protestants began to insist that the Scriptures alone were the source of doctrinal knowledge in the Church of Christ. In this way they hoped to eliminate the "new doctrines" which had grown up in the course of centuries and return to the purity and simplicity of the original Gospel.

Catholics countered this claim by insisting that tradition was also a means by which we obtain knowledge of God's revelation; and the Council of Trent stated definitely that revelation is contained "in written books and in unwritten traditions." And many Catholic theologians gave the impression that only part of revealed truth was found in the Scriptures, while another part could be known only through tradition.

Advances in scriptural study during the past fifty years have shown that these two positions are not as exclusive of each other as they once seemed; and a better mutual understanding of the meaning of tradition has made the chasm approachable even though it remains wide.

All modern students of the New Testament are agreed that our written Gospels and Epistles resulted from tradition. It was a short tradition, of maybe thirty to sixty years, and it was guided by the Apostles, who had seen and heard it all, and were filled with the Holy Spirit that they might teach it well. However, the stories had been repeated hundreds of times before they took their present inspired and written form.

Before we try to define tradition let us watch it working. We all agree that Christian belief and practice are based on a message which the Great God gave to His people on earth. He did not send an angel to engrave this message on plates of gold; He sent His only Son—He came Himself—to deliver it man to man.

There had been long centuries of preparation for the message brought by Jesus Christ. Its full meaning is understood only against the background of earlier revelation: the religion of Yahweh and the history of His close care of His Chosen People. This earlier religion and history is worth our study because it grew very largely from traditions—not short ones, not Apostolic ones, but the age-old traditions of tribal groups.

The central theme of Old Testament traditions was the Exodus: those years spent in the desert, the Covenant God made with His people, and the Law He gave them on Sinai. Each year the Passover was celebrated, and a main feature of the feast was the recalling and handing on of these ancient stories. The head of the family taught the traditions to his children, that they might learn and love them, and thus hand them on to their children.

You will tell me, of course, that all this is found in the Bible, where it is inspired by God. It is His Word. And you are right, but we must not forget that it had been tradition for many centuries—for dozens of generations—before it was written down in its present inspired form.

The same is true—much more notably true—of the earlier stories of the patriarchs: Abraham, Isaac, Jacob, Joseph,

Benjamin, and the rest. We would never know about them at all if tradition had not kept their memory alive for a thousand years or so, until the Holy Spirit found the right man to put it all on paper—or parchment, or papyrus.

If we go back to the stories of creation, and of Adam and Eve in paradise, we find the results of a tradition even more ancient, more symbolic, and more imaginative. No man was around to see the early aeons of creation; no man claims to have received a precise description of it from God. But ancient tradition had preserved basic truths in fanciful language; and these the author of Genesis sifted to form a prelude to his story of God's Chosen People.

We do not exaggerate at all when we say that the entire belief and worship, and most of the ancient customs, of Judaism were based on an oral religious tradition, which was written down only after the principles and practices had been crystallized. Modern scriptural studies make this very certain.

Now just one more example, linking Judaic tradition with Christian times. The Masoretes were Hebrew scholars, versed in the traditions of their people. (The word "Massora" means tradition.) They worked from the sixth to the tenth centuries A.D., to preserve, write down, and hand on the traditions which permitted a proper understanding of the sacred text. In particular they added the vowel points to the ancient Hebrew text, lest the tradition of how to pronounce the words be lost. Much of our knowledge of the original Hebrew Bible comes to us through these Masoretes who kept Judaic traditions alive deep into Christian times.

Into this religious context, based on ancient traditions, Jesus Christ gave us the message of God. We call it the Good News. The word "Gospel" comes from the Anglo-Saxon "god spel"—good spell, or good tidings. It has always been called the Good News, even by the Apostles, who used a combination of two Greek words: "eu," good, and "angelia," message, news.

Now, how would you expect good news to be spread in those early days, before printed books, radio, TV, or telephone, when hardly anyone could read? It was shouted in the markets and preached in the streets; and St. Paul traveled across Asia Minor and Macedonia and Greece to tell everyone about it. No one had time or inclination to write anything down for many years.

Of what did this Good News consist? Not merely of the words of Christ, but much more of the astounding fact of Christ. The Messias had come. God became a man, and lived with men. "We have known and seen and heard him; and these are some of the things he said to us—some of the marvelous deeds he performed! He died on the Cross to redeem us, and in his sacrifice we are saved; his blood washes our sins clean. And He has risen from the dead: We have seen him with our own eyes, and talked and eaten with him. And He has gone now to the Father, but He will come again in glory to establish his kingdom. And meanwhile He has sent his Spirit to guide and console us; and we have come to give you that same Spirit: to baptize you as the Lord commanded, that you may have faith in him and be saved."

That Good News was a tradition: something given by Christ to the Apostles, and handed on by them to all who would listen—handed on by others who received it from them: by Stephen and Philip, Titus and Timothy, Mark and Luke, Silas and Barnabas.

Then in due time, after the stories had been retold so many times that they had taken on definite forms, some of the Apostles and other disciples found time to gather them together and write them down, with the Holy Spirit inspiring their work. We are told that Matthew was the first to write; he used his native language—the language of our Lord—Aramaic. It is sad that this earliest written account of the Good News is entirely lost; we can only surmise what Matthew wrote, and probably find much of it repeated in Mark, Luke, and our present Matthew.

Mark was the next to write the Good News. He had heard it from various Apostles, no doubt, but especially from Peter. And later the Gospel as preached by Matthew was written in Greek; and then Luke wrote it down the way he had heard it so often from St. Paul. They all tell the same Good News as it was known from thirty years of tradition: of preaching and practice, of memory and repetition, and probably some scribbled notes. At times Matthew and Luke seem to be a sort of commentary on Mark; they fill in between his brief lines and change the order of his narration. They seem to say: Of course that is right, but this is more precisely the way we heard it.

There was only one Gospel, but it was told by three writers, and much later they were joined by a fourth: the Good News as John had preached it. Surely this book does not contain all that John had taught through so many years, but it makes a special point of bringing out stories which John particularly liked, and which the other Gospel writer had omitted.

Even before any of our present Gospels were written, St. Paul was writing letters based on the Good News which he had preached in various cities. His Epistles offer interpretations of the Gospel, even before it was written, and apply its teachings to special problems. The Thessalonians or the Corinthians could have made no sense out of his letters if they had not had a tradition of the Good News of Christ.

I am not trying to give you a history of the New Testament. My point is that tradition plays much the same role for us that it did for the Thessalonians and the Corinthians. The Scriptures are the inspired Word of God, to be held in highest reverence and read with intelligence, faith, and devotion; but they must not be pulled out of the context in which they were written. They must be interpreted and understood as the written version of the Good News which was preached and believed by the Church of Jesus Christ under the guidance of the Holy Spirit. That preaching, believing, and divine guidance did not abruptly cease when the Apostles died. The Scriptures did not deprive it of validity; they are merely the inspired record of it.

Now maybe we should consider technical meanings. Just what do we mean by tradition? One trouble with the word is that it applies to many things. It comes from the Latin verb "tradere," to hand over, transmit, surrender. A Roman might use this word if he gave you some money, gave his daughter in marriage, entrusted his family to you, or betrayed his friends to the enemy. The same verb might indicate that he devoted himself to a good cause, bequeathed his property to his heirs, delivered a message, or taught a science.

As we use the word for religious tradition it means to teach and to hand down from one generation to the next. It is a special kind of teaching, based on authority. If I teach something I have learned by experiment or observation, I do not call it tradition. Religious traditions may be divided into two classes: those which rest on the authority of God—which find their validity in revelation—and those which rest on the authority of ancient custom. This division is important; the first is usually called divine or Apostolic tradition; and the second, ecclesiastical tradition.

Only that tradition which is based on divine revelation imposes by its nature an obligation of acceptance and continued transmission. Those who discredit it, often do so because they confuse it with ecclesiastical tradition. Church traditions, when they are ancient and uniform, often result in an obligation of conformity; most of our Church laws have been induced by them. They resemble the common law growing into a statute; or a belief or practice which has the venerable backing of centuries of acceptance. Traditions of this kind are: the use of holy water and the sign of the cross; women wearing hats or veils in church, and priests shaving off their beards; the ritual ceremonies of the sacraments and the Mass; Veronica's veil and St. John's cauldron of oil; fasting and abstaining, and going to Mass on Sunday.

Certainly traditions like these are not placed on the same basis as Holy Writ. Even the Apostles had customs of this type: community of goods, and abstaining from blood and from strangled things. The traditions which help to form our doctrines are those teachings of the Good News—the same traditions which were written down in the New Testament and were not destroyed by the writing. They continue as a constant, active witness—under the guidance of the Holy Spirit—providing a background for the understanding of the Scriptures—even as it did for the Thessalonians, Corinthians, Ephesians, and Romans, who understood the Epistles of Paul because they already had the tradition of the Good News. Christians throughout the centuries have understood the written Gospels and Epistles because they read them in the light of this living tradition.

As I said before, Protestants and Catholics tend to come a little nearer to each other in their understanding of the role of tradition. Protestant scholars now accept this early Apostolic tradition which I have described—the oral giving of the Good News; but they tend to limit it to the time of the Apostles. Once it was written down, the oral teaching lost its validity for future generations. We hope that they will gradually see how arbitrary are these restrictions. We believe that the Good News went on being loudly shouted and widely proclaimed by successors to Paul and Peter, by heirs of Timothy and Barnabas, and that it remained alive and reliable because the Holy Ghost remained active in the Church of Christ.

The Orthodox Christians accept tradition as thoroughly as we Catholics do. But they have a little different concept of it. They tend to limit it to the Fathers and the early councils; so that it has long been static: something you find in historical sources. And for them tradition is a bit more diffuse than with us: it spreads quite evenly throughout the entire Church; every teacher and every believer is a witness to it—with the orthodoxy of the whole Church correcting local errors.

For us, tradition has two aspects: passive and active. The passive part is found in the sources: in the writings of the Fathers and the early councils, in directives of the Popes and formulas of Faith, in prayers, liturgies, attested customs, and archaeological remains. Active tradition keeps leading the Church on to a better understanding of the original revelation, to a more complete living of the spirit of Christ—always under the alert guidance of the Holy Spirit. The inspired and written Scripture never changes; but when we read it in the light of a living tradition we keep probing its meaning more deeply and seeing its implications more clearly. So for the Catholic, while the deposit of revelation in the Good News never changes, a constant growth in dogma is simply a manifestation of the life of the Church and of the activity of the Holy Spirit in it.

Also for us tradition tends to concentrate its effectiveness. We agree with the Orthodox that it spreads through the

81

whole Body of the Church, but it is more evident and intense in the bishops, who are successors of the Apostles, and particularly in the Bishop of Rome, who succeeds Peter as head of the Church.

In our understanding of tradition we remain conscious of the promise of our Savior: "And mark: I am with you at all times as long as the world will last" (Matt. 28:20). It is His presence which gives life and validity to tradition; and He clearly did not limit that presence to Apostolic times—but "as long as the world will last."

We also rely greatly on another promise of our Lord: "And I will ask the Father, and he will grant you another Advocate to be with you for all time to come, the Spirit of Truth" (John 14:16-17). And this "Advocate, the Holy Spirit, whom the Father will send in my name, will teach you everything, and refresh your memory of everything I have told you" (John 14:26).

In Apostolic times the Good News was alive and reliable because of the Holy Spirit who had come on Pentecost; in our day it retains its life and validity because of that same Holy Spirit who remains with us "for all time to come."

In recent years, besides the insights obtained from Scripture studies, Catholic theologians have been restudying the whole question of tradition, and especially the history and meaning of its definition by the Council of Trent. In the face of Protestant claims that the Scripture alone had value as a source of God's word, Catholics were tempted to reply: "Only part of our knowledge of revelation comes from Scripture; the rest is from tradition—as though from a different source."

Now we realize more fully that Scripture and tradition are one: the same Good News transmitted to us in different forms. And modern theologians incline to the belief that all doctrines are found in the Scriptures, at least implicitly or by intimation. Tradition helps us to discover meanings which might otherwise remain hidden. You need the background to get the message; you should not read the sacred words out of their true context. The same Spirit which inspired the writing of the word should guide the receiving and understanding of it. That Spirit was promised to the Church by its Founder,

82

was sent to the Church on Pentecost, and remains with the Church for all time.

Jesus promised that the Spirit would teach everything and refresh our memory of everything He had told us. It is this teaching and refreshing of the Holy Spirit which keeps the tradition of the Church alive and active—inquiring, delving, grasping and applying it to new problems, new needs, and the new frontiers opened by science and philosophy.

Yes, Kay, traditon is on the same basis as the Holy Word because they are both witnesses to us of the same Good News.

11

BRETHREN OF THE LORD

THE QUESTION

Although I am a non-Catholic, I enjoy reading the *Catholic Digest*. I became interested in it during a recent illness. As a result of my illness, I lost my job, found time heavy on my hands, and turned to reading more. My Catholic landlady was wonderful to me, and it was she who brought me the *Digests*.

I have been studying and comparing the differences between religions other than the one I was brought up in, and as yet haven't come to any conclusion as to the one I would like to join.

One of the beliefs of the Catholic Church is in the Virgin Mary. What I would like to know is this: How can you still call her a virgin when after Christ was born she had other children from her happy union with Joseph? I refer to the Bible text about Christ talking to the people and His disciples coming to Him and say that His Mother and brothers wanted to see Him. Perhaps you can explain to me why you still call Mary a virgin. Granted, she was one before Christ was born and immediately after, but that's no sign she remained a virgin. She had a husband who loved her, and he naturally would want children to bless their union.

Please help me if you can.

Birdie Harvey

THE ANSWER

I am glad you gave me the opportunity to answer the question in your pleasant letter, Miss Harvey. Pious Catholics

84

are often shocked to find that most Protestants simply take it for granted that Jesus had brothers and sisters. And some Protestants are equally surprised to learn that we hold that He was the only Son of His Mother.

When we read the story of Bethlehem, the stable, the shepherds, and the Magi, it never occurs to us that the intimate joy of Jesus, Mary, and Joseph might have been distracted by other children in the family. Of course, we know that Jesus was the firstborn Son of His Mother (Luke 2:7) and that Joseph had not known his wife "till she brought forth her firstborn Son" (Matt. 1:25). But throughout the centuries some Scripture students have held that Joseph had a number of other children by a previous marriage.

When we read about the anxious search made by Joseph and Mary in Jerusalem and their relief in finding their twelve-year-old Son in the Temple, we would have no reason to think that they might have been surrounded by other youngsters. Yet many non-Catholics take it for granted that Mary and Joseph, after the birth of Jesus, lived together as husband and wife and had at least seven other children.

Even when we read that Jesus at twelve years of age went to Nazareth and was subject to his parents and that He "advanced in wisdom and age and grace before God and men" there is no reason to suspect the presence of other children in the Holy Family. However, in later years we learn that Jesus did have a number of close relatives, and that they were not always helpful to Him and His divine mission.

St. John tells us that Mary had a sister, and as the majority of Scripture scholars read the text, this sister was also called Mary and she was the wife of Cleophas.

The first appearance of any "brethren" of Jesus was right after His first miracle at the wedding feast of Cana of Galilee, where He had "manifested his glory, and his disciples believed in Him." From Cana He went down to Capharnaum, "He and his Mother, and his brethren, and his disciples. And they stayed there but a few days."

From that time on these brethren are fairly prominent in the life of Jesus and in the history of His early Church. They were apparently rather closely associated with Him at home.

When He was preaching at the synagogue in Nazareth, His fellow townsmen were astounded at His wisdom and His power, and they exclaimed, "Is not this the carpenter's son? Is not his mother called Mary, and his brethren James and Joseph and Simon and Jude? And his sisters, are they not all with us?" (Matt. 13:55-56).

It is evident that there were at least four "brothers"; from the casual way in which they are named the list is not necessarily complete. And there must have been at least three "sisters," since they are *all* with us."

These brethren saw many of the miracles which Jesus worked, but they were very slow to believe in His mission and in His claims to divinity. On the feast of the Tabernacles, about six months before the Crucifixion, His brethren challenged Him to go into Judea and manifest Himself and his works to the world, "for not even his brethren believed in Him."

However, after they had been thoroughly shaken by the Crucifixion, Resurrection, and Ascension, the brethren seem to have had a change of heart. We find them with the Apostles in the upper room in Jerusalem, continuing "steadfastly in prayer with the women and Mary, the Mother of Jesus."

From that time on the prestige of the brethren was considerable in the life of the early Church. St. Paul indicates that they had special privileges comparable to those of the Apostles. And probably some of them were Apostles; St. Paul tells how he spent fifteen days with Peter in Jerusalem, "but I saw none of the other Apostles, except James, the brother of the Lord." This James is quite certainly that James the Less whose mother was at the foot of the cross of Jesus, and the same one who became the first Bishop of Jerusalem. He would be the one whom St. Matthew calls James, the son of Alphaeus; and there have been many theories to explain how he could be the son of Mary, the wife of Cleophas, and yet the son of Alphaeus.

It is commonly believed that Jude, who is called a "brother" of the Lord, was also that Apostle who is known as Judas Thaddeus. He would be the same one who wrote the Epistle in which he calls himself Jude, the brother of James.

86

There are some, however, who believe that he was not really a brother, but a cousin of James.

There is a theory also that Simon, the "brother" of the Lord, was that Apostle who is called Simon the Zealot by St. Luke both in his Gospel and in the Acts of the Apostles (1:13). Matthew and Mark call him Simon the Cananean, which derives from the Hebrew word for a group of "zealots." Hegesippus, an historian of the early second century, who was probably personally acquainted with some of the relatives of the Lord, is our authority for believing that Simon the Apostle was a "brother" of the Lord. He calls him Simeon and says that he was the son of Clopas, who was a brother of Joseph; consequently he was a cousin of the Lord, and after the death of James he was chosen to be the second Bishop of Jerusalem. This account of Hegesippus is recorded by Eusebius, the great historian of the early Church.

The fourth of these "brothers of the Lord," Joseph, seems to have disappeared, for there is no mention of him after he is named with the other three by his neighbors at Nazareth. Neither do we hear any more of the sisters; none of them has been otherwise identified.

If anyone without doctrinal background and awareness of Christian tradition would simply pick up the Gospels and read these references to the brothers and sisters of Jesus, I suppose he would take for granted that they were the children of Mary and Joseph. But it is a remarkable thing that none of the early Fathers or writers of the Church—except possibly Tertullian, who was a heretic—ever thought of considering these brethren as children of Mary. Some took it for granted that they were children of Joseph by an earlier marriage, but there was always a firm and constant doctrinal tradition that Mary had remained a virgin all her life. Origen and St. Basil are particularly strong in pointing this out.

It was not until the latter part of the fourth century that this early tradition was shocked. A Roman writer by the name of Helvidius made the bald and offensive statement that these brethren were the children of Joseph and Mary. St. Jerome, with all the force of his learned pen, tore into Helvidius with a complete refutation of all his claims.

Helvidius had a couple of prominent followers, one of them a bishop; but after the refutation by St. Jerome and a similar one by St. Ambrose, they were quickly condemned by several councils, and the whole question was considered settled for many centuries. It was revived, however, by the rationalist scholars of the nineteenth century, and following their lead today most Protestant Scripture students hold that Jesus had real blood brothers and sisters.

To Catholics, this idea is impious and defamatory. Not only do we believe in the divinity of Christ and the Virgin Birth, but we believe firmly in the perpetual virginity of the Mother of Jesus. We hold with St. Basil that "those who love Jesus cannot bear to hear it said that the Mother of God ceased to be a virgin." We consider it incongruous that other children, thoroughly human, should share the womb and the love which were given first to God's own eternal Son. We sense that those who hold otherwise are well on the way to denying the divinity of Christ.

It is not only piety which prompts us to these ideas. There is sound scriptural foundation for them. St. Jerome was the greatest student of Hebrew and Aramaic in the early Church —and one of the greatest of all time. In refuting the claims of Helvidius he pointed out that the Greek words for "brother" and "sister" used in the Scriptures stood for the Hebrew words "ah" and "ahoth," which were often used in the Old Testament to designate close relatives. Hebrew had no precise word for cousin. In the lands of the Near East, ties of kinship were intimate, and the closest relatives would sometimes be called brothers and sisters even though they were only cousins or nephews. So Abraham called Lot his brother, although he was really his nephew; Jacob calls himself a brother of Laban, although he was the son of Laban's sister Rebecca.

And St. Jerome also pointed out that it is ridiculous to argue, as Helvidius did, that the designation of Jesus as Mary's firstborn son implies that she had other sons. He would have been called that at the moment of His birth; the firstborn son is often the only son. And with the Jewish people the term had a technical, legal meaning. For instance, the firstborn son belonged to God and must be redeemed.

It is equally ridiculous to cite the words of Matthew that Joseph knew not his wife "till she had brought forth her firstborn Son" and argue from that word "till" that he must have known her afterward. The point being made is that the conception of this child was miraculous. It is entirely gratuitous to read into it any implication as to what took place later.

These might be called negative arguments. They simply show that there is no sound or irrefutable evidence in Scripture that Mary and Joseph had other children. There are also positive arguments, and one of them comes from the early origin of a firm and constant tradition that Mary remained always a virgin. It would have been plainly impossible for such a belief to establish itself in the very midst of Mary's own children and grandchildren. And we know that these brethren of the Lord were not obscure or forgotten; they were very prominent in the early Church.

Unless Mary were resolved to remain a virgin why would she have said to the angel at the Annunciation, "How shall this happen, since I do not know man?" Her surprise and wonder would have had no meaning because she was engaged to Joseph and ready to begin living with him. And if she had later broken the resolution here implied and proceeded to have other children, why would St. Luke have recorded her words?

Then I would have you recall the intense scene described by St. John in his Gospel. "Now there were standing by the cross of Jesus his Mother and his Mother's sister, Mary of Cleophas, and Mary Magdalene. When Jesus, therefore, saw his Mother and the disciple standing by, whom He loved, He said to his Mother, 'Woman, behold thy son.' Then He said to the disciple, 'Behold, thy Mother.' And from that hour the disciple took her into his home" (John 19:25-27).

If the brethren of Jesus were the sons of Mary these words would make little sense. Why would Jesus turn His Mother over to an outsider if she had sons of her own to look after her? And in the Greek of the Gospel, "Behold thy son" reads "Behold the son of thine"—implying the only son.

While Mary is often with these brethren it is never indicated by any word that she is their mother. She is always *His* mother, never theirs. "While He was still speaking to the crowds, his Mother and his brethren were standing outside, seeking to speak to Him." And after the Ascension, the Apostles were persevering in prayer "with the women and Mary, the Mother of Jesus, and with his brethren," not "with Mary and her children."

Not only is the Virgin Mary not named as their mother, but another woman is named in the Gospels as the mother of at least two of them. Compare that Crucifixion scene from St. John, quoted above, with this from St. Matthew: "And many women were there. Among them were Mary Magdalene, and Mary the mother of James and Joseph, and the mother of the sons of Zebedee." Mark has similar words: "Mary Magdalene, Mary the mother of James the Less and of Joseph, and Salome."

Of course, St. John does not mention his own mother, Salome, "the mother of the sons of Zebedee"; and Matthew and Mark do not make explicit mention of the Mother of Jesus; rather, they take her for granted. They certainly would not have designated her as the "mother of James and Joseph" when her own firstborn Son was dying on the cross beside her. But apart from these two omissions, traditional Scripture scholars have always believed that Matthew, Mark, and John name the same women: Mary Magdalene and Mary, the wife of Cleophas, who was the mother of James the Less and Joseph.

The prevailing Catholic tradition has always been that these brethren were really cousins of Jesus. It is true that some writers of the Church, especially the Greek Fathers, were persuaded by apocryphal accounts that the brethren were children of Joseph by a former marriage. But it must be pointed out that these apocryphal writings are entirely unreliable, that Joseph is never named as the father of these brethren, and that they are never in any way associated with him. His unique concern for Jesus and Mary at Bethlehem and on the flight into Egypt could hardly have been possible for the father of a large family with little children. In spite of the apocryphal stories there has developed in the Church a firm common belief that Joseph was also a virgin. Catholic piety is deeply shocked by the suggestion that the spouse of the Virgin Mary might have divided his loyalties with another wife and other children.

Whose children were they then? At least two of them, James and Joseph, must have been sons of Mary, the wife of Cleophas; and she is called a sister of the Mother of Jesus. Was she a full-blood sister? We have no way of knowing. There is a pious tradition that Mary was the only daughter of aged parents, and it is argued that two sisters of the same family would hardly be given the same name, Mary. Maybe she was only a half-sister; maybe only a cousin. Some authorities hold that she was a sister-in-law: that Cleophas was the brother of Joseph; and they identify Cleophas with that Clopas mentioned by Hegesippus as the brother of Joseph and the father of Simeon.

Jude is called the brother of James in Luke 6:16, and Acts 1:13. Was he also a son of Cleophas and of Mary, the sister of the Blessed Virgin? There are some who doubt it; they believe he was a half-brother, or a cousin. Possibly Simon was his real brother.

Much of this is speculation. We do not have the evidence to make us sure of exact relationships. And names like Mary, James, Joseph, Simon, and Jude were very common. That is why we cannot be certain that Simon, the "brother" of the Lord, was Simon the Apostle. And the spelling of names sometimes was altered in transcribing them from Aramaic to Greek. So it is just possible that Alphaeus and Cleophas could be the same person, explaining how Mary the wife of Cleophas could be the mother of James the son of Alphaeus.

Only on matters of doctrine have we no need to speculate. The perpetual virginity of the Mother of Jesus is a matter of faith. So we know that the brethren of the Lord were not her children. We are shocked to find so many Christians believing that they were—simply taking it for granted, without any awareness of the constant Christian tradition to the contrary or of the arguments so forcefully advanced by St. Jerome in 382, and still firmly convincing today.

12

SALVATION-JUSTIFICATION

THE QUESTION

I have been studying religion on and off for ten years, but only recently have I started to investigate Christianity, which I had always thought of as a somewhat negative religion emphasizing sin rather than union with God. Now I see, from reading the lives of the Saints, that union with God through prayer and self-discipline is the main teaching of the Catholic Church.

The only thing that confuses me is the requirement for salvation. I have heard Protestants say that it is a spontaneous act of faith in Jesus Christ which assures you of salvation no matter what you do, while Catholics seem of the opinion that you never really know whether you are saved because you can always commit another mortal sin despite your faith and be lost if you don't get to Confession before you die. This seems to imply that Christ died in vain, according to my Protestant friends; yet their doctrine appears to permit sin as long as they have faith.

I would appreciate it if you could clear up this very important question.

Anthony Harris

THE ANSWER

Anthony, your question is a very good one, but it is likely to inveigle us into deep theological waters amid the rough eddies of controversy. God's grace will be the central theme of my answer, and with the help of it I hope to remain calm, clear, and correct.

Our discussion concerns the process by which our human souls are made capable and fit to get into heaven and live there eternally in loving union with the God of all goodness. It is not a simple process; our spiritual jump from earth to heaven is greater in its own sphere than the rocket trip we vaguely plan to Mars.

Getting to Mars is complicated enough, but should we once arrive there our adjustment problems would be tremendous. Oxygen, food, atmospheric pressure, gravity, and temperature would be our most urgent concerns. So it is with heaven; getting there is a lifetime job, but living there would offer eternal problems, except that the all-capable God is there to solve them easily.

Our human difficulties with life on Mars and life in heaven arise from similar causes. By nature we are earth-bound beings, and living conditions are entirely different both on other planets and in heaven. Our bodies are designed to live under pressure of fifteen pounds to the square inch, to be nourished by three square meals a day, and to endure temperatures within reasonable range. And our souls are designed to know things through physical eyes and ears hooked up with a human brain.

We need not be detailed about Mars, but in heaven this earth-bound soul of ours will live in immediate and intelligent contact with the infinite God. We are not made to stand it. By nature we have no faculties for seeing or understanding God in this way, and no means of communicating with Him satisfactorily. Our nature is entirely different from His; yet our life in heaven will be that of adopted sons living in our Father's house, loving Him completely. And this despite the fact that our normal minds are unable even to know Him. How then can we love Him? And if we don't love Him how can we be happy with Him? We will be out of our natural element.

Many simple Christians have a concept of heaven similar to that of *Green Pastures:* it is a place of joy and singing, golden streets, winged angels, and levitating harps—the place of love and tolerance where we all meet after our exhausting climb up the devious roads of the mountain. And we secretly wonder if we will not be a bit bored with it all. For those good people, getting to heaven is a routine matter: Jesus Christ died for us so that we can get there. It is as simple as that. We believe in Him and accept salvation from Him, and if we are decent citizens, obey the law, and say our prayers, we will join all our good friends in a spiritualized happy hunting grounds when we die.

But heaven is infinitely above such simple concepts; it is the unlimited greatness and goodness of God shared directly with us. It requires a transformation of our human nature. We must be given a spark of the divine life if we are to share that life forever. We must be given some slight share in the divine nature if we are to be adopted children of God. Our faculties of mind and will must be enlarged and sharpened if we are to know God as He really is and love Him as His goodness deserves. We sum it up by saying that since our life in heaven will be supernatural (above our human nature) we must somehow be raised to that level of living and have our nature and faculties adapted to it. It is readily apparent that we can never raise ourselves above ourselves by our own power. God must do it for us. But how does He do it? That is your question, Anthony.

However, the problem you present is even more complicated than that. By our sins we have messed up our relation with the Divinity and fouled up our own nature, so that we are not only constitutionally unadapted to heaven but morally unworthy of its goodness. Everything there is holy, and we have made ourselves unholy. Everyone there is a Saint, and we will be in strange company unless we can somehow be rid of our unsaintliness. We must be changed into Saints, and that, you will agree, takes some powerful changing.

The process of changing us from sinners into Saints is called justification; it makes us just: good, holy. The majority of Christians are agreed that Jesus Christ is the one responsible for our justification; He made it possible by His death on the cross. He redeemed us, paid back to God the debt we had incurred by our sins, liberated us from our slavery to the Devil, opened the gate of heaven for us, and made possible our adoption as sons of God.

The argument starts, however, when we try to figure out the means Jesus uses to share the benefits of His Redemption with each one of us individually. How are your sins forgiven —and mine? The fact of the Redemption does not mean that you and I share in it automatically. Our share is there ready for us; but how do we get it? On the cross, Jesus acquired the means of making all men Saints. But not all men are actually Saints. What method does Jesus use to make living Saints out of you and me?

I keep posing the question in different words; it is time I began answering it. The basic answer is that some kind of effective spiritual contact must be established between Jesus Christ and ourselves. His human soul, now in heaven, is simply overflowing with the graces He obtained by His death on the cross. If our sin-shredded souls are united with His grace-filled soul, the overflow will come to us; and we will share His justice, His sanctity, and His union with the Divinity. We will be prepared for heaven.

There is no great discovery of theologians involved in this; Jesus made it clear by His own words: "I am the vine, you are the branches. He who abides in Me, and I in him, he bears much fruit; for without Me you can do nothing. If anyone does not abide in Me, he shall be cast outside as the branch and wither."

Thus far most of us are still together: Lutherans, Calvinists, Catholics. But the next question separates us: By what means is this effective contact with Jesus Christ established? Yet even here the separation is not readily apparent because we all agree that faith is the fundamental means of contact. We could hardly doubt it since Jesus Himself taught it (Mark 16:15), and St. Paul insists upon it all through his writings, especially in the Epistle to the Romans.

However, when we say "faith," we do not all mean exactly the same thing. For the Catholic it is a firm acceptance of the teachings of Christ, the Son of God. For most Protestants faith has much of the fiduciary in it; it is less an intellectual assent than a confident assurance. It is a firm conviction of the fact and effectiveness of personal justification through the merits of Jesus Christ.

Our real differences, however, center around the adequacy of faith alone to establish a thoroughly effective contact between ourselves and Christ so that His justice will come to our souls. And there are differences, too, in our various appraisals of the results of this justification in our souls.

Catholics hold faith to be the basic requirement, first in time and importance; but we believe that it must be a practical faith, animated by charity and productive of the works of love. Protestants generally, following Luther, maintain that faith is enough. They say that we Catholics take the credit for salvation away from Christ and try to hoist ourselves to heaven by tugging at our own bootstraps, with only a grateful nod to the Savior for a helpful boost. Some hold that we consider even this boost to be mechanical; He lifts us to heaven on a sacramental crane, and once we are there our good works earn us entrance. I will answer that charge later.

The Protestant concept of justification stems almost entirely from a tremendous subjective discovery made by Martin Luther in 1512 while he was in the tower of his monastery, meditating on the seventeenth verse of the first chapter of Paul's Epistle to the Romans: "For in it [i.e., the Gospel] the justice of God is revealed." From that discovery Luther evolved his own ideas of justification by faith; later Calvin followed him, but added emphasis on God's predestining choice of those whom He will justify.

Luther was a good theologian, but he was also a monk with a conscience; and that conscience troubled him. He was deeply aware of sin, without confidence of forgiveness. He longed for the interior peace which would come with definite assurance of his personal salvation. His anxiety of conscience had been stimulated by his frightening concept of God's justice; he had always understood it as the rigid justice of a stern judge who demands that we measure up—even though He must surely know that we can never do it. Then that day in the tower it suddenly dawned on him that the justice

96

of God is not a demanding thing, but a giving thing. It does not simply require us to be just; it makes us just.

This soul-shaking discovery should not have startled a Catholic theologian. It represented the traditional Catholic teaching; but for Luther it was delightfully new. Apparently his ideas on the subject had come from the Nominalists, especially Ockham, who had distorted the Catholic notion of justification into a kind of Pelagianism, the notion that we work out our own sanctification. In any case, in the light of his new understanding, Luther went on to meditate on other words of St. Paul, like Rom. 3:28: "For we reckon that a man is justified by faith independently of the works of the Law." And from such words, interpreted in the light of his personal needs for comfort and security, he evolved his doctrine that our justification comes entirely from the merits of Christ through our faith in Him, and without our personal efforts having any effective part in the process.

We Catholics believe that Luther simplified the process of justification too much. He had attained his understanding of spiritual freedom by a long, hard struggle within his own conscience; so that it was very deep and personal with him. The force of his inner conviction made the idea dynamic: other tortured souls, struggling with guilt and anxiety, must know the comfort of this discovery.

Luther's ideas of justification were determined also by his notion of original sin. He believed that man had quite ruined his nature by sin, to the point that he is incapable of doing anything good. Since our whole nature has become sinful, our every act exudes from sin—no matter how good our intentions or how strong our efforts. Furthermore, original sin destroyed our free will, so that we are determined to sin in spite of ourselves.

How then was it possible for this sinful nature to be justified? Can sin be made holy? Obviously not. But when sin is covered up by the merits of Jesus Christ, God can overlook it, and not impute it to us. We must recognize our sinfulness in true humility, repent sincerely, and then when we believe in Christ with firm confidence He so thoroughly hides our sins beneath His goodness that He justifies us in spite of them. We remain sinners underneath, but He tucks us under His own cloak and takes us through the gate of heaven with Him.

It would seem, as you suggest, Anthony, that, if followed with thorough logic, this idea of justification would overthrow the practical basis of sound morality. Our will is not free and we are incapable of good, and no matter what we do we contribute nothing to our salvation. Jesus sanctifies us in spite of our sins. Where is the incentive to goodness? Apparently, in Lutheran practice, such logic is short-circuited. Lutheran morality has always been rigid; and whether you have free will or not, most Protestants will hold you to personal accounting. None of them believes, in a practical way, that it doesn't matter what you do. They simply insist that Jesus saves us, no matter what we do, if we have real faith in Him. And if we have that faith we will be inspired to live by it.

There are two good aspects to Luther's doctrine: (1) It gives due importance to the justice of God and the merits of Jesus Christ; by de-emphasizing the human factor it emphasizes the supernatural nature of our justification. (2) Psychologically, it should liberate us from our scruples and worries. It leaves the work of justification entirely up to someone else; except for our trusting faith we remain passive in the process, with no need for fear of failure.

So much for Luther; now back to the Catholics! What do we Catholics believe about this process of uniting sinful man to holy God? How do we participate in the merits of Christ's death?

The Catholic idea of justification is not based on any single text of Scripture. We give full attention to Romans 3:28, but we give equal consideration to many other statements of St. Paul, to various words of Jesus Himself, and even to the Epistle of St. James. We fit them all together into a complete doctrine. It is not a simple doctrine, but it gives due weight to all the truths which enter into it: to God's goodness, power, and love, and to man's free will; to the evil of sin and the effectiveness of grace; to the essential role of faith and the requirement of love; to man's complete dependence on grace and the necessity of his co-operation with it.

Obviously, space does not permit me to quote many texts; here are only a few typical ones.

Jesus sent His Apostles into the whole world to make disciples of all nations, and He told them: "He who believes and is baptized shall be saved; he who does not believe shall be condemned." The point is that in addition to believing we must be baptized.

A lawyer inquired of Jesus: "Master, what must I do to gain eternal life?" And then, under questioning, he gave his own answer: that he should love God with his whole heart, soul, strength, and mind, and his neighbor as himself. And Jesus told him: "Thou has answered rightly; do this and thou shalt live." "This" is in addition to faith.

A certain ruler asked Him: "Good Master, what shall I do to gain eternal life?" He was reminded that he should keep the Commandments and was advised to practice poverty and charity, and then to follow Christ.

The words of St. James have always entered sharply into this controversy. He tells us that we must "be doers of the word, and not hearers only," and his challenge is direct: "What will it profit, my brethren, if a man says he has faith, but does not have works? Can the faith save him?"

The most rewarding source of study on justification is St. Paul, not in an isolated passage or two, but in all fourteen Epistles and particularly in those shorter letters of love and union: Ephesians, Philippians, and Colossians. He tells us how we are buried with Christ in Baptism and rise again with Him that we may be dead to sin but alive to God, in Christ Jesus. He reminds us that we must strip off the old man with his evil deeds and put on the new, with his heart of virtue and forgiveness, and above all charity, which is the bond of perfection.

In eloquent repetition St. Paul shows his delight in the effects of grace in our souls: it transforms, elevates, and unites. It permits us to do all things in Him who strengthens us; it permits us to walk worthy of God and please Him in all things, bearing fruit in every good work; and it permits us to grow in union with Christ by every work of truth we perform in love.

Looking at the whole picture of justification, in all its love and beauty, we might sum it up this way:

Our justification comes entirely from Christ. The basis of our effective union with Him is faith; but this faith is supernatural, and we cannot acquire it by our own efforts. It is a gift of God. We believe in response to His grace.

Then after faith we are normally joined to Christ in Baptism, the instrument He gave us to effect our union with Him. Love, which is grounded in faith, is the effective bond of this union; and from it we receive a share in His divine life which will permit us to live with Him for eternity, and enough of His divine nature to permit us to share, by adoption, in the paternal love of the Father.

(By way of exception, the essential effects of justification may come into the soul before actual Baptism. The strong faith which God gives us may produce an active love of God, which is also His gift; and thus we are brought into sanctifying union with Him by the ardor of our desire. With a child the process is reversed; Baptism gives him the faith, hope, and love which fit him for heaven, even though he is not able to make present use of them.)

When this sanctifying life of grace has come into our souls we are so thoroughly incorporated into Christ and so elevated and transformed by His presence in us that we live and act on a supernatural level, on the plane of heaven. Everything we do has value for heaven as long as it is a work of truth, done in love. We grow in union with God by living and acting with Him. Our natural acts could have no value for heaven, but they are given value by the grace of Christ. They share so thoroughly in His merits that they please God, and He attributes merit to them.

In all of this we recognize the devastating effects of original sin and the intrinsic evil of our own personal sins. But we do not believe that original sin destroyed our free will; it only weakened it badly. It did not make our nature essentially sinful; it only immersed us in sin. The grace of Christ, in our justification, pulls us out of the sticky slough of sin and cleanses us by immersion in God's love and goodness.

We believe that the process of justification has its effects deep within the soul. Sins are not covered up; they are removed, as regards their guilt. The essence of sin was separation from God; justification unites us to Him. But the taking away of sin is hardly more than a preliminary feature of justification; it gives us the life of heaven, the faculties for knowing and loving God in heaven, and for loving and serving Him meritoriously here on earth.

This Catholic doctrine cannot give the ironclad internal assurance of salvation which comes from a conviction of predestination or an experience of trusting faith, but it does teach a loving confidence in the mercy and goodness of God, in His effective desire for the salvation of all men, and in the abundant opportunity He provides for each of us. Understanding of the Catholic doctrine should not only bring tranquillity of conscience in the certainty of forgiveness, but also that peace and happiness which comes from awareness of God's love for us and His presence with us. Furthermore, it offers that ardent incentive for good works and self denial which can come only from awareness of love and confidence in our ability to return love in a manner acceptable to the One loved.

13

GIFTS OF THE HOLY GHOST

THE QUESTION

I believe Jesus Christ to be the Son of God. And I believe that there is no other way of salvation than through His shed Blood on the cross.

I would like to know how and what is the Catholic idea concerning the Baptism of the Holy Ghost, according to Acts 2:4, and the outward evidence of speaking in tongues. What I want to know is: Do you (the Church) believe it is for today?

In chapter 10 of Acts, St. Peter was preaching in Rome: a Roman household to whom Peter was preaching remission of sins through faith in Jesus received a mighty, spontaneous blessing (Baptism) in the Holy Ghost. Peter was sure of this, "for they heard them speak with tongues and magnify God" (Acts 10:46).

We Pentecostalists join with St. Peter and declare with confidence, "This is that"; and furthermore "that" is "this," which will perpetuate the work of Christ upon the earth, until Christ return for his Saints.

A Brother in Christ, Rev. Mitchell Blackburn

THE ANSWER

First let me ask you a question. How should I address you? Should it be Brother or Reverend or Mister? I am serious. We hear much talk of a dialogue between representatives of the different faiths. I think a good start would be for us to find out the proper, polite, and pleasing title for each other. I have noticed that some Protestants fumble a bit with "Father" when they speak to me; and I am often at similar loss when I speak to a minister. "Reverend" is an adjective; it seems clumsy as a title. "Brother" is fine in some areas and some denominations. "Mister" seems secular.

I like it when the minister has a degree and I can call him Doctor—until I get on a first-name basis, and then I find that my own formidable title of Monsignor frightens him from such familiarity.

In the army we got by easily: everyone could be Chaplain or Padre (much easier to say than "Father") and everyone shared a snappy, irreverent "Sir."

Since you sign yourself "A Brother in Christ," I will presume to call you "Brother," even as Paul addressed Philemon (7), as he claimed the Israelites (Rom. 9:3), and as he wrote to the Romans (e.g., 1:13; 10:1). I call you Brother in the same spirit of benevolence with which Stephen addressed the members of the council (Acts 7:1), but with no suspicion that you accuse me of blasphemy or want to stone me as the council did Stephen. I use it as a sign of our union in our mutual Brother, Jesus, who tells us: "Anyone who nurses anger against his brother must be brought to judgement. . . . if he sneers at him he will have to answer for it in the fires of hell" (Matt. 5:22).

Do you note a lack of familiarity in my quotations, Brother? I am using The New English Bible. It gives a modern clarity to the familiar verses. I don't know how Pentecostalists may accept it, but I plan to read it through once, at least. (And for my Catholic readers, I cite Canon 1400 which permits the use of a translation of this kind to a person who is in any way a student of the Bible or of theology. I am an amateur student of both.)

I presume, Brother, that your reference in your final paragraph is to the words of St. Peter in his first public sermon (Acts 2:16), but The New English Bible rather spoils your play on words; it says simply, "This is what the prophet spoke of"—instead of "This is that which was spoken by the prophet Joel."

Of course, I agree entirely with the statement you make

103

in the first paragraph of your letter: that we are all redeemed, sanctified, and saved through the sufferings and death of our Lord Jesus Christ. So I will devote my time to the questions raised in your next two paragraphs.

I shouldn't quibble about unimportant details, but chapter 10 of Acts says explicitly that Peter preached his sermon to Cornelius and his Roman household at Caesarea, a seacoast city of Palestine; not at Rome. My new translation says that Cornelius was "a centurion of the Italian Cohort," and he is generally considered the first Gentile convert to Christianity.

The point of your reference is that "Peter was still speaking when the Holy Spirit came upon all who were listening to the message." The Jews who had come with Peter "were astonished that the gift of the Holy Spirit should have been poured out even on Gentiles. For they could hear them speaking in tongues of ecstasy and acclaiming the greatness of God" (Acts 10:44-46).

You call this "a mighty, spontaneous blessing (Baptism) in the Holy Ghost." I question only your word in parentheses. If this is a Baptism then what does Peter mean in the next verse: " 'Is anyone prepared to withhold the water for Baptism from these persons, who have received the Holy Spirit just as we did ourselves?' Then he ordered them to be baptized in the name of Jesus Christ" (Acts 10:47-48).

And now to go back to your first reference (Acts 2:4): "And they were all filled with the Holy Spirit and began to talk in other tongues, as the Spirit gave them power of utterance." We consider this also "a mighty, spontaneous blessing," a special gift of the Holy Ghost. Only in most figurative language could you call it a Baptism; as you know that "to baptize" in Greek means to dip, or to dip under. The technical name for these special gifts of the Holy Ghost is charism, a word we borrow from the Greek, where it means a grace, favor, or a free gift.

Now your main question is this: Does our Church believe that we get these special gifts of the Holy Spirit today, in the normal course of our sanctification? The answer is that we do not get those extraordinary charisms like speaking in tongues, prophecy, healing, discerning spirits, and working miracles. We do get an abundance of those ordinary, practical gifts, graces, favors and charisms which we need to maintain a loving, sanctifying union with our Savior, Jesus Christ.

In some ways the Catholics and Pentecostalists are about as far apart as two Christian groups can be. And yet we do have much in common. Not only do we agree that our salvation comes uniquely through our redemption by Jesus Christ, but we also have a common faith in the supernatural. And that, as you know, is an attitude which many of our Christian brethren shun. They try to wring it out of their creed, and to find a "sensible" explanation for everything right in the natural order.

I want to make it clear that we Catholics share with you a firm belief in the extraordinary charisms given to the early Christians, and in the recurrence of these and similar special gifts in the lives of many Saints and mystics.

Our main disagreement would be on the frequency and purpose of these startling manifestations. We do not believe that they form a normal part of our sanctification. They were frequent in the early Church, where they were needed to bolster the witness of the Good News in a pagan world; or as in the case of Cornelius, where they were needed to teach lessons to the disciples themselves.

You must be very familiar with I Cor. 12, in which St. Paul explains the charisms and gifts of the Holy Ghost. Does he not make it clear that they are given for a special purpose? They are not given equally to all, but with much diversity; so that each person may be equipped for specialized functions in the mystical Body of Christ.

On one point you and I are in agreement; as human beings we need tangible, external evidence to convince us of the fact of our sanctification. We differ in the nature of this evidence; you seek it in ecstatic manifestations: in tongues, healings, and prophecies; we find it in the signs of the sacraments. We believe that Jesus was aware of our human need for evidence. He had healed the sick, raised the dead, and risen from His own tomb, to show His divinity. He had

105

equipped His Apostles with tongues and prophecies to bring His message of love and meekness to a proud and hateful world. But as enduring signs through the centuries His sacraments would be enough, bolstered occasionally by an attractive miracle, to serve a special purpose.

At the first Pentecost the Holy Ghost came down in visible form and scattered His gifts profusely. But we do not call that a Baptism. You need water to baptize, as St. Peter said in the home of Cornelius. When Philip had given the Good News to the eunuch from Ethiopia, "they both went down into the water, Philip and the eunuch, and he baptized him" (Acts 8:36).

Jesus Himself said to Nicodemus, "In truth I tell you, no one can enter the kingdom of God without being born from water and spirit." My new translation fails to capitalize the word "Spirit" here, as you and I both know it in our familiar versions; but otherwise, by omitting the article "the," it shows how water and Spirit combine in one efficient principle to produce rebirth. Reference is probably made to the words of John the Baptist: "I baptize you with water . . . but the one who comes after me . . . will baptize you with the Holy Spirit and with fire" (Matt. 3:11).

For us Baptism is not a noise from the sky, "like that of a strong driving wind" (Acts 2:2). It is not the sudden striking of "tongues like flames of fire" (Acts 2:3). It is not "a light flashed from the sky" on the road near Damascus (Acts 9:3). It does not cause us to speak "in tongues of ecstasy" as the family of Cornelius did (Acts 10:46).

Baptism is rather that action which our Savior commanded His Apostles to perform: "Go forth therefore and make all nations my disciples; baptize men everywhere in the name of the Father and the Son and the Holy Spirit" (Matt. 28:19). It is that which Peter counseled in Jerusalem on the day of the first Pentecost: "Repent and be baptized every one of you, in the name of Jesus the Messiah for the forgiveness of your sins, and you will receive the gift of the Holy Spirit" (Acts 2:38).

It is that which the Apostles did a few moments later, after Peter had "pressed his case and pleaded with them:

106

'Save yourselves from this crooked age.' Then those who accepted his word were baptized, and some three thousand were added to their number that day" (Acts 2:40-41).

Baptism is that which Philip did for the eunuch. It is that which Peter ordered to be done for Cornelius and his family after the gifts of the Holy Spirit had come upon them (Acts 10:47-48). It is that which was done for Saul at Damascus after the Lord had blinded him by the lightning of conversion, and after the scales had fallen from his eyes. "Thereupon he was baptized, and afterwards he took food and his strength returned" (Acts 9:19).

For us Baptism is an external action and sign, given us by Jesus Christ Himself and used by Him to sanctify our souls. In Baptism we receive the Holy Spirit just as effectively as the family of Cornelius did, and He comes to us with His most precious, but hidden charisms: faith, hope, and love; and He remains in our souls quietly and effectively as long as we want Him to stay. Seldom does He make a fuss in His busy work of making Saints of us; seldom does He display such startling gifts as tongues or prophecy.

After Baptism we have another sacrament which is a personal little Pentecost for each of us. We call it Confirmation. It gives us each the graces and gifts necessary to be an effective witness to Christ, as Jesus promised to His disciples before His Ascension into heaven: "You will receive power when the Holy Spirit comes upon you; and you will bear witness for Me in Jerusalem, and all over Judea and Samaria, and away to the ends of the earth" (Acts 1:8).

This sacrament lets each of us share personally in that promise which Jesus made to His Apostles at the Last Supper. "I will ask the Father, and He will give you another to be your Advocate, who will be with you forever—the Spirit of truth. The world cannot receive Him, because the world neither sees nor knows Him; but you know Him because He dwells with you and is in you" (John 14, 16-17).

Often in the Scriptures we find that an external action—a sign—was needed to bring the Holy Ghost. Philip the Deacon had preached in a town in Samaria where many had listened to his word and had been baptized, but "until then the Spirit had not come upon any of them." So the Apostles "sent off Peter and John, who went down there and prayed for the converts, asking that they might receive the Holy Spirit. . . . So Peter and John laid their hands on them and they received the Holy Spirit" (Acts 8:4-17).

It was on this occasion that a magician named Simon wanted to buy the power to give the Holy Spirit. He was sternly rebuked by Peter: "You and your money, may you come to a bad end, for thinking God's gift is for sale" (Acts 8:20).

This is the sacrament which Paul administered to a dozen disciples at Ephesus. He found that they had never heard of the Holy Spirit, that they were not really Christians, since they had received only the Baptism of repentance administered by John, as a preparation for the coming of Jesus. So then and there "they were baptized in the name of the Lord Jesus; and when Paul had laid hands on them, the Holy Spirit came upon them and they spoke in tongues of ecstasy and prophesied" (Acts 19:1-6).

As we go through the Scriptures we find that the laying on of hands was only one of the terms used for this sacrament. St. Paul probably referred to Confirmation when he wrote to the Corinthians: "And if you and we belong to Christ, guaranteed as his and anointed, it is all God's doing; it is God also who has set his seal upon us, and as a pledge of what is to come has given the Spirit to dwell in our hearts" (II Cor. 1:21-22).

St. Paul reminds the Ephesians: "And you, too, when you had heard the message of the truth, the good news of your salvation, and had believed it, became incorporate in Christ and received the seal of the promised Holy Spirit" (Eph. 1:13).

St. John has similar reference in his first Letter: "You, no less than they, are among the initiated; this is the gift of the Holy One, and by it you all have knowledge" (2:20). A footnote tells me that the original Greek expression is translated as "you . . . have an anointing." It is this anointing which is the gift of the Holy One and numbers them among the initiated.

Our sacrament of Confirmation has all three features: a laying on of hands, an anointing, and a seal. And using these signs as an impressive instrument, the Holy Ghost gives us Himself, His graces and His gifts, especially those sound, unspectacular charisms which are listed by the Prophet Isaias (11:2): "And the spirit of the Lord shall rest upon him: the spirit of wisdom and of understanding, the spirit of counsel and of fortitude, the spirit of knowledge and the fear of the Lord."

Confirmation also gives us that harvest of the Spirit which St. Paul lists in Galatians 5:22: love, joy, peace, patience, kindness, goodness, fidelity, gentleness, and self-control.

It also gives some of those gifts listed by St. Paul in I Corinthians 12: not often the charism of inspired preaching, or of wonderworking or healing; but always that greatest gift, which St. Paul extols in chapter 13: love, which gives meaning and purpose to all the rest, and keeps us from being "a noisy gong and a clanging cymbal."

Confirmation gives us all the supernatural aids we need to become witnesses to Christ in our modern world; and for being witnesses few of us need the extraordinary charisms given to the Apostles and to many of the early Christians. Possibly we are better off without the gifts of healing, of miraculous powers, prophecy, and ecstatic utterance (I Cor. 12:10), which would make us an oddity in the world, and leave less range for a firm and simple faith.

The next sacrament which has obvious connection with the Holy Spirit is that which we call Holy Orders: it makes us ministers of the Spirit, to teach and baptize, to bring the Good News of salvation and the aids for attaining sanctity.

Jesus gave the graces and powers of Holy Orders to His Apostles bit by bit, and His Church confers them today in successive stages: first to a deacon, then to a priest, and finally to a bishop.

First Jesus called His Apostles. He told Simon and Andrew: "Come follow Me and I will make you fishers of men" (Mark 1:16). At the Last Supper, He reminded them all: "You did not choose Me: I chose you" (John 15:15). At that same Last Supper, He gave them the greatest of their powers: St. Paul reminds the Corinthians of it: "The Lord Jesus, on the night of his arrest, took bread and, after giving thanks to God, broke it and said: 'This is my Body, which is for you; do this as a memorial of Me.' In the same way, He took the cup after supper, and said: "This cup is the new covenant sealed in my Blood. Whenever you drink it do this as a memorial of Me. For every time you eat this bread and drink the cup, you proclaim the death of the Lord, until He comes" (I Cor. 11:23-26).

After the resurrection, Jesus sent His Apostles to preach and minister. "Go forth to every part of the world, and proclaim the Good News to the whole creation. Those who believe it and receive Baptism will find salvation" (Mark 15:15-16).

At about the same time He told them, " 'As the Father sent Me, I send you.' He then breathed on them, saying 'Receive the Holy Spirit! If you forgive any man's sins, they stand forgiven; if you pronounce them unforgiven, unforgiven they remain' " (John 20:21-23).

After Jesus had returned to heaven the Apostles began giving these gifts to others. They first chose Matthias to take the place of Judas (Acts 1:15-26). Then the disciples chose seven men of good reputation, men full of the Spirit and of wisdom: "These they presented to the Apostles, who prayed and laid their hands on them" (Acts 6:6)—and they became deacons.

At Antioch the Holy Spirit made it known that He wanted Barnabas and Saul set apart " 'to do the work for which I have called them.' Then after further fasting and prayer, they laid their hands on them and let them go" (Acts 13:1-3).

After these two missioners had brought the good news to Antioch, Iconium, Lystra, and Derbe, they went back through each city, "heartening the converts and encouraging them to the true religion. . . . They also appointed elders for them in each congregation" (Acts 14:21-23).

St. Paul reminded his disciple Timothy: "Do not neglect the spiritual endowment you possess, through the laying on of the hands of the elders" (I Tim. 4:14). And also, "I now remind you to stir into flame the gift of God which is within you through the laying on of my hands."

So in our Church today our bishops choose men carefully, lay hands on them solemnly, and send them out filled with graces and gifts of the Holy Spirit, to preach and minister, to baptize and forgive sins, and to re-enact the realities of the Last Supper.

We have four more sacraments; and two of them, at least —Holy Eucharist and Penance—find abundant witness in sacred Scripture. I would like to discuss them, but my space is used up; maybe another time. The sacrament of Extreme Unction is described by St. James: "Is one of you ill? He should send for the elders of the congregation to pray over him and anoint him with oil in the name of the Lord. The prayer offered in faith will save the sick man, the Lord will raise him from his bed, and any sins he may have committed will be forgiven" (James 5:14-15).

We believe that this Last Anointing brings the graces and gifts of the Spirit also—those specially needed by the soul which faces death at close range. And Matrimony, too, brings its gifts: those needed by husband and wife for their many obligations to each other, their children, and God.

Our sacraments are signs of the life and sanctity they put into our souls, as instruments designed by Christ and used by the Holy Ghost. The human lover gives proof of his ardor by a kiss or an embrace. Our Redeemer shows His sanctifying love for us in the signs of the sacraments.

111

14

THE CATHOLIC CHURCH

THE QUESTION

The Catholic Church teaches that the only true religion is the Catholic one; however, I failed to see any reference to the word "Catholic" in either the first or the second Testament.

I would be interested in knowing who first used the word, and when.

Mrs. J. Sokolowski

THE ANSWER

What's in a name, Mrs. Sokolowski? Wouldn't you still be the same person if I decided to call you Mrs. Smith? You were once Miss Somebody, and your identity did not change when you acquired your husband's name.

In the earliest days apparently the organization which Jesus had established was called simply "the Church." It had no rivals; so it didn't need a surname. Then out of reverence it came to be known as "Holy Church"; and it was so designated in the earliest versions of the Apostles' Creed.

As far as we know, St. Ignatius of Antioch was the first to apply the adjective "catholic" to the Church. In a letter which he wrote about the year 110 he used the Greek word "katholikos," which means universal or general. By that time the religion of Christ had spread widely, and St. Ignatius may have meant the word "catholic" to designate the world-wide Church. Many think, however, that he used it in the sense of "one and only"—the true Church. Anyway, it soon

112

came to have that meaning: the catholic Church was the true Church of Christ, as distinguished from various heresies of those early days.

At first "catholic" was just a common adjective, of the type we use without a capital letter. Gradually it came to have a specific, technical meaning—the one-and-only Church of Christ; gradually it became a proper name, in much the same way in which men have acquired surnames in the course of history: the miller and the smith became Mr. Miller and Mr. Smith.

The word "Catholic" first began to appear in the Apostles' Creed about 357: "I believe in the Holy Ghost, the holy Catholic Church. . . ." This wording is still used by most Christians.

In the centuries prior to the Eastern Schism the name "Catholic" simply designated a true Christian—one not a heretic. Then it acquired a more specific meaning: it was opposed to the "Orthodox." And finally, after the Reformation, it became even more restrictive, especially when written with a capital letter: it designates principally that Church which has its headquarters in Rome, with the Pope as its head. This is especially true in Europe, where the adjective *Roman* is considered superfluous.

However, the name is also used today to designate several non-Roman churches which claim historical continuity with the Catholic Church of earlier centuries, for example, Anglo-Catholics and Old Catholics.

This same word is often used by Protestants today—always with a small "c"—to designate that undivided Christian Church of early centuries—the one which gave us the New Testament, the martyrs, and the catacombs. And sometimes "Catholic" is used rather loosely to embrace the conglomerate diversity of churches which we find in the world today—all claiming to be the Church of Jesus Christ.

It might seem that I have answered the question; but I ask you to read on, because there is little meaning in a name unless we know the reality which it designates. You say in your question that we Catholics believe our religion to be the only true one. I want to explain why, and to give you an idea of what we mean by the Church. It is a notion quite different from that which most Protestants have. When we are giving instructions in Catholic doctrine we often find Protestants agreeing with us through the early lessons on God, creation, the Incarnation, and Redemption; this is just what they learned in Sunday school. But we warn them to wait until we get to the Church; then they will hear something new.

To understand the Church we must keep in mind the purposes for which God became man: for which Jesus Christ lived, preached, died on the cross, and rose from the dead. The Church continues those same purposes and makes them effective in the life of each of us.

Jesus came to redeem and sanctify all men, of every land and time. He said He was the way, the truth, and the life; He opens the way for us to get to heaven, provides the truth to lead us there, and shares His life with us that we may live with Him for eternity.

Too many people have a vague sort of notion that the work of Jesus was finished after He had redeemed us by His death on the cross; they forget that His graces cannot be effective in our individual souls unless we receive them. They are not forced upon us against our will. So we must be taught the truths of Christ that we may be prepared to receive Him; the way must be pointed out to us; and we must be brought into union with Jesus that His life may flow to us.

The Church is the means our Savior uses to continue on earth the work He began at Bethlehem and on Calvary: our sanctification and salvation. On Ascension day He left this old world in His visible, human form; but through His Church He remains with us in a real and effective manner, extending Himself to all lands and all centuries.

This is what we mean when we say that the Church is the mystical Body of Christ. It is a new form of body, continuing the work of His physical Body; it reaches out in a spiritual way and embraces all of us who are members of it, giving us the teachings, guidance, and graces which Jesus bequeathed to us while on earth.

The Church is a means of sanctification precisely adapted

to our human nature. We are social beings, dependent on our fellow men for most of our normal needs; we are born, raised, fed, and educated by parents, community, and state. Why should things be different in our spiritual life? Should we not learn our faith, receive guidance, and take spiritual nourishment with the help of others: parents, teachers, and priests who make up the Church of Christ, and serve as agents of the Master in leading us to God?

We are human beings, not angels. We have both body and soul. God made us this way; so it is not likely that He would ignore our bodies in the process of our sanctification. We learn naturally through our senses. Would He teach us divine truths otherwise? And normally we learn by having others teach us.

Nothing can make an impression on us unless it comes to us through our senses. Our sanctification should be impressive; we should be aware of it, that we may appreciate it and co-operate with it. Would the wise Master choose a means of sanctification which could never reach our minds and hearts sensibly?

Considerations like these convince us that we need the Church for our salvation, and that Jesus, wishing to save us effectively, must have established it. But how do we know that He actually did establish it?

This is asking the question backwards. Actually we know about Jesus only through the Church. As we go back through history we find the Church first, and it leads us to the Master, who established it and remains its head. We reach Him because His Apostles followed His command to preach His Gospel. He wrote nothing Himself, and apparently nothing was written about Him for a score of years after His death. The Apostles, the leaders of the early Church, provided in their preaching the material from which the Gospels were written, under the inspiration of the Holy Spirit.

You may well agree that the Church was there, active and growing in those first decades after Christ. But how do we know that He established it? Maybe it just grew up to fill a need.

The Apostles are the key to the establishment of the

115

Church. Next after Jesus Himself, they form the most prominent feature of the Gospels. Why are they there? Were they merely friends and companions? Did they follow the Master about in order to provide a claque?

During the course of His ministry Jesus assigned to the Apostles definite functions. He taught them, trained them, gave them a part of His ministry, the daily benefit of His example, and friendship.

To them was given the privilege of understanding the secrets of the kingdom of God. They were told to go out and make disciples of all nations, and to preach the Gospel to all creatures. They were given authority to govern the flock of Christ, to bind and loose, to feed the lambs and to tend the sheep. They were told to baptize and to forgive sins.

Jesus sent His Apostles out to minister to the people of Israel, gave them specific instructions for their mission, and had them report their success to Him on their return. He promised that He would remain with them all days, even to the end of the world; and that He would send the Holy Spirit, who would teach them and help them to remember all they were to teach.

Jesus told His Apostles that He was sending them just as He had been sent by the Father. They were to teach their disciples to observe all that He had commanded, and "he who hears you, hears Me; and he who rejects you, rejects Me."

The Apostles evidently realized that they had a definite mission to perform, to carry on the work of the Master; and as soon as the Holy Spirit came on them at Pentecost they started preaching, baptizing, ministering, and organizing. The book called the Acts of the Apostles tells how the Twelve put into effect the commands of Jesus; it is the history of the early Church.

We believe that the true Church of Christ—call it what you will—must be the Church of the Apostles. No church can be Christ's unless it dates back to Him. He did not establish His Church by delayed reaction; we see it functioning right after the Holy Spirit came on it.

That Church which Peter preached in Jerusalem and which Paul established at Antioch is the same one which we know

116

from the catacombs in Rome, the one which grew from a persecuted sect to the official religion of the empire. It gradually acquired the name Catholic, and is still around today using that same name.

It is bigger today, better organized, has developed its doctrines and polished its ceremonies, but it has never moved from the Rock of Peter on which Christ built it. It is like a gnarled but thriving old oak which still grows from the same roots it had twenty centuries ago as a sapling. It still has the same cell composition, the same vitality, the same essential nature. It is the mystical Body of Christ now, just as it was then.

For more than nineteen hundred years this same Church has been preaching Christ's Gospel, offering the Sacrifice of the Mass, distributing the sacraments, giving guidance and admonitions, and fighting for its life in a world of indifference and persecution. At no point in its harried history can you find any break in its Apostolic succession, in the continuity of its Popes, bishops, teachings, or membership. Now and again some of its members have left, but that simply meant that they were outside the Church, which was still there as before. Often its properties have been confiscated by the state or turned over to heretical sects. But a man who is injured or robbed does not lose his identity thereby.

This continuity of the Church, its identity with the Church of the Apostles, is one of the marks by which we identify it as the Church of Christ. Change its name, if you wish; it will remain the true Church as long as it is the body of which Christ is the head, as long as the Pope is successor of Peter, as long as its bishops are faithful disciples of the Apostles.

Maybe I labor my point, but we recognize the Church of Christ not so much by its name as by the marks of its resemblance to the Church which Jesus established on the Apostles. I have pointed out one such mark: Apostolicity. There are others which I do not have space to develop for you now; I will just mention them briefly.

1. Unity. Jesus established only one Church; He taught only one doctrine; He provided one Redemption for all men;

117

He has only one heaven to which we are all invited. He prayed that His disciples might all be one—even as He was one with the Father and the Holy Spirit. He talked of one sheepfold, one flock, and one shepherd. His own sanctifying body should not be split into contending bits.

Any observer must recognize that the hundreds of sects of today, vying and disputing with each other, condemning, suspecting, and deriding each other, do not represent the true Church of the loving Master. We believe that only the Catholic Church has the unity of doctrine, worship, and organization which the mystical Body of Christ should have.

2. Universality. Jesus died for all men; He does not exclude any race, class, or group from His graces. He told His Apostles to preach to all nations, to make disciples of all men, and to teach them to observe all things He commanded. One of the principal reasons our Church is called Catholic is that it fulfills these requirements of universality so well. And it is the only one to meet them. The word "catholic" means universal.

3. Holiness. The Body of Christ must surely be holy, because its head is holy and its purpose is holy. But this is not a clear and conclusive mark like the others, because natural goodness can often be mistaken for sanctity; and it is not the policy of the Savior to erect barriers to the flow of His graces; partial faith, good intentions, and generous love may attach nonmembers to the Church by bonds of sanctifying desire, so that holiness shows in them.

Then, too, the human element in the Church, the perversity of individuals, often obscures the basic sanctity of the organization. You have to know the Church well to appreciate the holiness in her doctrines, her religious practices, and her sacraments, and the striving dedication of many of her members. Her roster of great Saints gives a clue.

4. Durability. By promise of Christ the Church is imperishable. He will remain with her until the end of the world, and the gates of hell will not prevail against her. That Church which we call Catholic is the only one which has lasted out the centuries with growing size and vigor.

From all this you may sense how different is our concept

of the Church. It is an external, functioning, visible organization, with teaching and governing authority.

The Church has tangible instruments to be used in our sanctification, the Mass and the sacraments. By our membership in this Church we are spiritually grafted onto the mystical Body of Christ in such way that we share the life of its head, our divine Redeemer.

There is another important phase of the question which I have not been able to touch upon. Peter, the Rock, had a basic role in the foundation of the Church, and his successors in office are the key to its unity, sanctity, catholicity, and durability—as well as the most obvious sign of its Apostolicity. Maybe we can talk of that another time.

15

PRIMACY OF THE POPE

THE QUESTION

In a recent issue of your magazine you asked non-Catholics to submit any questions we might have about the Catholic Church. It seems to me that we can have only one overriding question: "Is the Catholic Church the one and only true Church of Jesus Christ?" If it is, then the answer to all other questions is simply: "The Church teaches that it is so."

The proof of this overriding question revolves around whether or not the Pope is the direct and only successor to St. Peter. How can we be sure that St. Peter intended that the Bishop of Rome be his successor with all the authority given him by Jesus Christ? How can we be sure that St. Peter did not intend that one of the other bishops (earlier converted and established) or a council of bishops should have his authority?

If the Bishop of Rome was designated by St. Peter as his successor, why is it that it was several hundred years before a Bishop of Rome claimed this distinction? The fact that St. Peter died in Rome does not, I think, prove that the Bishop of Rome is the "Vicar of Jesus Christ and successor to the Prince of Apostles."

Please believe me that I am not asking this question with an antagonistic attitude. Nothing would give me greater peace of mind than to have this answered definitely, one way or the other. I married a Catholic, and my children are being raised as Catholics (with my permission). If the Roman Catholic Church is the "true" Church, then I should be worshiping with my family. If not, then we should all be searching elsewhere.

Angelo Adams

THE ANSWER

Your letter is logical and sincere, Angelo. Jesus Christ was God who came to earth to redeem us and take us back to heaven with Him. He established a Church to continue His work of leading us to heaven; and He appointed Peter head of that Church. He made it clear that He wanted us all to belong to this Church. All these things you take for granted; and your conclusion is very sensible: if we find that the Catholic Church is the same Church which Christ established we should most certainly belong to it. If there is no way of finding which Church He established then I don't see why we should belong to any, unless we specially like to listen to sermons or enjoy choir music.

I suppose you know, Angelo, that many people who are trying to find the Church of Christ do not take as many things for granted as you do. Your first point of concern is whether the Popes of Rome are really the true and lawful successors to St. Peter. I don't want to disturb your more basic convictions, but I am sure you must know that some people have wondered whether Peter, himself, was ever Bishop of Rome—and whether Christ ever appointed him head of His Church—and even whether Christ ever established a Church at all.

So maybe we might briefly review these earlier questions. Since you already agree with us on them we will not go into detail, but simply indicate our line of reasoning:

First, Jesus Christ did establish a Church. One of the first things He did in beginning His public ministry was to select His twelve Apostles, and then for three years He taught and trained them carefully. He told them that they must go out and make disciples of all nations, "baptizing them in the name of the Father, and of the Son, and of the Holy Spirit" (Matt. 28:19); and that they should go into the "whole world and preach the Gospel to every creature. He who believes and is baptized shall be saved, but he who does not believe shall be

121

condemned" (Mark 16:15).

He gave them the power of binding and loosing, and made them shepherds of his flock (Matt. 18:18; John 21:16). He prayed for a united flock: "that all may be one, even as Thou, Father, in Me, and I in Thee" (John 17:21).

He frequently compares this Church of His to a body, a kingdom, a sheepfold, and a city. Later, St. Paul calls it a body, of which we are all members and Christ is the head (Rom. 12, 4; I Cor. 6, 15). And Jesus promised that He would remain with His Church "all days, even unto the consummation of the world" (Matt. 28:20).

Second, Christ made Peter the head of His Church. An organization was essential to the work Christ wanted done: teaching, baptizing, binding and loosing, and tending the flock. An organization was particularly necessary because this was a long-term work of tremendous extent and importance. It had to continue for centuries—twenty of them, at least. And it had to extend to every nation and every creature. And heaven depended on it. Souls would be saved by it, or lost if it failed.

An organization was essential; but no organization can be effective or dependable or enduring unless it has a head. How would you hold it together and keep it united and stable and purposeful? If it had no head you could never tell which way it was headed! Feeling the need for authority and leadership, it would either have to grow its own head or else sprout a hundred little nubbin heads which would lead it off furiously in a hundred directions. And then how would Jesus ever keep His promise of remaining with His Church? Since it is divided, would He divide Himself? Would He give His divine blessing to each contradictory teaching as though it were His own Gospel?

Actually, it is very evident from the Gospels and the Acts of the Apostles that Christ did give His Church a head, and that this head was Peter. You have to read the whole story to see how prominently and consistently Peter stands out. He is always the first named in lists of the Apostles; St. Luke even refers to the Twelve as "Peter and his companions" (8:45; 9:32); and the angel at the tomb, after the resurrection, told the women that they should "go, tell his disciples and Peter" (Mark 16:7).

St. Peter is a natural leader, and takes his leadership for granted. The other Apostles accept it without objection, and the Master approves and confirms it. Peter was present at the Transfiguration and in the Garden of Gethsemane. He walked on the water. He took the miraculous catch of fishes, and was told that thenceforth he would catch men. He helped prepare the paschal supper, and was unfortunately prominent at the trial of Jesus. He was the first to enter the tomb on Easter morning.

The texts of Matt. 16:13-20, and John 21:15-17, are so well known and often quoted that we do not need to repeat them here. (On the first occasion, Jesus received a profession of faith from Simon, changed his name to Peter, and promised that he would be the rock foundation of His Church, with the keys of the Kingdom, and the power of binding and loosing. On the second occasion, after His resurrection, Jesus obtained a profession of love from Peter and made him the shepherd of His flock.)

The Acts of the Apostles tell us of many occasions on which Peter exercised his leadership in the early Church, especially in making important decisions on doctrine and policy. We simply haven't space to go into detail.

I don't believe there is any modern historian who doubts that Peter went to Rome and met his death there. So we can take that for granted. You and I rather take it for granted, too, that he was in Rome as an Apostle, doing the Lord's work—not merely as a tourist.

However, there have been some outstanding non-Catholic authorities, like Dr. Adolf Harnack and Bishop Lightfoot, who were not so sure. They readily admitted that Peter was in Rome and died there, but they either doubted or denied that he was bishop there. We can't brush aside eminent scholars like these and pay them no notice, but really it does seem that their arguments and claims are rather gratuitous, based on theories rather than on historical evidence. We might take a brief glance at some of that historical evidence, especially in the early centuries.

123

St. Cyprian was an Easterner, a Cypriot, who became Bishop of Carthage. He was a strong advocate of local authority and an outspoken critic of the Pope in certain matters. However, about the year 250 he wrote that Pope Cornelius had "succeeded to the place of Fabian, which is the place of Peter" (Ep. 55:8).

Firmilian was a contemporary of Cyprian, and Bishop of Caesarea in Cappadocia. He was in violent controversy with Pope St. Stephen on the subject of the re-Baptism of heretics, and he objected that Stephen claimed the right to decide this controversy because "he held the succession from Peter" (Cyprian, Ep. 75:17). Firmilian would have been the first to deny this succession if he could have found any reason for doing so.

Tertullian, a great theologian and historian of the early Church, had become a heretic by the year 220, when he wrote (*De Pudicitia* 21) acknowledging the claim of Pope Callistus that Peter's power to forgive sin had descended in special manner on him. Like Firmilian, Tertullian would have preferred to deny this claim, and he had been at Rome, where he would have found defects in the claim if any had existed.

There are other testimonies. But these which come from enemies of the Pope or opponents of his policies have special value. In those early days, although you argued with the Pope, you had to admit that he was the successor to Peter, the Bishop of Rome.

Now, Angelo, we come to a couple of points on which I may disagree with you a little. You rather take it for granted that St. Peter had the free choice of naming his successor or of deciding on the line of succession in the papacy. Maybe he did, but I am not so sure. Possibly, our Lord, Himself, determined the manner of succession to Peter's office and power. Neither of us has positive evidence, but I believe my theory is as good as yours. At least we both know that there had to be a succession, that the authority and leadership had to continue—that there had to be a head. Where is that head?

If a head is going to be any good it must act like a head. It must lead. It must show its authority. Can you name anyone except the Bishop of Rome who even pretended to be a head during the first eight or nine centuries? A head is no good if it hides. Peter could hardly have left his authority in Jerusalem or Antioch. He still needed it after he left these places and went on to Rome. He gave it up personally when he died, and it is rather natural to suppose that his successor in office would take it up where he laid it down. Any other supposition would have to be proved; and there is no evidence. My own supposition needs to be proved too, and there is much evidence.

St. Clement was the fourth Pope. Linus and Anacletus had filled in the years between Peter and himself. He was a disciple of the Apostles. About the year 95, he wrote an epistle to the Corinthians. He spoke with such tone of authority that Bishop Lightfoot called it the "first step toward papal domination." So you see, Angelo, I can't go along with your supposition that the Bishops of Rome did not even claim for several hundred years the distinction of being Peter's successor as head of the Church. Here is Clement, in the very first century, claiming that distinction and authority, and finding his claim accepted. His epistle was held in such reverence at Corinth that it was read in the churches as Scripture was. St. John the Apostle was still alive at the time, and was certainly much closer to Corinth than Clement was. But here was a bishop of the West directly intervening in the affairs of an Eastern Church and claiming authority to settle the matter, saying that the "word of God comes through us . . . and the Holy Spirit speaks through us" (Clem. 1, 70).

St. Ignatius of Antioch wrote a letter to the Roman Church, in the year 107, in which he acknowledged it as presiding over all other churches, "over the brotherhood of love." Remember that this same Ignatius was a successor of Peter himself—in the see of Antioch. But he made no special claim to distinction for that reason.

St. Irenaeus was very close to the Apostles. He was a disciple of St. Polycarp, who had been named Bishop of Smyrna by St. John. Irenaeus wrote a great work against the Gnostics in which he appeals to the superior authority of the Church of Rome, which has "preserved the traditions of

125

the Apostles" (*Adv. Haereses,* 3, 3, 2). He advises that Christians everywhere should conform to the traditions of the Church of Rome. And he also lists the Popes by name from Linus to Eleutherius, Pope at that time.

St. Victor (189-198) made the clearest assertion of papal authority of those early days. During his papacy there was a violent quarrel between Asia Minor and the rest of the Christian world about the date of Easter. Victor stepped in to settle it; and when a certain Polycrates of Ephesus objected on the grounds that their local traditions came straight from St. John the Apostle, the Pope threatened to excommunicate him. St. Irenaeus intervened, and argued that the Pope should not cut off these churches in Asia Minor from the rest of the Church, because the subject under debate was not a matter of faith. So Pope Victor withdrew his penalty; but the force of his authority remained.

Much later, in the middle of the third century, about 257, St. Denis of Alexandria wrote to Pope St. Sixtus II, asking his advice and a doctrinal decision. At that time, Alexandria was the most important see in the world, next to Rome, but it made early admission of the authority of Peter's see.

In your letter, Angelo, there is a note of urgency and need. You want the proofs to solve your doubts. We can sympathize with you, but I doubt that we fully understand. We are relaxed about these historical proofs. Our faith in the supremacy of the Pope is, in a way, independent of them. We know from the Scriptures that Jesus established a Church and made Peter its foundation and its head. The foundation must last as long as the Church which is built upon it; and if the Church were to lose its head it would certainly be a senseless organization. So Peter must still be there in his successor, and there is simply no question or doubt as to who that successor is.

Since we are sure of that already, we can examine the various proofs with relaxed interest, and note with pleasure how they confirm our faith. You need the proofs as a foundation for faith. We have the faith, and simply watch history back it up. Your sincerity makes us more appreciative of our own blessings, Angelo, and we pray that in God's goodness you may share them.

126

16

INFALLIBILITY

THE QUESTION

I read all I see on Pope John XXIII's plan for a world conference on Christian unity. Many Protestants and Catholics agree that the major item of disunity is papal infallibility. We know there is no substitute for right, and the one in authority must be accepted as right. But there have been a few bad Popes. Many would enjoy having the topic discussed soon.

Ermon Minton

THE ANSWER

Along the highest peaks of the Rocky Mountains runs the line of the Great Divide. A drop of water falling on one side of this line will end in the Pacific Ocean; a drop falling an inch away, on the other side, will end in the Gulf of Mexico. In your question, Ermon, you have put your finger on the vertex of the great divide between Catholic and Protestant thinking. Those who accept the notion of infallibility find Catholicism reasonable and attractive in its totality; those who reject this notion find the Church authoritarian and see no sense in some of her teachings.

Your question mentions only the infallibility of the Pope, but that is merely one aspect of the infallibility of the Church, and a minor aspect in many ways. We must first consider the broader doctrine, and then see how the infallibility of the Pope forms a necessary part of it.

And we should keep in mind the fact that infallibility, itself, is not an isolated doctrine. It makes no sense when it stands starkly alone. It is an integral feature of the Church which Jesus Christ established to continue His work of teaching and sanctifying in the world.

And in all our study of this subject we should remember that infallibility is a supernatural thing. The objection most frequently proposed against it maintains that error is natural to man, and that therefore infallibility is humanly impossible. We have no argument against this claim, but we counter it with the proposition that error is unnatural to God, and that infallibility is easy for the Divinity. This doctrine supposes that God is active in the world, and that He takes a direct personal interest in the affairs of men.

Infallibility is based completely on the fact that Christ established the Church as a teaching instrument to be used by His own divine hands, and that He remains with it and protects it as He promised. Jesus is the eternal Son of the Father; He became man for a definite purpose. He wanted to redeem and sanctify us, to prepare us to share His home in heaven forever. A basic part of His plan was teaching. He wanted to reveal God to us, that we might know and love Him. He wanted to tell us truths essential to our happiness: the glory of our goal, and the safe and sane route to that goal.

Jesus remained on earth only a third of a century to accomplish all His purposes for men. His personal contact was with a few hundred people, mostly of one nation, and all of one or two generations. How was He to bring His teachings and the benefits of His Redemption to billions of other men through twenty centuries and a hundred nations?

It was for this that He established His Church. It is like an extension of Himself through time and space. It brings His teachings and His sanctifying graces to all people of all lands and ages. It brings Jesus Himself to them, and permits them to be united to Him.

In the Incarnation, the Second Person of the Trinity created for Himself a human body, and He made use of this body of flesh and blood to teach the men of Palestine and to die on the cross. Then Jesus created for Himself a mystical Body, and He uses it to continue His teachings and to make His Redemption effective in the soul of each one of us. This mystical Body is his Church, and we the members of it are component cells of His spiritual Body, cemented into living unity by the encircling strands of faith and love and grace.

Jesus is the head of His mystical Body, the pervading source of its light and life. But He does not remain physically on earth to perform the routine human functions of heading up an organization. He appointed Peter and his successors to do this daily work in His name and with His help; and He promised to remain with them all days even to the end of the world.

Once we have this notion of the Church—the Catholic notion which we get directly from the words of Jesus and from His Apostle Paul—then infallibility becomes a normal, integral feature of it. Jesus came to teach men, all men, and the Church is His appointed teacher. Would we expect Him to appoint a teacher that would be undependable, that might be wrong as often as right, that would do a poor job of teaching? Why should He fail miserably in this important work? Success should be easy to Him.

Infallibility simply means that Jesus was just and fair when He required all men to believe His Apostles and His Church. "He who hears you, hears Me; and he who rejects you, rejects Me." "But if he refuse to hear even the Church, let him be to thee as the heathen and the publican." "Go into the whole world and preach the Gospel to every creature. He who believes and is baptized shall be saved, but he who does not believe shall be condemned."

If the Church of Christ had all human capabilities of error the Master would have been unjust in demanding that we hear her under pain of condemnation and accept her teachings as a condition for saving our souls. It sounds like blasphemy even to say it in plain words: "He who believes your teachings will be saved; you are as prone to error as any human institution; so you will probably be teaching insensate drivel half the time; but as long as they believe you they are all right. On the other hand, if they do not believe all the doctrines you dream up and put out, then they shall be condemned. Of course, this doesn't make sense, but I am not asking that they be rational; I just demand that they believe."

129

We hold that the doctrines Jesus taught are of supreme and vital importance to us. He did not go to the trouble of the Incarnation simply to throw out a few pungent nosegays which we might take or leave alone. His teachings are the guide to salvation. If He came to teach us things so important is it not reasonable to suppose that He would have taken precautions to assure our getting His teachings straight?

Infallibility means that Jesus treats us according to our human nature, recognizing our normal need for a teacher. When we were children our parents taught us to speak and to read. In school we relied on our teachers for science and philosophy. And we had confidence in them. We realized that they might make mistakes, and we were sometimes critical and questioning. It is not necessary that a science teacher be infallible; we can check up on him by experiment and observation. He helps us to learn, but he is not the only source of our knowing.

Jesus knew the difficulty of the lessons He came to teach. He put them in simple words, for simple listeners. But they involved doctrines profound and sublime. Man's natural curiosity would try to explore the depths of those doctrines. Man would encounter mysteries to baffle him; and there would be constant danger of his being fouled up in errors. He needs a teacher in theology more than in science. And that teacher must be thoroughly reliable, because there is no natural way of checking up on her. She teaches revealed things. If she is capable of error we can have no confidence in her.

We believe that Jesus is faithful to His promises. He told the Apostles that they should go into the whole world and teach His doctrine to all people, and that He would be with them until the end of the world. But what would be the use of His presence if He could not keep His Church from teaching error? He, the God of all truth, would be ashamed to abide with a Church which teaches error about divine things. We believe that His presence in the Church is not futile; infallibility results from it.

Jesus promised that the gates of hell would not prevail against His Church. The gates of hell represent the forces of evil. And error is the greatest evil that can come to a

130

teaching organization. If the Church is capable of teaching error then the gates of hell have already prevailed; she is a failure because no one can trust her.

Jesus promised to send the Holy Spirit, the Spirit of Truth, to abide with His Church forever, and to teach her all the things she should know. Shall we say that the Holy Spirit is a failure? Yet He would be, indeed, if He did not accomplish the purpose for which Jesus sent Him—if He could not keep the Church teaching what Jesus wanted it to teach.

Either these promises of Jesus were false, or He actually does keep the Church from error—and that is what we mean by infallibility.

We are even more convinced of the infallibility of the Church when we consider the alternatives.

If there is no infallible teaching authority on earth, then we can have no certain knowledge of what Jesus actually did teach. We would be forced to conclude that He did not consider it really important that we have sure knowledge of eternal things. Why then did God become man to teach those things? And why was the Master so forceful in requiring that we must believe to be saved? Would He have us believe errors or uncertainties?

Some people are quite frank about it; they say it is impossible for man to know about God and eternity. He must be content with educated guesses. Consequently they hold that objective truth in these matters is not highly important. As long as our conscience is right we need not worry, no matter how far out in left field we may be.

Some pious people seek to avoid such radical conclusions by making the Bible their rule of faith. In this holy and inspired book they hope to find and understand all that God wants them to know. Of course, there are problems of interpretation; the Bible was written ages ago, in a strange language, on profound and difficult topics. But many people believe that the Holy Spirit solves all these problems by personally guiding and inspiring each one of us in our reading, so that we understand rightly.

This solution offers several difficulties. It would seem to reserve the truths of salvation to the intelligent and the lit-

131

erate, those who can read and understand ancient and profound literature. And through the centuries such learned people have been in the minority. Simpler people have to learn from others, if they are to learn at all. So these others become teachers, without divine appointment, and without infallibility.

Persons who take their faith from Scripture alone must face a dilemma: either they run the danger of error in their private interpretations, or else the Holy Spirit makes them severally and individually infallible. And that would seem a much more complicated process than making a teaching Church infallible.

Even casual observance makes us wonder whether private interpretation actually works the way it is supposed to. It has resulted in myriad conflicting notions and hundreds of denominations; and there is no logical basis for reunion, except the unsavory one suggested earlier: that truth doesn't really matter.

In the Catholic Church, infallibility is the key to unity and security. If you were to make a survey throughout the world you would find the Church everywhere believing and teaching the same doctrines and following the same norms of morality, just as she has believed and taught and followed down through the centuries. Obviously infallibility does not keep every Catholic from error, nor does it keep each priest and bishop from teaching false doctrine, but it does provide a corporate guidance which will see and dispel these errors, or make it clear that the individuals who hold them are cutting themselves off from the teaching of the Church.

We usually find that the general infallibility of the Church causes less difficulty to non-Catholics than the special doctrine of papal infallibility. And one of the reasons is indicated in your letter, Ermon: you don't see how the Pope can be infallible, since some bad men have held that office. The answer is that infallibility does not keep the Pope from sin. It does not depend on the morality or the intelligence of the man, but is inherent in the office.

Neither does it inspire him, as the writers of sacred Scripture were inspired. It does not give him a revelation; it merely helps him teach the revelation already given by Jesus Christ.

And it does not keep him from personal error in matters of doctrine and morality; it only keeps him from leading the Church into error in this area—and uniquely in this area, because he is humanly capable of leading the Church through some dark and devious routes in practical policy.

The bishops at the Vatican Council, who defined the doctrine of papal infallibility, knew all about those bad Popes. They also knew about the good and saintly ones. But the Pope is infallible because he is head of the Church, not because he is a holy or learned man. In some inscrutable way the Holy Spirit guides him so that the Church, under his leadership, faithfully teaches the doctrines of Jesus Christ, without fear of error.

Pope Alexander VI is popularly considered a notorious example of a bad Pope. His family name, Borgia, has become a synonym for vice, even though it was also borne by saints and statesmen. He became Pope through politics, and he was a poor example to his people; yet the doctrinal integrity of the Church was never for a moment in danger. He was actually an efficient administrator as well as a sound believer. And the Holy Spirit probably hovers closer when the helm is in wobbly hands.

Even the personal orthodoxy of the Pope is not essential to infallibility. Pope John XXII is an interesting example. He was one of the Popes at Avignon in the fourteenth century, and the last legitimate Pontiff to bear the name of our Lord's beloved disciple until it was taken by our present Holy Father.

John XXII was not a bad Pope, but he had some strange ideas on the nature of life after death, and he was not reticent about expressing his opinions. His attitude caused disputations and confusion among theologians; but out of it all came clarification of doctrine and a humble admission of error by the Pope. The Holy Spirit probably smiled through it all; His task of keeping the Church on the straight doctrinal path was hardly put to the test.

These instances may be helpful to those who, like yourself, Ermon, think papal infallibility is much more comprehensive than it actually is. The Vatican Council was rigidly restrictive

133

in defining it as a doctrine. In general, the Pope's infallibility is confined to matters of faith and morality—to those pronouncements which set forth the teachings of Christ, or the immediate and necessary implications of Christ's teachings. And even in these doctrinal matters the Pope is infallible only when he speaks in a solemn and official manner to the whole Church, as head of the Church.

The technical name for such formal declaration is "ex cathedra"—from the chair. A king gives solemn decrees from the throne; a judge pronounces sentence from the bench; the Pope speaks officially from the chair of Peter, who was appointed head of the Church by Christ.

The Pope is not infallible for his own benefit, but for the sake of the Church. He participates, in a special manner, in the general infallibility of the Church. He is the head, and the Church follows where he leads. If he were not restricted he might lead the whole Church astray. For sake of clarity we might define papal infallibility, in a negative and partial way, as that protection which Jesus Christ gives His Church so that the Pope cannot lead it into error. It is a negative definition because the Pope actually leads the Church to positive understanding of the teachings of Christ; and it is an inaccurate definition because it considers the Pope as an entity separate from the Church. He is actually the head, an integral part of the body.

Seldom does the Pope make formal use of his infallibility for the definition of doctrine. In 1854 Pope Pius IX declared the doctrine of the Immaculate Conception. In 1950 Pope Pius XII made solemn pronouncement of the Assumption of the Blessed Virgin Mary into heaven. Both definitions had been carefully prepared by several years of repeated consultation with the bishops of the world, by the profound study of theologians, and by the formal recommendations of the cardinals. And neither doctrine was controversial. The definitions were merely solemn statements of things the whole Church believed without question.

In the course of centuries the Church has found it necessary, at various times, to define doctrines which were the subject of acute controversy. This has nearly always been done in a general council, like that which Pope John XXIII has recently called. Twenty councils of this kind have been held in the course of the Church's history.

It is doubtful that our next general council will make any important doctrinal definitions; there are no controversies which need decision. But like the other councils, it will be a practical and impressive example of the infallibility of the Church. Assembled there will be all the official teachers of the Church, acting as a unit, with the Pope as the head. The bishops who will be there are the successors of the Apostles, whom Jesus sent out to teach His doctrines to all nations, to make disciples of all men. And as Peter was the leader of the Apostles, the one to whom Jesus gave the keys of authority, the one whom He appointed shepherd of His flock; so the successor of St. Peter, Pope John XXIII, must convoke the council to make it official; either he or his delegate must preside over it, and he must approve any definition it makes to guarantee its infallibility. The body acts in union with the head, not at variance with it.

17

PAPAL SPLENDOR

THE QUESTION

I was baptized a Catholic when an infant but was never reared in the Catholic faith. I've been studying the Catholic Church, and believe that all its teachings point to the true Church. The problem I have is in regard to the Pope.

I've never been able to understand all the grandeur given to the Pope. As I see it, the Pope should be the humblest of the humble; instead, he rides on a gold chair, and our Lord rode on a donkey. Catholics kiss his feet and our Lord washed the feet of His Apostles. He lives in a palace, and our Lord had no place to lay His head. He is called Most Holy Father, and our Lord called Himself a servant of servants. The Pope sits on a throne, and our Lord, because He is humble, refused this offer given Him by Satan.

I hope you can give me some help on these points of Catholic teaching.

Mrs. C. E. Lowder

THE ANSWER

You know, Mrs. Lowder, that we Catholics consider the Pope to be the successor of St. Peter, the rock upon whom Jesus built His Church. He inherits through a long line of two hundred and sixty predecessors those "keys of the kingdom of heaven" which Christ gave to the first Pope; he has the power of binding and loosing, of ruling the Church on earth, as Christ's Vicar and representative; and he is the shepherd of the entire flock of Christ, through the appoint-

136

ment given Peter: "Simon, son of John, dost thou love me? ... Feed my lambs ... Feed my sheep."

It is important that we the members of the flock of Christ recognize and accept our appointed shepherd, that we appreciate his position and authority, hear his voice and heed his teaching, and pay proper reverence through him to the One whom he represents. We might learn these things from books and sermons; but ceremonies and symbols will teach us better.

We have both body and soul, and our intellect does not operate well without our senses. We understand best what we see, and find it difficult to believe without external evidence. We can form an abstract idea of papal power and position, but that idea is cold and unconvincing compared to the lively impressions of a visit to the Vatican. There you see the authority and dignity of Christ's Vicar proclaimed in sign and symbol which teach and attract.

All the riches and beauties of the world belong to the Lord; He made them to serve His purposes and proclaim His glory. We must not despise them or hold them evil. They can serve us both materially and spiritually, as God made the whole world to serve man. They can make us better and wiser and happier here on earth and help fit us for heaven later. But we can abuse precious and beautiful things, too, even as we can use the base and ugly for our destruction.

Glory, honor, power, dignity, respect, veneration, splendor, and pomp are all good things in themselves. They can impress and edify, bring happiness and joy, teach profound lessons, and lead to sanctity. It is for these purposes that the Church uses them in her ceremonies. But they can also be emblems of pride and vanity, symbols of tyranny and injustice, and implements of indolent luxury.

It is a basic principle of Catholic thinking that all God's creatures are good. Even snakes and poisons have their purposes. "God saw that all He had made was very good." But the angels could rebel, and man could use God's choice tree, in the middle of the garden, for his own destruction.

In American minds the royal trappings of pomp and power have long been associated with autocracy, oppression, and despotism. We have seen them often misused, and we are likely to forget, unless we stop to think calmly, that these things can and do serve good and pious and practical purposes. Yet we readily accept the stars of the general and the robes of the judge. We protest that clothes do not make the man, but we know that the stars give force to orders and the robes add dignity to decisions.

Even in a democracy formalities are requisites of human respect. Why does a good officer demand a snappy salute? Why change the guard at Buckingham palace? Why the ceremonies of diplomatic protocol?

Are they so much tomfoolery? Or so many trappings of vanity? We know that they are neither. They can be readily abused, as can all human things: but they are essential to the smooth functioning of human relations.

The Church learned in early centuries the need of ceremony: of vestments, candles, music, and beauty in all its forms; these ceremonies were needed to teach and impress and inspire, to symbolize and emphasize the deep truths of faith and the needs of man in prayer.

For similar reasons the Church learned in early centuries that there must be ceremonies and symbols attached to an office of authority and dignity; otherwise that office will not be generally recognized. It is true that a strong man will reveal his power in a subtle, unobtrusive manner to those who know him well, or even to those who come into direct contact with him. And it is equally true that critical courtiers quickly see through the glittering pretense of a weak sovereign, and spread the word abroad. But how many people know the man of authority well enough to discern his hidden power?

Royal splendor, when rightly used, manifests to the people the dignity and authority of the king's office. And though the human element may show through, either sadly or gloriously, he is honored, in principle, not for his personal qualities but because he is the head of the nation, the figure of its power and unity. God grant that either the king or the Pope be a strong and good man personally; but if he fails to measure up, the established dignity of his office may carry him through.

The Bible gives us evidence that God does not repudiate pomp and glory. When Solomon built the Temple of the Lord at Jerusalem his dimensions were vast and lofty, his construction sumptuous, and his decorations rich with pure gold, "most precious marble of great beauty," "a veil of violet, purple, scarlet, and silk," and "an altar of brass twenty cubits long." The Lord approved all this richness and elegance and was pleased with the sacrifices offered to Him from the splendid midst of it. The glory of the Temple taught the people loudly that the Lord is the greatest and that nothing is too good for Him—in our own love and service, as well as in His house.

While Jesus proclaimed the virtue of poverty by the simplicity of His personal life, He gave evident approval of the splendor of the Temple. He frequently visited it; out of zeal for its sanctity He drove out the money changers; He paid the Temple tax even though not personally obliged; and He praised the poor widow who gave her two mites to its treasury.

In thorough accord with His perfect humility, Jesus was not averse to showing forth His glory and accepting the homage due His divinity, when such manifestation or tribute served the purpose of His Messianic mission. He took Peter, James, and John up a high mountain with Him that they might see the glory of His Transfiguration. He was definitely pleased with the signs of honor and love shown Him by the sinful woman in the home of the Pharisee. He praised Mary of Bethany for her personal attention to Him, and He strongly defended her when she poured on His head the precious ointment from her alabaster jar.

These are small symbols of honor and glory, of course, but they were far from negligible in the simple surroundings in which they occurred. And even the event cited here as an example of Christ's humility, His riding on a donkey, was actually His greatest public triumph. It was His only open acceptance of the homage due the Messias, and it was impressive enough to precipitate His trial and execution.

Our Lord rode on a donkey, but He rode in triumph, in the manner the prophets had foretold, while the crowd greeted Him as King and Savior. In His country the gentle ass was a creature of nobility. With its solemn gait it had given faithful service to the ancient kings of Israel. There were no limousines in those days. It is true that a noble Roman on his powerful horse might have found our Lord's royal mount ridiculous; but that was just as well, since the crowd did not want to give offense to their Roman masters with a parade. But to the leaders of the Jewish nation there was nothing of the ridiculous about it. They recognized it as the symbol of the Messianic triumph of the promised King of Israel, a procession worthy of the Son of David. To them it seemed that "the entire world" had gone after Him.

With their limited facilities the crowd at Bethany and Jerusalem gave Him all the pomp, ceremony, homage, and acclaim they could. They gave their cloaks as a saddle and spread their best garments along the road as a carpet. They cut branches from the trees to garnish His path and carried other branches as symbols of honor and welcome. They crowded round Him singing and shouting out, "Hosanna! . . . The King of Israel!" They ran on ahead in joy and enthusiasm that they might wait to greet Him again and again.

The glorious ceremony of the Pope, his being carried into St. Peter's on his golden chair (which is really not gold at all), is reminiscent and strongly symbolic of the triumphal entry of Jesus into Jerusalem, and the response of the crowds is in many ways similar. The great difference is that the tribute to the Pope, while aroused by his gracious personality and encouraged by his personal virtues, does not end with him but is paid through him to the One whom he represents.

On his triumphal day in Jerusalem Jesus accepted the humble homage of His enthusiastic people, and was pleased with it. When some of the Pharisees told Him to quiet his disciples His reply was, "I tell you that if these keep silence, the stones will cry out." In the triumphal ceremony of His Vicar in St. Peter's He accepts similar homage through His representative, and is pleased with it. He accepted the homage at Jerusalem because it was rightly due the Messias; because it proclaimed His mission to the world; because it was a lesson and inspiration to men and served the plans of God.

140

He accepts the tribute to His Vicar because it is an acknowledgment of the office which He established on Peter; because it proclaims His Church and its mission in the world; and because it teaches men and inspires them with love for His mystical Body, the earthly means of their salvation.

In principle, the Popes are humble men, like the Master they represent, and the majority of them have been so in actuality. Daily meditation teaches them that the gentle Savior whom they should imitate is better known for Calvary than for Bethany; and that they are successors of a rough, blustery fisherman, whose only importance came from the choice of the Master. They never forget that their own most fitting title is the age-old one of "Servant of the Servants of God."

When a good and saintly Pope is carried down the marble aisle of St. Peter's in all the color and splendor of a pontifical procession and receives the enthusiastic acclaim of his people, it may well make him the humblest man alive, deeply aware by painful contrast of his own personal unworthiness. And a holy Pope living amid the historic magnificence of the Vatican may well preserve in his own soul the spirit of poverty, reserving for his own use a few simple rooms, as recent Popes have done, eating frugally, limiting his comforts, working hard, and letting responsibilities crowd out personal friends and normal pleasures.

We know that not all Popes have been like this. Some have gloried in their power and used it ruthlessly for ambition and gain. Some have lolled in their luxuries. And some have built costly monuments to their own memory, grasping to themselves the honors paid to their office. But these were the Popes of sordid periods of history, not likely, we hope, to occur again.

Men, however, remain human in all ages, and the Pope is a man centered in the spotlight, burdened with the highest office, and expected to portray every virtue. Some may again falter. But Christ's Vicar will still be honored.

Whether the Pope is good or bad, whether he humbly accepts homage as due his office, or avidly seeks it for his personal glory, the Catholic people demand that proper recognition and respect be paid to the office which Christ established, and through it to Christ Himself. If the ceremonies of St. Peter's were suppressed they would have to be restored because of the pressure of popular petition. If the Vatican did not exist it would have to be built as a necessary symbol of the Pope's position in the world.

It may not seem like a fair way of answering your question, Mrs. Lowder, to ask you whether or not you have ever been to Rome, seen a pontifical ceremony in St. Peter's, or had the memorable thrill of an audience with the Pope. The tenor of your question indicates that you would have to answer, "No"; then I could say: "Well, you have never been there, and I have; so I know more about it than you." I might squelch you by such argument, but I would hardly convince you. And yet I must say that I am sure the experience would give you a different attitude.

The first time you would see the Pope carried into St. Peter's amid the blare of trumpets and a blaze of lights, you would probably be overwhelmed with the brilliance of it all, maybe a little annoyed with the noise and crowding informality of the spectators, and certainly impressed by the affable, friendly, gracious, sincere personality of the present Pope. And then, as you became more familiar with the ceremony, you would realize how unforgettably it teaches to all the people the sanctity and importance of the Church, which Jesus established for our sanctification, and the dignity and authority of the Pope, who is the personal represenative of Jesus Christ as the head of His Church.

And the first time you entered the Vatican you would probably be amazed at the size and splendor and complexity of it all, but as you became more familiar with it you would realize that its very antiquity teaches forcibly of the ancient Church which comes from the Apostles, while its vastness and variety point out the universality of the Church which was established for all men of all ages.

Personally I know that having seen the Pope carried in solemn procession on his colorful chair I would not want to see him come into St. Peter's any other way. If he decided to walk—or come on a donkey—I would join the Roman crowd in disappointed protest. And I would feel very sad if the splendor of the Vatican were to be decreased or the colors of the Swiss Guards toned down.

While the Vatican is one of the greatest palaces of the world, it is by no means a place of personal luxury for the Pope. It houses many of the administrative offices of the Church; has one of the most ancient and valuable libraries in the world; contains a great museum of classical sculpture and medieval craftsmanship, a gallery of precious paintings, rooms decorated by Raphael and other masters, and the Sistine Chapel with the famous frescoes of Michelangelo. Most of these things of value and beauty now belong to the world, and are made available to thousands of daily visitors.

Splendor and magnificence can be a mere pretense, a whitened and glorified sepulcher to hide the vacuity or fetidity within. And some persons, recalling sad days of past centuries, think that the pomp of the Pope is like that. But splendor and magnificence are also the good things of God which can be used for His glory and can be external symbols of inner truth which they teach with impressive clarity. They can even be a humble shield for personal poverty, simplicity, and deep spirituality; and with recent Popes that is what they have been.

18

EASTERN RITES

THE QUESTION

While visiting Washington, D. C., recently, I had a chance to attend a service in a Greek Uniate Catholic church. I understand that this is one of several groups owing allegiance to the Pope at Rome.

I would be interested in knowing more about these rites. How many are there? How do their Masses and worship differ from those of the Roman Catholics? How did they come about?

Wayne Kastl

THE ANSWER

At least twenty groups of churches in the world, Wayne, are generally called Eastern rites. They are thoroughly Catholic but differ widely from the Western or Roman rite in language, ceremonies, customs, and traditions. The Eastern churches are usually classified into five general rites because of similarities of history or ceremonies: Byzantine, Alexandrian, Antiochian, Armenian, and Chaldean.

Many American Catholics are surprised to learn that there are ten million real Catholics in the world who receive Holy Communion under the forms of both bread and wine; baptize their babies by immersion and confirm them as part of the same ceremony; and make the sign of the cross from the right shoulder to the left. Many of their priests are married men, and most of them wear long beards. Many of them still use the old Julian calendar, which is thirteen days behind our Gregorian calendar; thus, they celebrate Christmas on our

144

January 7. And when they recite the "Our Father" they conclude it: "For thine is the kingdom, and the power, and the glory. . . ."

A study of the Eastern churches would greatly broaden our grasp of history and geography, give us a better understanding of the unity and universality of the Church of Christ, and teach us needed humility. Members of the Roman rite belong to a majority group; they are forty times as numerous as all Eastern Catholics together. And majorities are likely to be proud.

It would be salutary for Roman-rite Catholics to realize that these Eastern rites are as sacred and venerable as our own, and that some of them are more ancient. They are no less Catholic, no less pleasing to God, and no less a part of the mystical Body. Only in numbers are Western Catholics more important than they. And in the early centuries they outnumbered Catholics of the West.

The majority of these Eastern Catholic churches are well represented in the United States; it is strange that so many of us know so little about them. You live in Illinois, Wayne, so you would have to travel only a few miles from your home to find a variety of Eastern churches: Chaldean, Melkite, Maronite, Ukrainian, and Ruthenian, including Hungarian and Croatian. They are all in Chicago.

A Roman-rite Catholic might go to Confession, receive Communion, or assist at Mass in any of them. He would find their ceremonies strange at first, and would be confused by their use of Syriac, Arabic, and ancient Slavonic languages; but he would probably find several of them using English, too, at least for part of the Mass, which they call the Sacred Liturgy.

If the visitor watched carefully he would find in their liturgy many of the same features which are in the Roman Mass: readings from the Scripture, the Creed, the Sanctus, the Consecration and Elevation, the Pater Noster, the breaking of the Sacred Bread, and the Communion. Most of the churches use leavened bread, which they mingle with the species of wine; and they give Communion with a golden spoon. But no matter what the rite, it is the same Sacrifice

145

which Jesus first offered on Calvary; and He is received whole and entire under one species or two.

A Roman-rite Catholic would not be permitted to have his children baptized or confirmed in one of the Eastern churches, except for a peculiar reason and with special permission. But neither could a member of one of these churches bring his children to a Latin parish to be baptized, without similar permission, as long as there is one of his own churches nearby. The Church is strict about this so that the different rites will be kept intact, and so that no efforts may be made to take members from one to the other; Baptism is a sign of membership.

A Latin Catholic might wish to marry a girl of Eastern rite. The Church would bless such a marriage joyfully, but she would insist that it take place in his parish rather than hers. On the other hand, if his sister wished to marry a man of Eastern rite the marriage would take place in the parish of her fiancé. In either case, the bride might join the rite of her husband, or retain her own rite, according to her preference. But the husband could not join the wife's rite without special permission from Rome; and the children would belong to the rite of their father.

In general, every Catholic belongs to the ancestral rite of his fathers; and no one can transfer to another rite without permission of the Holy See.

I once knew a young woman of Eastern rite who wished to join the Carmelites. She had grown up in a Roman-rite parish, and knew nothing of her own Eastern Church, but the Carmelites could not accept her until she had received sanction from Rome. She obtained it easily, but it was so worded that when she later left the convent, before profession, she returned automatically to her Eastern rite.

Two groups of the Ruthenian Byzantine rite are represented in Washington, D. C., and throughout our country generally.* The larger group is called Ukrainian. Its members

* The Byzantine rites are those which developed in various lands and languages under the influence of the Church at Constantinople—ancient Byzantium. They are often called Greek Churches, but the name is inaccurate. Byzantine is better.

came to this country from Galicia, on the northern slopes of the Carpathian mountains. It was a part of the Austrian empire when our early immigrants came from there, about 1880. Then, after the first World War, it was given to Poland. Now it is divided between Poland and the Ukrainian state of Soviet Russia. Its members have known much persecution.

Two Ukranian dioceses ,more properly called Apostolic exarchies, exist in the United States, one in Philadelphia and the other in Stamford, Conn.* They have 177 parishes in 21 states, besides the District of Columbia, with nearly 300 priests and more than 300,000 members. They are the largest Eastern-rite church in the world; before the second World War they had five or six million members.

The other Ruthenians in Washington came originally from the southern side of the Carpathian mountains. Their early immigrants came largely from the kingdom of Hungary, that area which is now eastern Czechoslovakia. Their Apostolic exarchy, at Pittsburgh, includes also Byzantine-rite Hungarians and Croatians. They have 188 parishes in 14 states, with 214 priests and nearly 150,000 members. Before the war they numbered well over a million throughout the world.

The Ukrainians and Ruthenians are very similar in rite and racial origins, but quite distinct in national traditions and customs. Both use the Old Slavonic language in their liturgy, but the Ruthenians retain the original forty-three letters which were devised by Sts. Cyril and Methodius in the ninth century, while the Ukrainians have simplified it to thirty-four letters. The Ruthenians in the United States now use English for many parts of their liturgy, and have generally adopted the Gregorian calendar.

Numerically the next most important rite in the United States is the Maronite. I first learned of this rite when I was studying canon law in Rome. On my right in class was a dark-bearded young priest from Lebanon, who had sharp eyes, quick wit, and a friendly manner. His breviary reminded me of the Koran—though I had never seen the Koran. He told me that it was printed in ancient Syriac, a language akin to the Aramaic used by our Lord. They use this language

* A third Ukranian exarchy has recently been established in Chicago.

147

together with Arabic in their liturgy. He was proud of the fact that no heretics or schismatics use his rite; all Maronites are Catholic. They are the largest Christian group in Syria, and have forty-three parishes in the United States.

After the Ruthenians' the next largest Byzantine church is the Romanian. Their rite is very similar to the Ruthenian, except that they use their own Romanian language in it. They have seventeen churches in the United States; the original members came from Transylvania, which was then a part of the Austro-Hungarian empire.

An outstanding cardinal during the conclave which elected Pope John XXIII was Gregory Peter XV Cardinal Agagianian, Patriarch of Cilicia of the Armenians, and successor to Cardinal Fumasoni-Biondi and Cardinal Stritch as Secretary of the Congregation of the Propagation of the Faith.

Cardinal Agagianian's rite is quite distinct from all others, and his people are widely scattered in various parts of the world. Their original homeland is now part of the U.S.S.R.; their chief center is now Syria. Before his recent return to Rome, Cardinal Agagianian lived near Beirut. The majority of Armenian people are schismatics who use the same liturgy as the Catholics. They all use the Armenian language in their ceremonies. There are six Armenian Catholic parishes in the United States.

Cardinal Tappouni also helped elect Pope John. Tappouni is the Syrian Patriarch of Antioch. In the seventh century, after the Arab conquests, most of the Syrians became Mohammedans; but there are still many Christians there, of one rite or another, and about half are Catholics. Cardinal Tappouni's rite is sometimes called "pure" Syrian, or West Syrian, although it is also found as far east as Iraq, where the cardinal was born, and in India, where it is the rite of some 75,000 Thomas Christians, called Malankarese, who came back to the Catholic Church about thirty years ago, under their archbishop, Mar Ivanios.

The Syrians use the ancient Syriac language for the principal parts of their liturgy, but much of it is in Arabic or, among Indian Catholics, in a dialect called Malayalam. Between five and six thousand Catholics of this rite live in the

United States, but they have no church of their own.

Tradition tells us that St. Thomas the Apostle went to India, and from earliest times evidences of Christianity have existed along the west coast of that great country. One large group, called Malabar Catholics, came back to the Church more than three hundred fifty years ago. They now number a million and belong to the Chaldean, or East Syrian rite, which is also used by the Chaldean Catholics of Iraq. The United States has two Chaldean churches, one in Chicago and one in Detroit.

The Near East offers a variety of rites. Go to Beirut and you will find most of them in the same city. Many Catholics of the Near East, in Syria, Palestine, and Egypt, belong to the Byzantine rite. They are called Melkites. Although they are scattered in various countries they are unified and well organized under the Patriarch of Antioch, who probably has best claim to being the direct successor of St. Peter in that ancient and venerable see. The language of their liturgy is Arabic. In the United States there are twenty-five Melkite churches in fifteen states.

In the early centuries of the Church the Patriarch of Alexandria was widely influential. His city was one of the largest in the world, capital of the rich province of Egypt. But heresies injured the Church of Egypt, and then Mohammedanism dealt it a stunning blow. Today there are only two small groups of poverty-stricken churches which are direct descendants of the Alexandrian rite. One is in Egypt, where the native Catholics are called Copts. The other is in Ethiopia, where they are often called Abyssinians.

The Copts use the ancient Coptic (Egyptian) language, with a few Greek words and increasing amounts of Arabic. The Ethiopians use an ancient Semitic language, called Ge'ez. They use drums, cymbals, and bells to maintain the rhythm of their chant. There are no Coptic or Ethiopian churches in the United States.

I have mentioned most of the larger groups of Eastern churches; but there are still several Byzantine churches I have not named. These churches are often called Greek, but only one should be given this name, and it is very small, indeed. If

149

you searched closely, you would find a few Byzantine-rite Catholics in Greece, on Cyprus, and at Istanbul. They are really Greek Catholics; there are a few in the United States, but they have no church.

There are still a few Russian Catholics scattered through the world. They have two churches in California and a chapel at Fordham University, in New York. A few years ago one of the priests from the Russian center at Fordham visited our parish and celebrated the Sacred Liturgy in the Byzantine rite. Our people packed the church, and with a little instruction were able to follow the ceremonies intelligently, to join in the responses and the chant, and to receive Holy Communion under both species.

No church has a more fascinating history than that of the Italo-Greeks, who are now often called the Italo-Albanians. The southern part of Italy had been settled by the Greeks from the ninth century B.C. Pythagoras lived in Calabria; Archimedes was a Sicilian. The Church in southern Italy claims foundation by the Apostles themselves; and it is quite possible that Sts. Peter and Paul both landed in that part of the world on their way to Rome. In the eighth century the Byzantine rite and influence spread in that area, and the people became subject to the Patriarch of Constantinople.

After the Eastern schism, in the eleventh century, the Byzantine church in southern Italy gradually died out, but then about the year 1500 it was revived by immigrants from Albania. Today about twenty towns in Calabria have Byzantine churches, and about five in Sicily. Many members of this Italo-Albanian church came to the United States, but they found no churches of their rite here, and they did not feel at home in the Latin churches; so many of them lost their faith.

That about completes the list. Bulgaria has a few Catholics of Byzantine rite, and a few Catholic Serbs live in Yugoslavia. In theory, the Georgian Catholic Church still exists; but even the Georgian Orthodox have been largely suppressed by the Communists. Most of the Slavic Catholics have been severely persecuted, and their churches have become largely disorganized behind the iron curtain.

In Rome, a special congregation takes care of the needs of the various Eastern churches. Our former Apostolic Delegate, Cardinal Cicognani, was secretary of this congregation before he became Secretary of State. During the past dozen years various books of a revised canon law have been issued by the Holy See for all Catholics of the Eastern rites. This new law does not aim to change their ancient and proper customs. It rather tries to preserve intact their traditional differences of rite, and keep them from becoming Latinized —especially in countries like America where the Eastern Catholics are a small minority, and are often subject to Latin bishops.

A rite is a collection of services or ceremonies by which we seek to worship God and sanctify our souls. Jesus gave us the essentials of the Mass and the sacraments; these can never be changed; they are common to all rites. But He did not give the ceremonies which surround these essentials to make them solemn and impressive. These developed by popular practice; but in the course of centuries these popular practices gradually became uniform in certain areas—standardized by the influence of the great centers of authority: the Patriarchates of Rome, Alexandria, Antioch, Constantinople, and Jerusalem.

The Church has never tried to impose general uniformity of rite. Her essential unity requires that all her members, everywhere, have the same faith and morals, belong to the same mystical Body, and be united to the same visible head on earth. Languages, ceremonies, specific prayers, and popular customs are not essential. It is the Church which counts, not the rite. The motto of the Church has always been, in words which I think come from St. Augustine: "Unity in essentials, freedom in nonessentials, and charity in all things." Her individual members would do well to follow her lead in all three phases of her motto.

19

SALVATION OUTSIDE THE CHURCH

THE QUESTION

In the August, 1956, issue of the *Catholic Digest,* I read, with a lump in my throat, "Farewell to a Chaplain." A Catholic priest was preparing a Lutheran to die a happy death. "If a Lutheran were really sick, what prayers would he want a Catholic priest to say for him? Ernie, we're going to say those prayers, together, and then I'll help you make an act of contrition; and if you don't mind, I'd like to say some prayers out of my own ritual."

The article does not say that the Lutheran chaplain was baptized, but I pray that he has gone to heaven.

A few years ago, five American Protestant missioners in the jungles of Ecuador gave their lives in their zeal to spread Christianity among the savage Indians of that country. If they had been Catholics they would have been martyrs to the faith.

They were not baptized into the Catholic Church, but again I pray that they have gone to heaven.

The Catholic Church is adamant in its attitude that there is but one Church and that it is the weighty responsibility of everyone to belong to it. "Outside the Catholic Church there is no salvation." But can we believe that the Lutheran chaplain and those five Protestant missioners were not saved?

Catholic priests whom I have asked concede that good Protestants will go to heaven as surely as bad Catholics will go to hell. The Baptism of desire, they say. Well, all of us desire to go to heaven.

152

Then, why all this bother about conversions into the Catholic Church and why all this worry about proselytism? Do not all Christians confess the brotherhood of man and the Fatherhood of God? Does this not make all religions the same?

Rafael F. Alcazar

THE ANSWER

With confidence I join you in prayer, Rafael, that this Lutheran chaplain has gone to heaven; and in the midst of my prayer I can hardly restrain a smile as I think of his astonishment in passing through purgatory on his way there.

It may interest you that many of the Catholics of Ecuador do consider those American Protestant missioners to be martyrs—rather unwise martyrs (at least in their missionary methods), but sincere, brave, and generous. They died for the love of Christ in an heroic effort to make His love known to savage pagans. If they who died with such sacrifice and devotion are not in heaven with Jesus, whom they loved so ardently, then despair might well run rampant amid the rest of us.

So, just as you imply, Rafael, we Catholics are pretty sure that innumerable non-Catholics go to heaven. Your question is: How do we account for their getting there since we keep insisting—with St. Cyprian and the Fourth Lateran Council— that "outside the Church there is no salvation"?

We stress the fact that the Church is necessary to salvation precisely that we may avoid the conclusion you imply in the final paragraph of your letter: that all religions are essentially the same; boil them down to their least common denominator and take your choice. The Church would rather seem intolerant than give her approval to the proposition that error is equal to truth.

The doctrine of no salvation outside the Church is understandably offensive to those who are outside the Church. Their immediate impression is that we are condemning them, personally, to hell. And then, when we start explaining that we don't really mean them, individually, they decide that we

153

are hedging, and that in our clumsy efforts to apologize we contradict ourselves and fail to make sense. Actually, this doctrine is full of good, sound theological sense, when we understand it as the Church has always taught it; and it need not give offense to anyone who grasps its full meaning and its logical necessity.

It might help to clarify our explanation if we could make it clear from the beginning that the Church's intolerance (if you wish to call it that) is directed toward error itself, and not towards the person who is in error. It is directed toward false institutions, posing as churches of Christ, rather than toward the people who belong to these institutions. The Church tries to imitate the love of Christ without letting charity blind her to the importance of truth. She recalls how He blasted the errors of the Pharisees, and then made friends with individual Pharisees like Simon and Nicodemus.

To emphasize this distinction we might state the doctrine in terms of the institution: Jesus Christ established only one means of salvation, His Church. He established no other churches as rivals or auxiliaries. And His Church is essential in His plan of sanctifying and saving men; not merely helpful, but necessary. He could have worked out a plan of salvation without the Church, but He actually chose to sanctify men in a unified group, using one to help the other: "Go and . . . make disciples . . . baptizing them in the name of the Father. . . . He who hears you hears Me. . . . If he refuse to hear even the Church, let him be to thee as the heathen and the publican."

We believe that the Church is the unique means of salvation because the New Testament and the early history of Christianity make it clear that Jesus established only one Church.

We believe that the Church is the one means of salvation, because our Lord prayed for unity: "Yet not for these only do I pray, but for those also who through their word are to believe in Me, that all may be one, even as Thou, Father, in Me and I in Thee; that they also may be one in Us, that the world may believe that Thou hast sent Me" (John 17: 20-21). And He also yearned for unity: "And other sheep I

154

have that are not of this fold. Them also I must bring, and they shall hear my voice, and there shall be one fold and one Shepherd" (John 10:16).

Our belief in this doctrine is based on the exclusive nature of truth. The mathematician will not tolerate the proposition that two plus two equals five. Truths about God are far more important. Two churches cannot be equally good if one teaches truth and the other teaches something contrary to that truth. The teaching organization which Christ established must be zealous for the truth Christ taught.

We believe that the Church is the exclusive means of salvation, because she was sent to teach the entire doctrine of Christ to all men: "Go, therefore, and make disciples of all nations, . . . teaching them to observe all that I have commanded you; and behold, I am with you all days, even unto the consummation of the world" (Matt. 28:19-20). It is this constant presence of Christ with His Church which makes it unique. He made no such promise to any other organization.

The Church would deny her very nature and divine institution if she were to admit rivals on equal or similar basis. It is her task to incorporate all men of all times and places into the one fold of the one Shepherd. How can she seek to embrace all, as her divinely given duty, if she recognizes a right of other churches to embrace some of them? There must be "one body and one Spirit . . . one Lord, one Faith, one Baptism; one God and Father of all" (Eph. 4:4-6).

This quotation from St. Paul suggests the principal reason for our belief that the Church of Christ is the unique and unified and exclusive means of salvation: it is the Body of Christ. "For as the body is one and has many members, and all the members of the body, many as they are, form one body, so also is it with Christ. . . . Now you are the body of Christ, member for member" (I Cor. 12:12, 27).

If you try to split up Christians into many churches you seek to dismember the Body of Christ. The Church hates heresy because it tears the Body of Christ apart.

We are sanctified by membership in the mystical Body of Christ. He is the head of that Body, and life flows down from Him through the Body to all its members. There is only one

155

Redeemer, one Mediator, through whom we are saved: "I am the way, the truth, and the life. No one comes to the Father but through Me" (John 14:6). And we cannot come to Christ except through His Church, the Body of which He is head.

So you see that as long as we are speaking of institutions, this doctrine that "outside the Church there is no salvation" is rather simple. Christ established only one Church; it is the only means He gave us for our salvation. All others are false. However, when we consider the members of these churches as individual human persons, the problem becomes complicated. We run into questions of moral guilt and inculpable error, of sincerity and good faith and love. We need to be psychologists as well as theologians, and even then we can only estimate the relationship, in will and conscience, between a man and his Maker.

This fact we do know: that the evidences for the one true Church are not so apparent and convincing that they command immediate acceptance, especially in the mind of the man who has been raised from childhood to regard the Church as an ancient ogre. It is entirely possible for him to be wrong without guilt. And God will blame us only for the things of which we are personally guilty.

Each man's salvation is his individual concern. The Church cannot save him in spite of himself. Even almighty God will not do that. The Church is the means of bringing him to God, the instrument for bringing God's graces to him, but the rest is a matter of his own will. To her members the Church brings the means of salvation directly and fully, but some of them reject her offerings. To those outside her membership, the Church may bring these same means of salvation indirectly and partially, and many of them may accept all she brings.

If the Church is to distribute divine gifts to those who are not her members there must be some connection between her and them. There is such a connection, although it is sometimes rather tenuous. It is the bond of implicit desire of membership, which is embedded in good faith and honest unawareness of error. Good faith is faith of a sort; and good intentions cover a multitude of faults.

This membership in the Church by desire is similar to Baptism by desire. It is possible for nonbaptized persons to love God so completely for His own goodness that they attract the divine love in return, and that love sanctifies them. Likewise, the person who is not a member of the Church may be so good and so desirous of doing the will of God that he would not hesitate to join the Church if he really understood that it is the true and only mystical Body of Jesus Christ. Actually he is convinced that the Church is something quite different, and he spurns membership in it. Yet his good intentions amid his honest error bind him unknowingly to Christ's instrument of salvation.

This membership by desire is entirely subjective; it has none of the outward effects of real membership. But the Church, in her charity, fully recognizes its reality and effectiveness. She knows that it can often produce a devout and holy Christian life, and that Saints and martyrs may result from it. She would have us regard our separated brethren with humility and charity, with tolerance and hope. But she does not want our charity to blind us to the importance of truth. There is danger that we come to imagine that doctrine doesn't matter, that sincerity and honesty are the only things that count. That is why she insists so strongly that she is the only source of salvation established by Christ.

Among non-Catholic Christians, membership in the Church by desire is often bolstered by various links of truth borrowed from her and by some powerful means of grace retained from their former membership in her. They believe in God, the Father almighty; in Jesus Christ, His only Son; in the Redemption, and our sanctification in the grace of Christ; in a moral code based on justice and charity; and in an eternal life of reward or punishment. These great truths are terribly important, and they are all Catholic. The Church kept them alive and intact for fifteen centuries to give them as a priceless heritage to those who deny her. Those who believe them have much of Catholicity deep in their souls.

Besides these basic teachings, most non-Catholic Christians have kept some of the sacraments. Practically all have Baptism. Some schismatics have Holy Eucharist and Holy

157

Orders. All have Matrimony, even though many may not recognize its sacramental character. We believe that an infant validly baptized in a Protestant church is an adopted child of God, filled with the grace which makes it heir to heaven. Its spiritual position deteriorates only as it learns and accepts false doctrines. Its direct and internal relationship with God changes only as it becomes guilty of heresy. If its faith remains honest, firm, and undoubting it may never become guilty.

Even the pagan has something of Catholicity in him. It may not have come to him directly through the Church, but it is one in substance with the teachings of the Church, e.g., that there is a Supreme Being, that man has an immortal soul, and that there is such a thing as moral right and wrong, with reward and punishment as sanction.

These people outside the Church, then, are saved by what is Catholic in them, not by anything non-Catholic in their position. Their rejection of Christ's Church would ruin their chances of salvation if they did it voluntarily and intentionally —if they were guilty of it. Their good faith saves them, and their good intentions provide a sanctifying link with the Church of Christ.

Pope Pius IX summed it up in a talk he gave more than one hundred years ago. "It must be regarded as true that he who does not know the true religion is guiltless in the sight of God so far as his ignorance is invincible. Who would presume to fix the limits of such ignorance, amid the infinite variety and difference of peoples, countries, and mentalities?"

And we might add, in the same vein, who would presume to fix limits to the mercy and forgiveness of God? We do know that God wishes all men to be saved, and that to every man who has the use of reason He gives graces sufficient for salvation. Only a man who rejects those graces will go to hell. Who but God can read the heart of a man? The theologian can define invincible ignorance, but he cannot determine its prevalence; neither can he measure the effects of divine love in the soul of man. "He who has my Commandments and keeps them, he it is who loves Me. But he who loves Me will be loved by my Father, and I will love him and manifest

158

myself to him" (John 14:21). "If anyone love Me, he will keep my word, and my Father will love him, and We will come to him and make our abode with him" (John 14:23). When God makes His abode in the heart of a man, that man is holy.

20

THE CONVERT

THE QUESTION

For the past eight years my family has lived next door to a wonderful Catholic family. We are Protestant, but our two families have always been matter-of-fact and outspoken about our difference in religion, each observing his own devotedly.

My neighbor's son and I dated through high school and college. Now we have fallen in love, and I would be happy to become a Catholic in order to marry him. After living next door for so long I am aware of what this religious change might entail, but I feel it could work out because of our mutual love, respect, and long friendship for each other.

Our families would like to see us together for the rest of our lives, but they are concerned lest the religious transition prove too great an obstacle to our happiness. We both feel that our deep love for each other and our faith in God will help me to become a good Catholic wife and mother.

Please tell us if you think my willingness and sincerity is enough for the basis of a happy marriage with this Catholic boy. Is the emotional involvement of becoming a Catholic as great as my family seems to think?

D. Allen

THE ANSWER

Maybe you have noticed that I like to address my questioner by name; it helps to keep my answer direct and personal. But you do not give me your name; so I am going to call you Dee. I hope you do not mind. It is an abbreviation for

Dolores, one of the many titles of Mary, the Mother of Jesus; and if you are going to become a Catholic it is important that you get on familiar terms with her and learn to love her as your own spiritual Mother.

Let me answer your question in a general way first, Dee, and then we will consider the details and qualifications. Your willingness and sincerity alone are not enough, but they are the essential requisites. Starting with them, I am sure that you will be able to establish the basis for a happy marriage with your Catholic boy friend. And I am confident that the change in religion which you contemplate will not be an obstacle to your happiness, provided that your conversion is thorough, based on faith and conviction, and not just a change of convenience. Make sure that it is your love for God which draws you into the Church and not merely your love for the boy next door.

My confidence is based on experience. Each year I see many people make this change, and increase their happiness by it. Only rarely do I find one who shows regrets, and nearly always this is a person whose conversion resulted from expediency and was not complete, internal, and supernatural.

You know that changing your religion is not like changing your cloak. It is a major transformation within yourself; it requires effort, soul-searching, and adjustment; it needs prayer and God's grace; and it involves your mind, will, and emotions. It is bound to alter in some measure your relationships with your family and friends. It will change your attitude toward life and the world in general, and even toward yourself. And even more, it will deeply modify your relationship with God Himself.

That makes it sound formidable, doesn't it, Dee? Actually it is a gradual process, usually without serious shock. You are by no means ready to make the change yet; you will have to study and pray and receive instructions for many weeks. Right now, apparently, the motives which prompt you to become a Catholic are mostly good natural ones: your love for your future husband and your desire to establish a happier home through unity of religion. These are good beginning motives; you start taking instructions because of them. But don't let these motives alone lead you into the Church.

In the course of your instructions you will learn what the Church really is and what she teaches. You will see the evidence for the faith, and its reasonableness. You will be convinced by logic, attracted by the beauty of ceremony, inspired by doctrine, and consoled by prayer and the hope of forgiveness. Thus, gradually your motives will become faith and conviction, a love of Jesus and His Church, and a desire to save your soul.

Unless these supernatural motives do come to you in the course of your instructions, then you must not become a Catholic. The basic change involved in conversion is that of belief and conviction. If you are only halfway convinced that you are entering the one true Church of Jesus Christ, you can expect troubled times ahead. If you are only partly sure of the truth of Catholic teachings, you may expect your doubts to increase when you are challenged by the rigors of Catholic living.

Normally, most of your intellectual difficulties should crop out and be solved in the course of the instructions. Some problems and questions will remain, but they can be eliminated gradually by further study and prayer. Some of them will never appear until you have committed yourself, when they may arise out of perversity. But none of them will be serious if you will face them and seek immediate solution of them. Once God has given you faith He will not take it away as long as you make reasonable use of it.

For many converts the most painful change is external; it involves family, friends, customs, and social standing. Often, parents are violently opposed, even those who have no firm religious convictions of their own. They would tolerate anything but Catholicism. You have a great advantage here; your parents are understanding and tolerant.

But what about your friends? You must be patiently ready with a witty word or a gracious smile to fend off their digs. And you should be armed with ready answers for some of their stock objections. You will be told that you are forsaking freedom of conscience for authoritarian morality, imposed by the hierarchy; that you are sacrificing independence of

162

thought for the binding strait jacket of infallible doctrinairism; and that you will no longer be free to worship God in the intimacy of your own soul, but will be compelled by Church law to reach Him through the priest and the sacraments and the intermediaries of Saints.

By the time you are a Catholic you will realize how ridiculous these old chestnuts are, but how are you, an amateur, going to handle them when they are thrown at you red hot? You will be accused of narrow-mindedness by those experienced in bigotry, and you will be taunted with superstition by those who worship mirages. And even in this age of satellites, you may still hear whispers of convent horrors and priestly machinations. These things will not disturb your faith but they can readily ignite a slow burn.

The third phase of conversion is emotional. This emotional adjustment to Catholicism may well be the hardest and longest, and in your case it will be complicated by the fact of your adapting, at the same time, to a new life as wife and homemaker. However, it will be made much easier by the bolstering example of your Catholic husband, and by the encouragement of his family, with whose religious life you are already familiar.

You indicate that you have had a fairly firm adherence to some church, Dee; but if your religious background is typical of that of many converts, you have probably been a bit uncertain and indifferent about religious truth. If you become a thorough convert, your attitude will change. You will have firm doctrinal conviction and a clear and certain concept of the goal of life. You will have sureness in your steps toward that goal, awareness of sin, and certainty of forgiveness. In all this your emotional adjustment will be pleasant. You will delight in the serenity and security of it all.

If you have lived amid the usual prevalent prejudices, your acquaintance with the reality of Catholicism will be another emotional relief. About your only problem here will be that of restraining yourself. You will be fired with a driving enthusiasm to go out and convince your bewildered former associates that their prejudices are unfounded, their fears and hatreds unwarranted, and their misunderstandings im-

163

mense. Converts usually make the most enthusiastic apostles, in the manner of St. Paul.

Because of the good will you manifest you probably will have no great difficulty in adjusting to the traditional morality of the Church—to those phases of her moral teaching which most moderns disregard or repudiate: on divorce, birth control, abortion, sterilization, and various facets of sexual conduct. As a good and loving wife you will be as opposed to divorce as any born Catholic, and as an ardent convert you will accept Catholic ideas about birth control firmly. But don't brush this matter aside too lightly; later you might feel that you were not really warned. The rules are not easy; babies are quickly conceived, financial demands are real, and problems of health and fatigue cannot be ignored. Unless you fortify yourself with a thorough understanding of moral reasons you cannot hope to be a hero, and you can easily develop resentments which will break out in frustrated protests.

You know about the laws of the Church, Dee. In your personal observance of them they should offer you no particular difficulty. The born Catholic does not always find it easy to get up and go to Mass on Sunday; for you, the novelty of it, combined with your determination to learn to follow that missal, may well give added incentive. Catholics are likely to be prejudiced against fish; you probably grew up to like it. Lent will be a minor hardship, but it is not easy for us veterans, either. It is penance, not fun. And as for contributing to the support of the Church, that will be mostly your husband's problem—and, besides, it will involve the same kind of money you were accustomed to contribute as a Protestant.

It is as a wife and mother that you will find yourself burdened by Church laws. I hear that it is quite a problem to get a husband and six children out of bed, washed, dressed, variously fed, and on their way to church. Of course, some of them will not want feeding, because they will receive Holy Communion. But others will demand their breakfast. And, of course, you will have to get to Mass somehow, yourself.

If you take the entire crew with you there will be crying

164

or restlessness. Dowagers will glare; you will feel embarrassed; and your prayers will be distracted. But God will be pleased with you, even if some of your neighbors are not. On the other hand, if you leave some of the younger ones at home, it will probably mean that you and your husband will not be able to go to the same Mass. It will give you a feeling of separation in something intimate: your prayer, sacrifice, and Communion.

As a homemaker, you will find the laws of fast and abstinence a headache. Are you familiar with Catholic calendars? Better study one now; you will be consulting it often in years to come, trying to figure out whether it is a day of total abstinence or half abstinence, whether the children can eat meat even if you and your husband can't, and whether you can have three full meals or only one. And even if you get the law of it straight you still have the problem of menus: how to make fish appetizing fare for youngsters, in spite of the bones; or how to diversify salmon, select cheese, disguise eggs.

The marriage laws of the Church will offer you no problem personally. You will comply with them happily in a beautiful nuptial Mass, which your own family will find confusing but impressive. However, like most Catholics, you will find some things about marriage laws perplexing. Why cannot this particular neighbor of yours receive the sacraments? How can this divorced hussy get married in the Church? And too bad about that poor girl down the street; she cannot get married again, even though her first husband was a rat.

In time, you will learn that this whole marriage business is complicated. It will help to learn the general principles well, and then practice humility and charity, recognizing that intimate details of personal problems should not be grist for the gossips' mill.

About one thing I must warn you, Dee. It is Confession. I know that you have been warned before. My warning is less frightful than that of your friends, but more factual. As a convert you will not like Confession—at least not all aspects of it, and not right at first.

You will like the comfort it gives you after it is over—the assurances of forgiveness and love and grace. But this business of checking up on yourself and facing the seamy realities is no fun. Neither is it pleasant to admit your personal failings to someone else, even when that someone is a sympathetic priest, kind and understanding, hidden anonymously behind the confessional screen.

Born Catholics have only a passing distaste for Confession, as they might have for a healthy medicine. Their ease comes from familiarity. So my advice to you is to face up to the problem and conquer it by getting used to Confession as fast as you can. Go to Confession every week for several months. Then you will have the thing licked and you can enjoy its consolations in leisure and peace. If you keep putting it off at first, and dreading it, you will find it looming in fearful distortion.

And another warning, Dee: beware of scruples. Maybe you have no inclination to them, but some converts have. The intensity of their conversion, the firmness of their resolutions, the exaltation and novelty of their spiritual experiences, and their new awareness of sin in all its variety and repugnance, all combine to stir up latent anxieties. They begin to worry, to question past actions in the light of new knowledge, and to wonder just what is sin and what is not. If you should encounter fears and uneasiness go quickly to a good spiritual advisor, maybe the priest who instructed you, and tell him the whole story frankly.

A new car is advertised to give you joyful power and smooth mileage. If it fails to do so you quickly take it back to the garage for proper adjustment. Your new religion should give you peace and security; if it does not, you need some spiritual adjustments to help you fit better into it.

Some details of Catholic practice may not appeal to you. A few converts never learn to like the Rosary. I would encourage you to work hard at it, because your happy use of it will be rewarding. But if it never becomes your favorite prayer, don't worry! You can be a good Catholic without it. Some converts are slow in developing ease and familiarity with the Blessed Virgin Mary. Think of her always in association with her Son; she gave Him to us, and she gets all her meaning from Him. She will lead you closer to Him than you ever came before.

It will help, Dee, to keep a clear distinction between things which are essential and those which are merely good or helpful. You may be interested in pictures, medals, statues, and holy-water fonts; on the other hand, you may find most of them dreadfully poor art. Your attitude toward them need not affect the thoroughness of your Catholicity.

But the Mass: that is essential. You will be quite lost for a while in the intricacies of the missal and the unfamiliarity of Latin, but you will probably be intrigued, too, by the mysteries, vestments, and ceremonies. Whatever your difficulties, face them and work at them, because the Mass really matters. And the same is true of Holy Communion, and all the sacraments. They are essential to Catholic life and devotion. Try to understand them well and use them often.

Don't expect the Catholic Church to be as cozy and friendly as your Sunday school was. Catholics are rather businesslike about Sunday Mass. You may be slightly shocked by a certain air of efficiency and dispatch. But stop and think of the number of people to be served and the frequency of the services. It is possible that the Sunday sermon will lack the polish you have known. And you may hear more about money; after all there is the parochial school and convent, the central high school, and the diocesan seminary—to say nothing about Peter's Pence and the Propagation of the Faith.

Unless you belong to a little community parish you will probably not find much standing around and visiting in front of the church, and certainly not in the church. You may not find one of the priests at the door of the church to greet you as you arrive or leave. He is probably hearing Confessions, teaching catechism, meeting with the Holy Name men, or counting the collection.

There is one thing you will just have to find out for yourself: the intricate effects of the parochial school. What tales your children will bring back! Sometimes Sister would be horrified to hear herself thus quoted; sometimes she really said it.

And in summing it all up, I would have you notice this, Dee: you give up nothing of a spiritual or supernatural nature when you become a Catholic; and you acquire many spiritual advantages. There may be social losses, sentimental detachments, and material deprivations, but spiritually you will find everything on the plus side. Any positive spiritual values you had before, you can keep and develop. To them you will add the Mass and the sacraments, and regularity in prayer. Of course, you prayed before. But have you prayed regularly, at least twice a day? And have you fasted, and done penance, and made a retreat?

At first you may find it strange to recite prayers that you have learned, or to read them from a prayer book. But you will soon find that it is the only way to maintain regularity and frequency in your prayers. And remember that if there are some prayers you do not like, choose others which please you—and keep yourself always free to pray in your own words, as you did in your Protestant days.

There is really only one thing I would like to spare you in the fervor of your new conversion; it is the bad example of careless Catholics. Your ideals will be high, and you will be shocked by indifference to those ideals in Catholics who have evidently spent a lifetime blunting them. On the other hand, I am sure that you will be inspired by the exalted example of good Catholics, as numerous as the bad. And from them all you should learn one big lesson about the Church: every single member of it is a human being, from the Pope on down to you and me. We are weak, strong, good and bad, like all other men. We have great advantages; our Church is divinely founded, the Holy Ghost breathes life into it, and it is Christ's own mystical Body; it has the Mass and the sacraments, together with Christ's own teaching and example. But while some of its members are saints, others don't really try at all, and some don't try hard enough.

21

PRIESTS

THE QUESTION

I am a non-Catholic; I have many Catholic friends, and one of them gave me two *Catholic Digests,* as she knows I read a lot. Thus I came across the section, "What Would You Like to Know about the Church?"

I do hope my question does not hurt anyone; but it has made me wonder. My question is this: What have you a right to expect from your priest?

The way some of my Catholic friends speak when they talk of their priest makes them sound as though they are frightened, and also that they could not speak to their priest outside the Church.

I do hope this question doesn't sound as if I am finding fault. I would like to understand. I would like to feel I could go and talk to anyone doing God's work.

Mrs. Betty Jane Stapleton

THE ANSWER

My dear Mrs. Stapleton, your question certainly has no hint of faultfinding or offense. It seems sincere. And no priest will be surprised at it. We are all aware that there is something about the Roman collar, the life of celibacy, the eminence of the altar, and the reverse side of the confessional screen which sets us a bit apart. Most priests have encountered inquiring attitudes similar to yours amid the hearty friendliness of the locker room, the formal exchanges of the business world, and even in their own guest parlors.

We suspect that there are people who would like to visit us, to inquire about the Church or to discuss personal problems, who are kept away by a vague fear of the unfamiliar. They know they would not be entirely at ease with us—at least not right at first.

We would like to think that our own Catholic people are free of this timidity. From infancy they have been acquainted with priests. They have known them at catechism; in the school, confessional, the church; at social functions. Yet actually we know that not all Catholics are at ease with us. I cannot forget the painful awe with which I regarded my own pastor long ago, though he was kind and jovial—in an enigmatic way—and turned out to be one of the best friends I ever had.

A question like this one can hardly be answered by explanations. Personality relationships are involved. Each priest is different, an individual, just like the rest of one's friends. The authorities put us all in black suits, behind the same backward collar. They teach us all the same subjects in the seminary, and help us form our characters along the same spiritual principles. But they never pour us into molds.

There are all kinds of priests: staid and formal, friendly and jovial, polite and boorish. Some are intellectual and spiritual; others seldom crack a book, except their breviary and missal. Some are generous, others miserly. Most are reasonably good; a few are bad.

One of the greatest faults of priests may be that they are spoiled by respect. Our Catholic people have an ingrained reverence for the sacred dignity of the priesthood.

Priests have it, too. The disillusionments of human weakness have not dimmed our faith that we are the ordained ministers of Christ, empowered to offer Sacrifice in union with Him, sent out to teach in His name, and to confer His sanctifying graces through the sacraments. Our people keep us pleasantly aware of our eminence by their daily deference, occasional special honors, and frequent generosity. A person on a pedestal is not the easiest to approach—not in a close and equal way, at least.

The meshing of two personalities is a reciprocal problem.

170

I might be friendly and frank; but if you are timid and suspicious it will take us quite a while to become good friends. The priest's personality problems are not much different from those of the doctor. Both need to inspire confidence. Both must put a client at ease, mingling in right proportion respect and informality. Not everyone has by nature the bedside manner. Ordination does not change character. Reversing a collar does not invert natural traits.

Mrs. Stapleton, I think the only satisfactory answer to your question is for you to meet a priest personally. I am fully aware that you may not like the first one you meet. But since I must answer with words, let us speak of ideals.

Pretend you are a Catholic. What do you have a right to expect of your priest? First, that he be a saint, but a modern saint. He should have business acumen, social grace, oratorical skill, entertaining wit, good fellowship, and fatherly sympathy, combined with all the standard virtues.

Did you ever see a priest like that? If you do, show him to me. I will enshrine him as a paragon.

But you really do have a right to expect that your priest be a saint; by the ideals of his vocation he is a living, breathing replica of Christ before His people. He preaches the word of the Master. He should manifest in his own life the inspiring example which led the men, women, and children of Palestine to Jesus, which made them reform their lives and imitate His virtues.

You can expect your priest, as the modern representative of Christ, to offer Mass regularly and devoutly. Mass is a continuation of the Sacrifice which Jesus offered on Calvary. It is the practical daily means by which the people receive the benefits of that redemptive Sacrifice.

You can expect your priest to administer the sacraments carefully, generously, and zealously. The sacraments are divinely designed instruments for bringing souls into sanctifying union with Christ. They bring the Savior to men, with all His love, forgiveness, and grace.

You can expect your priest to be a man of learning. It is his task to communicate to his people a gleam of eternal wisdom. This can be done effectively only in terms of temporal knowledge. So the priest has been given a long and careful formation in intellectual things. But I should warn you, too, that sometimes the distractions of the ministry have dulled the acuity of his intellectual interest.

It is not directly indicated in the Gospels that the priest should be a businessman. But modern needs of the Church require that a pastor be a capable administrator, alert to raise money, pay bills, keep buildings in repair, pacify the janitor, keep the housekeeper happy, the Sisters content, and the assistants at work. The doorbell and the telephone, after the alarm clock, are the jangling monitors of the pastor's day.

Jesus did not send His Apostles out to be social lions. But the modern priest is expected to be a civic leader, organizer of campaigns, guide for the Boy Scouts, inspiration to the sodality, referee for the women's aid societies, patron of parties, hearty fellow on the street. And in all these activities he must be at once broad-minded and righteous, "good Joe" and saint, wit and mystic, genial and restrained, effusive and dignified. Something has to give!

Most of the things you can expect of the priest are summed up in his title: Father. He gives spiritual life in Baptism, and nourishes it to strong maturity with the food of the Holy Eucharist. He maintains the house of the Lord, the spiritual home of the Lord's children. He binds up wounds in Confession, hears complaints, helps solve problems, gives advice, with occasional reprimands, and sometimes loses patience with his brood.

I have been holding up shining ideals, but I do believe that this title "Father" actually means a great deal in the relation of Catholic people to their priest. It comes from them with entire naturalness and spontaneity. It conveys respect and affection. It implies a closeness of relationship which is usually a reality—in part, at least.

We fully understand that people who are not Catholic and have had little close association with priests will find us distant, puzzling, and a bit forbidding. Breaking through that barrier is one of our daily problems. But if Catholic people feel frightened and ill at ease with us, it must be largely that pedestal problem. They tend to keep us up there, even though they see us wobble and fall off occasionally.

Our people may criticize us and gripe about us; they may see our faults and deplore them; but they persist in endowing us, in their own minds, with most of the virtues, often more than we deserve.

We do have faith: an understanding and acceptance of the teachings of Christ and His Church. This faith bolsters us through the myriad problems of priestly and pastoral life. It is our duty to teach this faith to others, inspire them to hold it firm, and give them the example of living it faithfully. If our faith were to weaken, our daily lives would become dreary. The Mass would lose its meaning, prayer would be routine, and daily duty a harsh burden.

We do have hope: a confidence in God's mercy broad enough to embrace our whole flock. We hope that they will be forgiven and saved along with ourselves. The shepherd's hope must be broad, because he knows that he can get to heaven only by taking his sheep with him. He knows his personal unworthiness to serve as instrument of their salvation. Yet it is through his ministry that grace comes to his people.

Most of us do have charity: a sound practical love of God and our neighbors. Before us is the picture of the Good Shepherd, who loved his sheep so much that He laid down His life for them. It is charity which keeps our zeal alive, and makes us aware of the value of souls. And it is charity which maintains our position with our people. The pastor who really loves his flock can be less than ideal in many other respects and still accomplish much spiritual good, and his people will love him and find ready excuses for any failings they observe.

Our people expect us to be just, and generally they think we are. Justice is the basic virtue which regulates the relationship of one person to another, and a pastor's life is a constant succession of varied personal relationships, each requiring that he be fair. Even as with charity, a man may fail greatly in other virtues and still do a job acceptable to

173

his people as long as he treats them justly.

Fortitude, strength, courage, and perseverence are basic daily needs of the spiritual life. You have a right to expect your priest to be firm and consistent in his own life, that his spiritual force may sustain his people in their waverings.

Prudence comes next after faith and charity as an essential virtue for the priest. Even his justice must be administered with prudence or it will seem harsh and irritating. And even charity without prudence might become sentimentality.

Temperance is the virtue by which a man keeps himself under control. The priest has double need of it: for himself and for his flock. To the moralist, temperance is much more than sobriety. It has various divisions. First come modesty and chastity. So important are these virtues that the priest takes a vow to respect and foster them. They are the professed virtues of a priest. So you can be really surprised if you find him notably lacking in them.

You have a right to expect your priest to be sober, and maybe you know of some who have failed. Say a prayer for them; their weakness has made their ministry suffer, indeed.

If you visualize the priest as a copy of the Good Shepherd, you will expect him to be gentle, kind, patient, and tolerant towards his flock. His temper is often tempted, but it is not supposed to break control. His firmness need not be harsh; and anger, however righteous, should not flare beyond restraint.

The ideal priest is humble. He seeks the welfare of his flock, not his own glory. He knows himself and his abilities, and he uses his talents fully, but he never overestimates himself. He is not diffident or apologetic, but he seldom preens himself. For the glory of God and the good of souls he tries to do the best job he can: to preach forcefully, sing melodiously, talk engagingly, build beautifully, and counsel wisely; but he seeks not to exalt himself. He accepts criticism as readily as praise. He shows forth his true self without excuse or pretense.

When you meet that ideally humble priest, let me know. I have known a few, but I would travel far to meet another.

You have a right to expect your priest to be obedient to

his Master and to the Church. You can certainly expect that he be honest in speech and action. His word is usually accepted without question. He aims to be frank without being blunt. He hopes to inspire confidence, but never to betray it. He guards a secret as faithfully as he tells the truth.

Certainly the ideal priest must be a religious man, one in union with God. Religion is his business. So you can expect him to be faithful and devout in prayer, meditation, and the reading of the Scriptures. You will nearly always find a rosary in his pocket, and calluses on his knees.

The most prominent virtue of the ideal priest will be zeal, inspired by the love of God and seeking the good of souls. It gives the shepherd ardor for the safety, welfare, and increase of his flock; it sends him out to seek the strays and to help with problems; it makes him restless in striving for the spread of truth and virtue. It keeps him busily on the job, distracted by details of the ministry.

All these things, and many more, you have a right to expect of your priest. You will hardly find them all combined in any one. Yet our own people know that we should have these many virtues, and they tend to credit us with them. So if they are sometimes frightened of us, so that they can hardly speak to us outside the church, it may well be due to the reverence with which they mount us on that pedestal. Or it might also result from our gruffness, seeming arrogance, frowning mien, or rigid reticence. The collar changes not the man.

Now, after all those words, Mrs. Stapleton, if you really want your question answered, you should try to get acquainted with a priest. He won't hurt you; and the odds are that you will like him.

22

CELIBACY OF THE CLERGY

THE QUESTION

Recent news tells of a runaway priest who was found married and employed. I am a Methodist and my wife is a Catholic, and she hasn't been able to convince me that it wouldn't be best for all concerned if priests could marry. I feel that the law should be revised so that they could lead a more normal life, be more qualified to advise the married on their problems, and help do away with malicious stories that are made up about priests and nuns. If priests have a choice, more than likely they wouldn't marry anyway, but those who wished to could do so. Couldn't your law stand revising?

Jack Hilterbrant

THE ANSWER

I like your question, Jack, because it is asked with evident sincerity and sympathy. But it is a delicate and disturbing question for a priest to answer. Many of us know of someone who has sadly defected in the manner you describe. Thus the problem touches us closely, and we don't like to talk about it. Then, too, most of us have personal experience in the hardships of heroism in this matter, and we hesitate to bring our intimate experiences out into the open. Yet I think that most of the priests who know best the problems and casualties of celibacy would vote to retain it. Maybe we are just stubborn and idealistic, but we can hardly imagine the priesthood otherwise.

Anyway, your question must be honestly faced if we are to explain the Catholic Church, her beliefs and practices.

I should point out right in the beginning that our discussion concerns only that vast major branch of the Church which is called the Roman rite. In most Catholic Churches of Eastern rites a married man may be ordained, but a priest cannot contract a marriage after his ordination. In the Roman rite, however, laws of ancient standing and rigor refuse ordination to a married man whose wife is still living, and prevent an ordained man from marrying. Moreover, in all areas and rites of the Church, celibacy is an invariable requirement of monastic and convent life. Monks and nuns take vows before God and the Church that they will lead lives of unmarried chastity.

Most people outside the Church find such celibacy strange. There are skeptics who doubt that the vows are kept, and cynics who ridicule efforts to keep them. They hold such restrictions unnatural, and inviting frustration.

Catholics take clerical celibacy for granted. Like the priests, they could hardly imagine the priesthood otherwise. Centuries of custom and tradition bolster their personal experience, which dates from earliest childhood. They just can't picture a priest's wife or children, or a Catholic rectory with nursery and playroom.

Few social customs are entirely good; few established practices are entirely bad. We must balance the pros and cons, and then choose the better course. Thinking persons both in and out of the Church are aware of objections to clerical celibacy; I am not certain that all are aware of the reasons that favor it. So I will give a brief résumé of both. I will start out with the objections you propose and then add a few I have frequently heard or have realized myself.

I think that you have hit upon the strongest objection yourself: the great difficulty of chaste and happy observance of celibacy, at least for men who must live in a world geared to marital life and sexual indulgence. Only men of strong character, high purpose, and inspiring ideals can succeed at a task so tough; and these can hope for complete success only if they are constantly bolstered on all sides by God's graces. Such difficulties when they are bested for supernatural purpose become a source of merit for heaven. But they are not always vanquished readily; so there are two types of undesirable results:

1. The restlessness and frustration of some men under the chafing yoke of denial and restriction. There is a suspicion that alcohol may sometimes be used as an escape from tensions thus created; and failure to live up to ideals can cause a sense of guilt, with serious unhappiness, and bring ill effects to other people, as well.

However, experience makes us wonder whether celibates or benedicts are more involved in such problems of maladjustment. And to further lessen this objection I would point out that most priests have fairly well sublimated their sexual needs in work, prayer, sports, companionship with fellow priests, or a variety of hobbies. Their neurotic symptoms are not particularly frequent or notable.

2. Sad defections of the type you describe. A priest is the first to be touched by sympathy for a fellow priest who fails. We know that he was not really bad, but only unable to live up to his own high ideals. And most of us have personal experience with temptations, hopes, and discouragements which were similar to his. And yet such falls are seldom sudden; they are rarely a complete surprise. They were prepared by a long series of imprudent and nonclerical errors: neglect of prayer, slighting of study, shunning of work, evading priest friends, preference for female companionship, sentimental involvement in personal problems, and unwise choice of recreation.

Our brotherly sympathy for the fallen priest ends abruptly when we encounter the rare turncoat: one who has become embittered agains the Church because of his personal failure, or, even worse, seeks shameful profit from anti-Catholic prejudice through books and lectures. Most of those who carry on campaigns of hate against the Church have some slimy stories hidden in their past—and not as well hidden as they hope.

Honest men fail through weakness and accept the results of their failure in humility. They usually retire into relative obscurity and try to salvage some remnants of happiness in the midst of their conflicts. It is hard to estimate the number of such defections. They are tragic; and yet we know that failures are many in all walks of life. I have no way of knowing whether they are more numerous with priests than with others. If they are it is because ideals are perilous; when you scale the heights you risk a fatal fall.

Failure in celibacy is usually irreparable. You may recover from defeat in other professions, but for the man who has acquired a wife there is no return to the priesthood; and he usually finds it hard to adjust to another type of life. And even when he does adjust he knows that his spiritual welfare is in jeopardy.

Much could be salvaged from these personal disasters if the Church would mitigate her discipline; but the problem is one which does not admit of much leniency, if a celibate clergy is to be maintained at all. If there were an easy way out most of us might take it in moments of weakness.

3. Your next objection supposes that a celibate priest lacks understanding of marital problems. And many would add that he also fails to comprehend the problems of young people who are keeping company and preparing for marriage. There may be some truth to these arguments, though they are based on a flimsy premise: that there is no way of learning things except through personal experience. When you have heard both sides of enough marital stories, you begin to acquire the knowledge and sympathy needed for being helpful. And it may be that what the priest lacks from personal experience he gains by impartiality; one often gives prejudiced counsel when he bases advice on his own limited experience.

4. Your final objection seems to me less valid than the others. Malicious stories would only take on a new cast and flavor if priests were married. As it is, modern gossips have trouble finding anything new. Competent storytellers, like Boccaccio and Victor Hugo, have told most of the good ones long ago. And avid historians have dredged up all the clerical filth the centuries had to offer. Modern versions offer only changes of place and personality.

179

It is never possible to eliminate malicious stories. They have been told about the greatest saints. Husbands and wives are often the subjects of evil gossip. Should we then adopt polygamy as a means of eliminating it? And if we did, the gossip of the harem would surely be tart and spicy.

We can be quite sure that a married clergy would not be exempt from the venom of wagging tongues. Slanderers would merely add a spate of stories about the pastor's wife and children.

Little minds are seldom concerned with ideas; they are not even attuned to the great events of the world. They seek sensation in the aberrations, real or suspected, of their neighbors. Where they cannot find evil they invent it, or else they scornfully belittle the good which is too evident to deny. If celibacy is otherwise good we should not let gossiping little minds cause us to junk it.

Now let us take a look at other objections which are sometimes proposed.

5. The failure of celibates to live life fully in the area of sexual experience. This objection has complete validity only to a person who accepts a hedonist philosophy: that life's success is measured by the total of pleasures a man has been able to garner before death. It remains, however, a strong argument to any person whose basic interest is naturalistic.

The restraints of celibacy have full meaning only to a man who can appreciate the supernatural value of penance. From a natural point of view there is no purpose in giving up good things unless they harm our health, habits, or efficiency. But to the supernatural view all sacrifice made for love of God participates in the redemptive value of Christ's supreme sacrifice, so that it becomes an adoration of God, a purification of the soul, a source of eternal merit.

6. The loss of much of life's deepest meaning and happiness, in the peace and security of home, in the love, help, and personality fulfillment which a good wife contributes, and in the rewarding responsibilities of parenthood. There is something lacking to a man who does not leave a child to carry on his name, to perpetuate his skills and character traits, and to benefit from his wisdom and love.

The answer is that no man can have everything in life. He must make a choice of professions, giving up many to concentrate on one. He must choose between foods; he cannot eat them all—at least, not all at once. He cannot live everywhere; he cannot make close friends and companions of all men; he cannot choose all hobbies and diversions.

You cannot have all the benefits of wealth and yet practice poverty; if you indulge your tastes as a gourmet you lose your trim figure. The celibate deliberately gives up the good things of home, wife, and children for the sake of spiritual values which are not compatible with them, that he may work more freely and efficiently for God, the Church, and the souls of men.

7. Maybe the most regrettable result of clerical celibacy is that there are no children to profit by the heredity, environment, education, intellectual challenge, and spiritual stimulation which should be found in a priest's home. Some of the outstanding men in all artistic and intellectual pursuits have been children of ministers. From their youth they learned to appreciate the finer things of mind and spirit. It may well be deplored that priests cannot influence another generation in such intimate manner; though we may fondly hope that their impact may have greater total effect by being spread over a wider field, with less intensity.

8. Possibly vocations are diminished by this stringent requirement. Many ardent young men who would like to be priests are frightened away by the sacrifices involved in celibacy, or frankly admit after due trial, deliberation, and consultation that they do not have a call to such an exacting state.

We do need vocations badly; so we can only hope that we profit sufficiently in quality to compensate for our losses in numbers.

9. Celibacy is a subterfuge, a clever snare, a deliberate trap contrived by Rome to help her keep control over her clergy, so that she can juggle them like puppets to accomplish her nefarious designs.

With this ridiculous objection we terminate our list. Maybe you can think of more, but they do not come to my mind at the moment. So I turn now to the reasons which prompt the Church to retain this rigid discipline in spite of the objections we have seen:

1. Ancient custom and established tradition certainly play a major role; but I am sure that these factors alone would not be decisive. The Church is conservative, but she is not opposed to change when sound spiritual advantage indicates that it should be made. The Church has long been aware of the objections to celibacy; she has experienced its hardships and seen its tragedies through the ages. She does not retain it out of blind stubbornness, but rather from keen awareness of its great spiritual advantages, proved by centuries of experience.

2. At least from the time of St. Paul the conviction has prevailed in the Church that virginity and chastity are high ideals of spiritual aspiration. They make the soul reach constantly above itself; they assert repeatedly its mastery over the body. And when this striving and winning is done for love of God it has eternal value. It can lead to great sanctity. Consequently virginity has been held on a higher plane than marriage. It is exceptional; it is not for everyone; and a practical comparison of these two holy states is hardly possible. But in the abstract, apart from individuals, the ideals of sacrifice, dedication, love, and devotion which are involved in celibate chastity are higher in the spiritual scale than the love, giving, and fulfillment of marriage.

3. Mystical truths contribute definitely to the Church's attitude. These are truths which tantalize us by dancing just beyond the range of cold reason. They are exemplified in the fact that the Church is Christ's own Body extended to embrace within its spiritual fibers the many millions of us who are its members, making us one with Him. It is fitting that a pure priest should represent the spotless Master in the service of His mystical Body, that a chaste and restrained priest should handle the Eucharistic Body of Christ, and that a priest sanctified by sacrifice should be the one to offer the Sacrifice of Christ. (By this I do not mean to imply that celibacy is necessary to purity, chastity, restraint or sacrifice; or to hint that our married brothers of Eastern rites are any

182

less worthy than we are to offer the Eucharistic Sacrifice.)

4. One very practical reason for celibacy is the fact that the unmarried priest is much less fettered in mind and body. Family interests do not distract him from concentration on his work of the ministry. The good husband should give his wife and children first place in his thoughts, love, attention, and concern. The celibate can give priority to his priesthood.

5. Another reason is so practical it can be measured in dollars. It is much cheaper to maintain a celibate priest than a minister's family. And this advantage appears even more clearly when the priest is sent into the mission fields, where he is usually fed, housed, clothed, and supported by the faithful back home.

6. Other advantages show up sharply in mission fields and in time of war and danger. Celibacy permits the priest to live with natives as one of them, without concern for family comforts and security. He need not worry about wife and children when he encounters danger and disease. I have no statistics to prove that priests are greater heroes than ministers; I only know that they have fewer ties to hold them back. They are free to give themselves to their people and for their people.

In this area ideals inspire, and the example of the martyrs exercises an influence. When a husband and the father of a family is asked to give his life for his faith, he may well respond with courage, but he must be torn between two obligations.

You may object that this argument is hardly practical today. But consider those mission fields which have been taken over by the Communists. During the war I had a close friend who served as an army chaplain because he was excluded from his mission field. But his ardent desire to return made him restless; and in spite of obvious dangers he went back as soon as he could. He did such remarkable work that they made him a bishop—but not for long; the Communists got him, and he was never heard from again. I know he was ready to go; there was nothing to hold him back; and he died in union with Christ on the cross—but probably in very prolonged and exquisite agony.

7. From the earliest centuries the monasteries have challenged the secular clergy to celibacy. It is evident that monastic life would be impossible with wives and children cluttering up the cloisters. Secular priests do not want to be less than their monastic brethren.

8. It is hard for us priests to imagine how ministers ever get their Sunday sermons prepared. We know that they often outdo us in the pulpit; but what do they do with wife and children while they are studying and writing? We have trouble enough with the telephone, doorbell, janitor, housekeeper, school, and church.

9. We are convinced that our celibacy increases the confidence of our people in us. This belief has been called into question by critics who think that celibacy sets us apart; indeed, so sharply that the average person holds us in awe and hesitates to approach us. Our conviction, based on experience, is that this very difference gives our people greater confidence in us and permits them to reveal the secrets of their hearts more trustingly.

George Sand is not a likely authority to quote in favor of the Church, but when a famous French priest left the Church and got married, she wrote as follows. "Will the *Père* Hyacinthe still hear Confessions? That is the question. Is the secrecy of the confessional compatible with the mutual confidences of conjugal love? If I were a Catholic, I would say to my children: 'Have no secrets which cost too much in the telling and then you will have no cause to fear the gossip of the vicar's wife.' "

Maybe it is custom and habit of thought, but as a Catholic I would find it hard to even imagine myself going to Confession to a married man, however wise and holy. And yet I am sure that it must be a habit of thought, because the faithful of Eastern rites show no such hesitancy toward a married confessor. So take this argument for what you hold it worth.

10. No poll has been taken, but I am convinced that celibacy meets with the approval of the great majority of priests. They made the choice of it freely, after long soul-searching and preparation; they have fought to retain it personally

amid trying temptations; and almost daily they see its advantages as they struggle with their parishioners' marital and family problems. In exchanges of priestly wit, celibacy sometimes takes a jovial beating; but even in the midst of such banter we often arrive at the calm consensus that we are the most fortunate of men.

11. Again without benefit of polls, I am sure that an overwhelming majority of our Catholic people favor retention of celibacy for the clergy. Much of their conviction may result from established habits of thought; they simply cannot imagine married priests, and the novel idea is repugnant to them. The married clergy of our Eastern rites have great difficulty in doing any effective work in America because of this attitude of our people toward the priesthood.

12. A final reason is the training problem. Any priest can imagine the ridiculous confusion of a seminary which had wives and children all about. It would mean a total reversal of the Catholic concept of spiritual formation, handed down to us from the early centuries of the Church. And yet we know that the problem is very real in Protestant seminaries, where provision must be made for married-student housing and for the expenses and distractions of family maintenance.

Well, Jack, I have tried to list the pros and cons fairly. My personal prejudice may show in the fact that I have many more reasons for than against, and have proposed answers to most of the objections. There are hints of the possibility that we might someday have married deacons to assist the priests in various phases of their work. But without claiming power of prophecy we can be reasonably sure that during our lifetimes the Church will make no notable change in her traditional requirements for priests.

23

SISTERS

THE QUESTION

As another non-Catholic who reads the *Catholic Digest,* may I commend you upon your answer to: "What have you a right to expect from your priest?" (See p. 169).

Would you please answer a similar question for me? What has one a right to expect from a nun?

Mrs. John Scott

THE ANSWER

Some good old Sisters, Mrs. Scott, shake their heads, and say, "You never know what to expect from these modern young nuns. They are recent teen-agers put into Religious habits, and reluctantly deprived of their cigarettes."

Strangers to convents who see Sisters file by in uniform dress and manners may think of them as turned out in series by machine. They would naturally expect the same response from any two of them, like the electronic reaction to a push button.

There are doting mothers who think Sisters hate children by profession. But any number of hospital patients wonder if it is delirium which makes them see wings above those angelic faces and soothing hands.

In deciding what you should expect from nuns, keep some elementary truths in mind. They are evident when we mention them, but in our actual thinking we tend to forget them.

Nuns are human. Often you see only a carefully composed face peeking out through pleats of starched linen; and

186

the rest of their humanness is hidden by their habits.

They are women. We should expect in them the virtues and vices common to their sex. Naturally you may expect some of the virtues to be more consciously developed, and many of the vices to be firmly repressed; but nuns remain thoroughly women, for all that; and mere man should wisely say no more.

They are women of serious, dedicated, and sacrificing character. The lightheaded, selfish, frivolous, boy-crazy types seldom go into convents, or seldom stay long should unstable moments put them there. And yet, as the puzzled old Sister says, young nuns are modern girls who grew up on rock-'n'-roll, television, and early dating.

They are religious. So notably is this their character that it has become the proper name of their profession. You will expect them as Religious to be women of prayer. I guarantee that you will seldom be disappointed.

They have high ideals. Their sights were fixed straight on heaven when they entered the convent, and every day these sights are readjusted to that same focus as the turmoil of life jars them from their fix.

They are individuals. Don't let identical dress fool you. Sisters of the same Community are often drilled in similar mannerisms, but when you push the contact button firmly you must know the particular character to predict the response. Some are sad, others effusive, and most are complex mixtures in between. You will find the timid right beside the confident.

They are dedicated. You probably know that most Sisters take three vows, by which they consecrate themselves to the faithful service of God in poverty, chastity, and obedience. Their years of spiritual training are designed to adjust their lives to the requirements of these vows.

The average Sister spends two and a half years in preparation for her first vows. She goes into the convent as a postulant: a guest asking to be taken into the family. She must stay at least six months in this status, while she finds out what the life is really like, and submits to some judicious scrutiny herself.

Then if the postulant wants to stay and the Community finds her acceptable she is received. In an impressive formal ceremony, she becomes a novice. For the next two years she wears a habit similar to that of the other Sisters, except that usually her veil will be white. She practices the life of the Community, learns its details, and absorbs its spirit. She is in training and on trial; there is no definite commitment. She is free to leave at any moment, and the Sisters may tell her to leave if it becomes apparent that she is not going to fit into the life of the Community.

One year of the novitiate is particularly strict. It concentrates on prayer, meditation, the reading of the Scriptures and spiritual books, that rigorous self-restraint which is called mortification, and persistent practice of the basic virtues of community living. Those virtues are humble and ready obedience, charity, kindness, respect, promptness, diligence in duties, and constant decorum.

The second year of novitiate is often similar to the first; it is closely supervised by a novice mistress and guided by a spiritual director. But in some institutes much of this second year is spent in studies or in specific training for later tasks.

When the novitiate is over the Sister may take her first vows, but they must be temporary, usually for three years. And again at the end of that time she is perfectly free to leave. Before she may take her final vows she is interviewed by the bishop, or his representative, to make sure that she really wants to stay, and is not under pressure from any source, such as parents or Sisters. Similar interviews preceded her reception as a novice and her first vows.

After five and a half years it is expected that the young Sister will know her own mind. So now she is ready for final vows. After that she is bound to the Community by the solemn promise she made to God; and the Community is bound to her, also. This mutual bond can be severed only by the Pope, who can dispense the Sister from her vows when sound reasons urge it, for the welfare of all concerned.

The three vows have tremendous import; that is why such care is taken in preparation for them. They both bind and liberate. They bind the Sister much as a law would oblige her to fulfillment of the duties she promised; and they free her soul for its flight to God.

Most Sisters take simple vows—as distinguished from solemn vows. These are legal terms which I will not attempt to explain now, the difference is largely technical.

The vow of poverty is simplest of all. It frees the Sister from concern about personal possessions. She retains title to her property, so that it is waiting for her if she should ever leave the Community; but she has someone else, a brother, for instance, take care of it for her and dispose of any revenue from it. She seldom gives it a thought. Anything she earns by her own work belongs to the Community, which is permanently responsible for all her needs. She has no money, no worries, and complete social security. The Religious Order is communism at its best.

The vow of chastity frees the Sister from family worries, attachments, and distractions. Christ is her only spouse; the Community is her family; and the people she works with are her children. She can give them all her love. This vow obliges the Sister to lead a life free of active sexual interests.

Obedience is probably the most complicated of the vows. It is there all the time, and can be a daily irritant. The Sister must accept assignments, directives, and work at the will of her superior. Yet if she adheres to the spirit of this vow it may free her more than any other. In the rule of her Order and the commands of her superior she finds clear, detailed expression of the will of God. Obedience eliminates doubts and worry, gives her confidence, adds merit to her activities.

Obedience is the vow most notably at variance with our modern spirit. You have probably seen the film *The Nun's Story*. It showed the valiant but failing efforts of a strong modern girl to fit herself into the pattern of obedience required by an Order unusually strict. Many of us found in this film the honest portrayal of a conflict of soul, technical perfection, and beautiful photography. But some of our Sisters were perturbed by it; they thought it failed to grasp their spirit, and showed only the cold mechanics of spiritual formation, grim in its rigor, and devoid of the love and humor of real life.

189

Every day she is in the convent the Sister will follow a fixed schedule of work, prayer, rest, and recreation. Rising is always early, probably 5:30. The Sisters will assemble in the chapel at six for morning prayers and meditation. Mass will be at 6:30; and they will receive Communion. Then after Mass they will spend another fifteen minutes or so in thanksgiving.

Breakfast will be fairly simple, with food sufficient for the work to be done; probably there will be no talking, and maybe some public reading in the refectory. Then everyone will get ready for the work of the day; and all will assemble again in the chapel at noon for prayers, maybe the Rosary, and an examination of conscience. Except on special feast days dinner will be eaten without conversation, to the accompaniment of spiritual reading. If the schedule permits there may be a brief recreation, but usually it is back to classroom or hospital.

In the afternoon there will probably be more prayers in the chapel, and hopefully, time for private reading of spiritual books. There are sure to be Community prayers before supper, and night prayers before bedtime. After night prayers comes the period of the grand silence; there is to be no unnecessary conversation until after Mass the next morning.

That is a very sketchy notion of a Sister's day. And besides, it fits no known Community. My latest list indicates that there are 370 different and independent Religious Orders or Congregations of women in the United States, and probably no two of them agree in all details of their daily routine. Some Sisters, like those in hospitals, are up before 5:30, and may find that the demands of their particular duties often keep them from Community exercises, a necessity much deplored.

Others may spend the major portion of their day in prayer, spiritual reading, and meditation; for instance, those who have perpetual adoration of the Blessed Sacrament in their chapel. Many Sisters recite the Divine Office, or the Little Office of the Blessed Virgin, by chanting the various psalms, prayers, and hymns. This is usually done in the chapel, at fixed hours of the day, and may require an hour or more of time.

Some Communities insist on fasting and penance; others have mitigated the ancient rules to fit modern needs and temperaments. Some Sisters live in strict cloister, never leaving the area of their convent and garden, and receiving no visitors. Others drive cars, organize athletic events, produce plays, and lead orchestras.

You may wonder why all this diversity. The 370 Orders in America and many more in other parts of the world, grew up spontaneously from the plans of pious foundresses. Mostly the rules were designed by the Sisters themselves and then submitted to Rome. A special Congregation for Religious has general supervision over projects of most Orders.

Otherwise the life and business of each Community is in the hands of the members themselves. They elect their superiors; and if the Order is extended widely there may be provincial superiors in different areas, and over all a superior general, with an international council of advisors. The Sisters own their own property, gain their own living, pay their own bills.

In this modern day, you can expect almost anything from Sisters in the way of competence, interest, and activities. I don't know any Sister-bricklayers personally, but I am confident you could find them in mission lands, along with truck-drivers and printer's devils. You can easily find lawyers and doctors, artists and poets, scientists and musicians, and some capable orators. But I don't know of any politicians—though I have certainly met some diplomats among them.

I have seen lists of hundreds of activities in which Sisters are engaged, but mostly you will find them in various phases of teaching, nursing, and social work; and, of course, in the financing, building, and managing of their hospitals, schools, and orphanages—usually with remarkable skill and solvency.

Habitually when we think of Sisters we picture long dark robes, dangling rosaries, copious linen coifs, and a demure dignity. Popular movies have shown us that the dignity can give way to athletic skill, good humor, and fellowship. And several modern Orders have discarded the medieval robes, replacing

191

them with neat and practical uniforms, occasionally designed by fashion experts.

In recent years our Sisters have become increasingly aware of the need for advanced education and professional competence, along with their spiritual formation. Most of the Congregations in the United States have banded themselves together in a Sister Formation conference to study, encourage, and find ways of achieving this education and training.

The greatest obstacle to it comes from the insistent demand which is made on all sides for the service of the Sisters. The need for them has increased so rapidly that the vocations have not kept pace. Thus there is temptation to meet the present need at the cost of thorough professional preparation. The Sister Formation conference tries to resist this temptation with vision of longer range and goals of higher quality.

Above all else you have a right to expect virtue in the nuns. If you get to know them well, and are sensible in your judgments, you will seldom be disappointed. Rare is the paragon of all virtues—they are human after all; but frequent is the exemplar of much goodness.

Faith, hope, and charity you take for granted. Nuns' entire lives are built on and around these basic virtues and would have no meaning without them. You will also expect their love of God to show itself in love for their fellow men. You find it most evident in the self-sacrificing services they give. You will find it also in courtesy, which is a refinement of charity, and in gentleness, zeal, and devotion. You will even find it in patience, which is an elastic virtue: it stretches and stretches, and then sometimes snaps. Children in school know how to stretch it, and mothers resent its snaps.

In judging the virtues of Sisters, particularly their patience, we should remember that they never heard of a forty-hour week; sixteen hours a day is more their normal speed. They work in areas where conflicts are inevitable: with sick people, and young people, and those with many problems. Their work load is always excessive: they may have sixty or seventy in class. For them recreation is only a laugh—and a short one at that.

You may rightly expect Sisters to be honest, fair, and

tolerant. We should be the same with them. You may expect them to have fervor and humility. Usually you will find about them an air of tranquillity, which comes from peace within their own souls.

And now, Mrs. Scott, when we have lined up all the things we may expect from Sisters, we might remember that your question can be turned in reverse. What do the Sisters have a right to expect from us? They ask no compensation, little recognition, no luxuries, and few comforts. They are not seeking fame or honor, but trying to do good for all of us because they love us in Jesus Christ, their Spouse, who redeemed us. We can at least show them courtesy and understanding, and maybe a touch of gratitude. And the least we can do is say a daily prayer for them. They say many more for us.

24

MASS STIPENDS

THE QUESTION

I am not a Catholic, but having many Catholic friends and relatives, I have attended Catholic funerals. I have been impressed with the great number of Masses requested for the soul of a deceased. However, since a priest is allowed to say only a certain number of Masses a year, I am wondering how it is possible for so many Masses to be said for the dead, along with the Masses for anniversaries.

Also, why is it necessary to have a set offering? Or should there be an offering at all?

In regard to Masses for the deceased it does seem unfair that some persons who have more wealth than others will naturally have more prayers said than others of more limited financial means will. In God's eyes are we not all equal?

I hope these questions do not seem impertinent. I just desire a better understanding.

Mrs. L. M. Kelly

THE ANSWER

You are far from impertinent, Mrs. Kelly. Your questions are reasonable, and I hope I can answer them for you.

First, let us consider the basis and origin of Mass stipends. Such review will be useful to us Catholics, too, because stipends form a custom which we take for granted. We are a bit surprised each time we find them called into question.

Let's begin with the fact that the Mass is a sacrifice. It is our supreme act of worship and has a spiritual identity with the Sacrifice of Jesus Christ on the cross.

In Old Testament times animals were sacrificed daily in the Temple. The victims were actually immolated by the priests, but often some of the people had a special part in the offering by bringing their own animals to the altar. In a sense they were the ones who made the offerings; the priests acted as their agents. They gave the victims to the priest that he might give them to God.

In the Mass, of course, the victim is provided by God Himself. It is Jesus Christ, true God and true Man. Calvary is not repeated, but it is continued by the presence of Jesus under the appearances of bread and wine.

The people who want a special part in the sacrifice of the Mass cannot provide the victim, but they can provide the bread and wine. Like the faithful of the Old Testament, they give the material to the priest that he may give it to God in their name, after it has been transformed in the words of the Consecration: "This is my Body. This is my Blood."

The faithful of the early Church actually brought the bread and wine to the altar at the Offertory of the Mass. But in the course of time this offering became less direct; the people gave the priest money so that he could buy the bread and wine and have them on hand for the sacrifice. Even today Mass stipends retain much of this notion: I give you the materials of the sacrifice that you may offer it up to God in my name.

Another basis for Mass stipends comes from St. Paul: "Do you not know that they who minister in the temple eat what comes from the temple, and that they who serve the altar, have their share with the altar?" The priest's job was to offer sacrifice. A man should be able to live from his job, without "moonlighting," as St. Paul the tentmaker was content to do. Thus, the offerings which the first Christians brought to the altar at Mass always were more than were needed. The priest could take the surplus home.

Christianity spread, and its social life became more complicated. The simple directness of the Offertory was changed into an alms, or money gift. "I want you to offer Mass for me today; so take this penny and buy yourself enough to eat for the day."

Gradually customs became written rules. You see that where something as sacred as the Mass is concerned, the Church was anxious to avoid any shadow of abuse. If she didn't make strict rules some greedy priests might insist on more generous alms, or go out soliciting them, or maybe even take offerings from several people for the same Mass.

The Church holds today to the same notion: your Mass stipend is an alms to support the priest on the day he offers Mass for your intentions. Actually it is only token support; most of our laws were made long ago, and have not kept pace with inflation. The stipend varies between dioceses, but in our area the basic offering is still a dollar—and it is hard to stretch a shrunken dollar so that it will cover a day's living.

The Church law consciously uses two names for the Mass offering: it is a stipend or an alms. I have my own theory that "alms" is the more traditional name, but that "stipend" is a polite euphemism; it removes the hint of a handout.

Church laws are carefully designed to keep avarice from the altar. They give assurance that all Masses will be offered for the intentions agreed upon. Here is an outline of the principal rules:

1. The amount of the stipend is set by the bishop's written laws or by established customs.

2. The rules of my own diocese are fairly typical, although many bishops have increased the amounts in recent years. Our regular offering for a Mass is a dollar. If this Mass is to be said on a specified day or in a particular church the stipend should be two dollars. If a high Mass is requested the offering is five dollars, but out of this the priest must usually provide the expenses of an organist, and sometimes a vocalist or choir.

3. A priest may accept more, but he may not demand more. And usually he can accept less, too, just so he does it in a generous spirit, with no semblance of bargaining.

4. Once a priest has accepted a stipend he is gravely bound in conscience to offer the Mass as requested. If he cannot do it himself he must get some other priest to do it, and pass on the complete stipend to this other priest.

5. Masses must be offered in the time, place, and manner

196

specified; and where no special time is indicated by the donor the law says that any urgent intention must be taken care of forthwith (as soon as possible) and within the time indicated by the circumstances. If I am asked to offer Mass for the recovery of a sick person I cannot put it off until he is well— or dead.

Other Masses must be said "within a proper measure" of time. Much will depend on the number involved. If a man asks me to say thirty Masses for his intention he can hardly expect all this month. Others will want Masses said, too, and I will have some intentions of my own. But if he asks me to say one Mass, he won't expect me to put it off for a month, either, even if there is no urgency.

The law states further that under no circumstances may a priest accept more Mass intentions than he can take care of within a year.

6. A priest may take only one stipend for each Mass. In fact, he may accept only one stipend for each day. Often on Sunday, or other special days, a priest must say two Masses, sometimes three, to accommodate the people, but he may receive an offering for only one of those Masses. It is an alms for his living that day, and is not to be hoarded. The only exception is Christmas; special gifts are in order on that day, and each priest may say three Masses.

7. The priest who accepts Mass stipends must be a careful bookkeeper. His obligation to say each Mass binds him under pain of serious sin. Even if he were to lose the stipend or someone were to steal it he would still be required to say the Mass.

8. Pastors must offer Mass for their people each Sunday and on about thirty feast days each year. On such days they may not accept a stipend, even though they say a second Mass.

These are some of the general rules, but now I must get to some of your particular questions, Mrs. Kelly.

How is it possible for all these Masses to be said? Obviously the priests in a large parish cannot take care of all the requests. They must send the stipends to other priests.

In America are many small parishes where the priests can

easily offer Masses for more intentions than they receive from their own people. And there are many more similar pastors in other countries.

Often the diocese has a college or seminary. The priests there have little opportunity to receive stipends directly from people desiring Masses.

We have hundreds of monasteries, convents, and houses of Religious Orders in America; in these there must be nearly twenty thousand priests. They can use great numbers of Mass stipends; each one celebrates Mass every day.

There are about 3,500 American missioners in foreign lands. For them their Mass stipend can often be, very literally, their support for the day. Besides, Americans supply Mass stipends to many thousands of other mission priests.

So you see Mass offerings are a source of substantial support for the various works of the Church throughout the world.

I may send my extra stipends to some friend in a poor parish, a monastery, or the missions. When he acknowledges receipt I know that he has assumed my obligations, and I am relieved of them. But my conscience could not be at ease if I sent them to someone I did not know. So for practical purposes they are usually distributed through reliable organizations which keep close check on them.

As regards that set offering, Mrs. Kelly, you now see that the reason is to avoid abuse: to prevent any vying for big stipends and scorning of small ones.

Now for your final question. We are all, indeed, equal in God's eyes—except that He has indicated some preferences for the poor, humble, and unfortunate. Maybe the wealthy man really needs those extra Masses if he is to get to heaven as fast as the poor man who can't afford stipends!

I suspect that it works out something like this. The Church has its own intentions in every Mass, in addition to the particular request for which the priest offers it. You will recall that these intentions of the Church always include: adoration of God, reparation for sins, thanksgiving for God's favors, and petition for many needs. And there is always, in each Mass, special concern for the souls in purgatory. Those who could not afford to have any Masses said for themselves probably come first in reaping these general benefits.

I think of those hundreds of Masses which were requested for my saintly old grandmother. Probably she doesn't need one of them, but greatly enjoys seeing them offered, from her vantage point in heaven.

Really, we shouldn't be calculating about stipends. The good Lord doesn't really need any of our prayers, penances, and Masses to set His justice to work or release the bonds of His love. He merely gives us the privilege of co-operating with Him. Anyone who reaches heaven gets there by the graces which Jesus Christ merited for him on Calvary—and distribution of those graces is not tied down by the fickleness of his friends. There are mysteries involved in that, because we can certainly be of help to the souls in purgatory by our prayers, penances, indulgences, and Masses; but it is God Himself who makes the ultimate gift of His graces, and His justice sees the whole picture.

It is for our own good that we are asked to lend our co-operation. When we take part in the Mass we are united to Jesus Christ in sanctifying love, offering Him to His eternal Father as He offered Himself on the cross, offering ourselves in acceptable union with Him, and receiving His graces direct from the pierced hands of His crucifixion.

25

CONFESSION

THE QUESTION

I would like to know where in the Bible it says anything about Confession. Jesus does tell his disciples that whose sins they forgive are forgiven and those they retain are retained. But it seems to me an awful stretch of the imagination if Confession is based on this. This could mean if one wished to confess, he could do so. If the Church made it optional instead of compulsory, it would not be so hard to understand.

O. J. Lewis

THE ANSWER

Frankly, Mr. Lewis, I think you score a couple of good points in presenting your question. I cannot prove to you directly from the Bible alone that confession is necessary for the forgiveness of sins. And we have no evidence that Jesus ever heard anyone's confession.

Why then do we consider confession necessary? First of all, I think you know that we Catholics do not base all our doctrines on the Scriptures alone. We revere the Sacred Writings as the inspired Word of God—given us for our inspiration and instruction, and as the principal source of God's revelation to man. But we do not consider them the exclusive source of the things God wants us to know. We believe that Jesus Christ established His Church to be our teacher; to preserve the Bible, to tell us which writings rightly belong in the Bible, and to interpret its true meaning to us.

Right now, Mr. Lewis, I cannot attempt to show you all

the reasons why we accept the Church as the teacher, divinely appointed, of all the doctrines of Christ. It would divert me too far from your question. Briefly, our conviction is based on the whole picture of our Lord's ministry: His careful choice and training of His Apostles, the series of commissions He gave them, and in particular words like the following:

"Go, therefore, and make all nations your disciples, and teach them to observe all the commandments I have given you. And mark: I am with you at all times as long as the world will last."

"Go, into the whole world and preach the Gospel to all creation. He that believes and is baptized will be saved; he that does not believe will be condemned."

"And I will ask the Father, and He will grant you another Advocate to be with you for all time to come, the Spirit of Truth. You will know Him, because He will make his permanent stay with you and in you."

"The Advocate, the Holy Spirit, whom the Father will send in my name, will teach you everything, and refresh your memory of everything I have told you."

We believe that confession is necessary because the Church teaches that it is; and Jesus Christ remains with His Church at all times, just as He promised, that it may rightly teach all nations to observe all his commandments. When the Church tells us that confession is necessary we believe it, because we know that the Advocate, the Holy Spirit, is with the Church now and for all time to come, refreshing her memory of all that Jesus first taught her through the Apostles.

However, Mr. Lewis, I am sure that you will not be satisfied with this answer, since you are not yet ready to accept the teaching authority of the Church in all its implications. So let us see if we do find any indications of confession in the Bible.

The Old Testament prepared the way for the teachings of Christ, and is well filled with calls to repentance, reform, and works of penance, with a hope of forgiveness consequent on these preparations to receive the mercy of God. And confession comes frequently into the picture even in those ancient times. The first confession of the Bible was made by Adam and Eve. It was a reluctant one, seeking excuses and diverting blame; so it did not bring immediate forgiveness. Pharao confessed his sins to Moses and Aaron, but he was not sincere; so the plagues continued.

Balaam confessed his sins to the angel of the Lord and was permitted to continue his journey and speak the word of the Lord. The Israelites confessed their sins to Moses, and the serpents were taken away. At Masphath they confessed before Samuel, and the Lord helped them to defeat the Philistines.

David confessed with great humility, and Nathan immediately assured him that the Lord had taken away his sin. Saul, Solomon, Judith, Esther, and Job are others who confessed their sins. But, of course, you will tell me, Mr. Lewis, and I will agree with you, that none of these made a detailed declaration of sins, as we do in the sacrament of Penance. They were merely figures of the future, showing the way to humility and penance, illustrating the general principle that confession is good for the soul.

In the New Testament we also read of the confession of sins. First to John the Baptist: "They confessed their sins and were baptized by him in the Jordan river." And finally to St. Paul, at Ephesus: "Many, too, of those who believed came and openly confessed their practices." The Apostle John recommends confession to us: "If we openly confess our sins, God, true to his promises and just, forgives our sins." And St. James advises us: "So confess your sins to one another, and pray for one another that you may be healed."

God's mercy, love, and forgiveness are the theme of some of our Lord's best-known parables. When the scribes and Pharisees accused Him of attracting sinners and feasting with them He told about the shepherd who would leave his ninety-nine sheep in the desert and go in search of the one that was lost, and when he had found it would carry it back on his shoulders, joyfully: "I tell you there is joy in heaven over one repentant sinner."

Then, there was the prodigal son, who was received with paternal affection. He made a confession: "Father, I have sinned in heaven and before you." The father's response was to bring out the finest robe, put a ring on his finger, sandals on his feet, and then kill the fatted calf for a feast.

While it is probably true that Jesus never heard anyone's detailed confession, He did personally forgive sins on various occasions, as you know well. St. Luke tells the story of a sinful woman, a scandal in the town, who intruded on our Lord in the home of Simon, the Pharisee. Because of her dramatic evidences of faith and love Jesus told her, "Your sins are forgiven. Go home and be at peace."

The Master was teaching in the Temple one time when the Pharisees brought before Him a woman caught in adultery. He confused all her accusers by inviting the one free from sin to throw the first stone at her. When they had all slunk away He said to her: "Neither do I condemn you. Go, and from now on sin no more."

St. Mark tells the most convincing story of Christ's power and readiness to forgive. Four men tore the roof off a house so that they could lower a paralytic before the Master. When Jesus saw their faith, He said to the paralytic: "My son, your sins are forgiven you." Then, to prove to a skeptical crowd that He really had the power to forgive sins He told the paralytic to rise, take up his mat, and walk home.

The final act of forgiveness which Jesus performed personally was on the cross, only moments before He died. He promised the repentant thief: "I assure you, this very day you will be with Me in Paradise."

In view of these examples of personal and explicit forgiveness, Mr. Lewis, it is hardly an argument against our sacrament of Penance to say that Jesus never heard the confession of anyone. You could use the same argument with more force against Baptism. Apparently Jesus never baptized anyone. He sent the Apostles out to do that. But He did forgive sins personally, before He sent the Apostles out to do the same. Jesus did not need explicit confession; He could read the hearts of men; but the Apostles had no such perceptive power; they could use the power of forgiving intelligently and justly only if the sinner first told them his sins and his sorrow.

We cannot rightly appreciate the importance of confession unless we have a concept of the whole sacramental system which our Savior gave us for our sanctification. The seven sacraments are external signs or symbols which are effective means of bringing the graces of God into our souls. They are effective because they were established by Jesus for that purpose and because He works through them.

We are probably in complete agreement, Mr. Lewis, that Jesus obtained for us, by His death on the cross, all the graces we will ever need to make us holy and get us to heaven. But there remains the problem of getting those graces to us in a way which will induce us to accept them, give us confidence that we have them, and lead us to co-operate with them.

Certainly Jesus could have decided to give us His graces by direct spiritual contact with our souls, without any external sign. He does do that daily. But apparently He chose to give us the sacraments because He wanted to sanctify us in accordance with our complete nature, composed of body and soul. If He had ignored our bodies in giving us His graces He would have treated us as angels, not as men.

Jesus was a man, and He knew full well that you can't make an impression on a man except through his senses: sight, hearing, taste, touch, and smell. He wanted our sanctification to be impressive to us. So He chose external, sensible, tangible signs to accomplish it.

Jesus knew also that subjective things are often illusory and uncertain. We can never be quite sure of them unless we have some way of testing them by objective reality. External signs of grace give us assurance of internal sanctification.

We have seven sacraments to take care of our daily needs for grace from our Baptism in infancy to the Last Anointing before we die. Each sacrament is a sign of grace and puts grace into our souls. Jesus chose his signs carefully, so that each one would signify its special purpose—the particular type of grace it gives.

The washing waters of Baptism indicate the grace which cleanses the soul from original sin. The bread and wine of the Eucharist signify a nourishing grace which is the daily spiritual food of our supernatural life. The sign of the sacrament of Penance is equally appropriate. It is implied in those words of our Lord which you quote in part: "Receive the Holy Spirit.

204

Whenever you remit anyone's sins, they are remitted; when you retain anyone's sins, they are retained."

The power thus given to the Apostles is twofold, alternative. Its exercise requires a judgment. Justice requires that this judgment be informed and prudent, based on facts, not haphazard or arbitrary.

Sins are similar to crimes. In civil law, crimes are judged by judicial process: there is an accusation and arraignment, evidence is presented, and pleas are made for justice, leniency, parole, or pardon. The sacramental sign chosen for the forgiveness of sin is similar to a judicial process. The penitent accuses himself; he presents the evidence against himself; he makes his plea of guilty, but also asks forgiveness on the basis of his faith and love, his sorrow, and his determination to sin no more.

The confessor acts in the name of Christ and by the authority given him in the Savior's words. On the basis of the evidence presented he makes a careful and lenient judgment of the sinner's sincerity, even as Jesus did with the paralytic, the scandalous woman, the adulteress, and the thief on the cross. And when the confessor pronounces his judgment in words of remission, Jesus keeps the promise He made to His Apostles: the sins are forgiven.

Let me explain it another way: when I baptize you I use the external signs which Jesus established: water poured in the name of the Father, Son, and Holy Spirit. Through this sacrament Jesus fills your soul with grace, removing original sin. When I give you absolution in Confession I use the external signs which our Savior established: a judgment of forgiveness based on the evidence presented. Through this sacrament Jesus fills your soul with grace, removing the sins which you have committed but now repent.

There remains one part of your question which I have not touched, Mr. Lewis: Why is confession compulsory instead of optional? You might agree with me that our Lord established the sacrament of Penance, and that confession is necessary for the proper reception of that sacrament. You might agree that the sacrament is a good and useful thing, productive of grace, satisfying and comforting to the penitent, helpful in problems, and conducive to reform. And still you could protest: Why can't I skip it if I don't feel I have personal need of it? Surely, I can go straight to our Lord, tell Him I am sorry, and ask his forgiveness directly!

One point I wish to make clear: the sacrament is not a barrier to our personal contact with Jesus. It is rather an avenue to Him, a means of bringing Him to us. And it does not prevent our obtaining immediate nonsacramental forgiveness of our sins by an act of faith, love, and repentance, similar to that of the scandalous woman in the house of Simon. We call this an act of perfect contrition. It brings grace into our souls immediately, but it does not exempt us from confessing our sins later.

I might answer your question by proposing another. Why didn't our Lord make Baptism and Holy Communion optional? "Unless a man be born again of water and the spirit he shall not enter the kingdom of heaven." "Unless you eat the flesh of the Son of man and drink his blood you shall not have life in you."

If confession were optional the power given to the Apostles would be no real power at all. What value would authority have if those subject to it could evade it at will? Suppose Jesus had given us a choice of going to Confession or getting forgiveness in some simpler and less troublesome way. The result would be that pious souls who hardly need the sacrament would appreciate it and avail themselves of it, while big sinners who need it most would stay away in droves—making frequent acts of contrition in moments of remorse. But they would never really stir themselves up to a detailed awareness of their sins, a humble admission of guilt, a fervent, explicit plea for forgiveness, and a firm determination to reform—bolstered by sound advice and encouragement in the confessional and fortified by the grace which Jesus gives through His sacrament.

26

THE BLESSED VIRGIN MARY

THE QUESTION

My query is this. Just recently in our daily press I saw the announcement that His Holiness the Pope intended in the near future to declare the Virgin Mary as the *only* mediator between mankind and God. Is this true?

I am a non-Catholic myself, but have been deeply interested in your faith for the last three years. I have all that time subscribed regularly to a Catholic paper, but have never seen any hint of this in your press; but neither has there been a denial.

If, therefore, it is true, on what does your Church base the assertion? It seems to me that it cuts out Jesus the Christ completely, and renders His self-sacrifice null and void.

He was the one who devoted His life and gave it for mankind; surely then *He* is the mediator?

I am indeed puzzled and, I admit, somewhat shocked by it. I also feel this cannot be very good for your campaign of conversion.

I hope that you will be kind enough to enlighten me on this point.

Mrs. Gladys Cope

THE ANSWER

Someone has made a mistake, Mrs. Cope. Your reporter has mistaken the Mother for her Son. It is not the Virgin Mary who is the *only* mediator between mankind and God; it is Jesus Christ, her only Son.

We do call Mary the Mediatrix of all Graces. It is a title

which stresses the intimacy of her association with her Son in that work which she brought Him into the world to accomplish: the redemption and sanctification of our souls. Some Pope someday may declare it a doctrine of the Church that Mary is the mediatrix, in this sense; most Catholic theologians already hold it to be certain.

But you may be sure that such declaration would not "cut out Jesus Christ completely." On the contrary, like all the mysteries and glories of Mary, it would add greatly to His glory, increase our love for Him, and draw us nearer to Him in profound adoration. Every doctrine of Mary is because of her Son, and for the sake of her Son.

Nothing is more distinctly Catholic than devotion to the Blessed Virgin Mary, and it is largely because of this devotion that Catholics remain deeply convinced of the divinity of Christ, and vividly conscious of His humanity. We are able to understand Jesus better, because we know His Mother so well. It is easier to know and understand her than Him.

She is a human person—one of us. He is a divine Person. Of course, He does have a human nature, like yours and mine. But He also has a divine nature, entirely unlike anything we can ever imagine. A divine Person with two natures! How can we ever know Him and feel comfortable with Him? Thank God, we have His Mother. She brought Him to us in the first place, and she takes us to Him, and teaches us to know Him —and to love Him.

The early Christians, those of the first five centuries, found their knowledge of Mary very useful in clarifying their ideas about Christ. Right in the beginning they simply took Christ and Mary both for granted. The vision, memory, and love of their Savior so overwhelmed them that they did not stop to worry about the mysteries of His Person or His natures. Neither did they speculate about His Mother; she was simply there by His side, at the crib of Bethlehem, at the foot of the cross—and at the throne of heaven.

Never at any time did Mary occupy the middle of the stage; that spot was for her Son. But as those early Christians became more accustomed to the astounding fact of Christ's presence they began to inquire into the details of His Incarnation,

His Person, and His natures. And it was then that Mary helped them to understand rightly and avoid mistakes. Against the Arians, the Nestorians, and the Monophysites she guided them, through the Councils of Nicaea, Ephesus, and Chalcedon, until those early followers of her Son finally had a clear grasp of the full meaning of His divinity and humanity, and the union of His two natures in one person. And as their knowledge of Him became more definite they understood her better, too.

After the Fathers at Nicaea, in the year 325, had proclaimed the equality of Son and Father, it dawned fully on theologians that Mary was the Mother of a divine Person. The heretic Nestorius couldn't accept that.

So it became necessary for the Council of Ephesus to declare that she really was the Mother of God, *Theotokos*. And then again, when the full meaning of that term had dawned, there came further disputes about the distinction of the two natures of her Son. Another heretic, Eutyches, failed to understand that if Jesus had a real human Mother He must have been a real flesh-and-blood human being Himself. But the Fathers at the Council of Chalcedon understood, and they declared definitely that the two natures, divine and human, in Jesus were complete and distinct, even though they were united in the one identical Person.

There is considerable evidence that veneration of Mary began even in the time of the Apostles, and her praises grew more frequent as the Christian community grew. Early writers like St. Ignatius, St. Irenaeus, St. Justin, and Tertullian, made explicit mention of her, right after the time of the Apostles. We have a second-century picture of her in the catacombs. And even such unreliable apocryphal writings as the *Proto-evangelium of James* show how widespread was popular interest about her.

By the time of the Council of Ephesus, in the year 431, everything essential about the role of Mary had been firmly established as doctrine: there is only one person in Jesus Christ, and Mary is the Mother of that person; every privilege she enjoys, every title given her, and every honor paid her results from her divine maternity.

209

God's Mother is worthy of honor. He honored her Himself in choosing her from among all His creatures. We never forget the basic truth of our religion: there is only one God, and He alone is to be worshiped. But that does not mean that we are forbidden to pay reasonable, sensible honor to creatures. God explicitly commands you to honor your own father and mother. Is it then wrong to honor God's Mother?

From the beginning, the Church has given to Mary the highest form of honor that can be properly given to any creature. She is human, just as we are. We must never adore her; that is for God alone. But otherwise we cannot honor her to excess, because it is not possible to overestimate the privileges God gave her in making her His own Mother.

Most of the opposition to Catholic devotion to Mary results from a misunderstanding of the nature of that devotion. We do not try to deify Mary nor make her equal to God in any respect. We simply honor one of our own human race, in imitation of God, who honored her first. We are trying to imitate Jesus Christ, who honored His Mother.

We hear complaints that there are too many Marian doctrines, some of which are not apparent from the Scriptures. They are all logical consequences of the divine maternity. First of all, there is Mary's virginity. The Gospels make it clear, as the Old Testament had foretold, that Jesus was born of a virgin Mother. The Fifth General Council, in 553, and the Lateran Council of 649 declared her virginity to be a matter of doctrine. It was a necessary consequence of her divine motherhood, since the only Father of Jesus was God Himself.

Early Doctors of the Church, like St. Jerome and St. Ambrose, upheld the firm and constant tradition of the Church that the virginity of Mary was permanent. This was simply a fitting sequel of her divine maternity, since Christians from the earliest times had found it repugnant that other children should be born from the womb made sacred by the divine Child. Besides, this seemed the only reasonable explanation of Mary's statement, "I know not man."

The Immaculate Conception is a doctrine found in the traditional interpretation of certain texts: Gen. 3:15; Luke 1:27. Mary is called "full of grace," and the doctrine of the Immaculate Conception simply takes those words without restriction. She was full of grace at every moment of her life: from the moment she began to live, from her conception. This privilege, too, is given her because of her divine motherhood: the flesh from which the innocent Body of Christ was formed should not be stained by sin. He who came to conquer sin was appropriately born of a sinless creature. Since He was God, He could keep her free from sin. So He did. Her sinlessness was the result of the Redemption; but it was by prevention rather than by cure.

The Assumption, defined by Pope Pius XII on November 1, 1950, is the most recent formal doctrine of the Church. But it is far from new. It is found in early tradition, and was the first feast of Mary in the Church celebrated since the fifth century. We don't find it directly mentioned in the Scriptures, but the Gospel and the Acts of the Apostles do present the Mother of God as always closely united to her divine Son, always sharing His lot, especially in His fight against Satan, which resulted in complete victory over sin and death—two words always joined together by St. Paul. The Assumption follows from her sinlessness, and that was because of her motherhood.

We honor Mary as the Mother of Men, our mother. She conceived her Son by her own free consent. And by that consent she accepted Christ whole and entire, not only the physical Christ, but also the mystical Christ. And we are members of Christ, as St. Paul says, part of the mystical Christ. So we, too, were accepted by Mary, at the moment of the Incarnation, as her children, spiritual brothers of her Son. Her consent and acceptance of us was ratified, in the full realization of its burdens, at the foot of the cross, when she united her personal sorrow with the sufferings of her Son for our redemption. We owe Jesus to Mary; and so, indirectly, we owe the grace of the cross to her. This grace makes us children of God. So she is, indeed, the spiritual Mother of all men.

I am not avoiding your question about the mediatrix. I have been trying to give it a background, so that my explanation will have more meaning. It is the common and explicit teaching of the Church today that every grace given to men comes

211

to them through Mary. She is the almoner for her generous Son. She hands out His treasures, as a Mother's right. Being mediatrix is simply a Mother's privilege. She was intimately associated with her Son in everything pertaining to our Redemption and salvation while they were both on earth. Why should He change the order of things now that they are both in heaven?

Jesus Christ is the only mediator betwen God and Man. He brought God to us when He became man. He takes us back to God with Him through His redemptive grace. He permits us to understand something about God, first, by bringing God down to the human level, in the Incarnation; and second, by giving us a bit of divine intelligence, in Faith.

Mary, the mediatrix, brought Jesus to us, and brings us to Jesus. She permits us to understand Him, first, by making us realize how thoroughly He is one of us, as her own Son; and second, by reminding us that she, though human, is the Mother of God. Her Son is a divine Person.

No one who really understands Mary can misunderstand Jesus. But if we reject her, as many moderns have done, we will come to doubt the divinity of Christ, or the reality of His human nature, or the personal union between those two natures. Without her, we become confused about her Son, and if we are confused we may reject the true Christ. Let Mary, His Mother, lead you to Him, and teach you to know Him completely and to love Him intimately. That is the way to become a saint. And it is evident from your letter that you want to be a saint.

27

SAINTS AND STATUES

THE QUESTION

I am not a Catholic, but my husband is, and therefore the *Catholic Digest* finds its way into our home each month. I read your magazine and have attended Mass often.

This always stirs up a question in my mind about the statues in church, such as those of St. Joseph and the Blessed Virgin. I see people kneeling before these statues and praying, I understand, not to the saints but to God through the saints.

The First Commandment specifically states: "I am the Lord thy God; thou shalt not make unto thee any graven image, or any likeness of anything that is in heaven above, or that is in the earth beneath, or that is in the water under the earth. Thou shalt not bow down thyself to them nor serve them; for I, the Lord thy God, am a jealous God. . . ."

On what basis, then, does your Church permit kneeling before statues, and, for that matter, how can you even make and possess them? I have asked this question many times of the clergy and of Catholic lay people, and I get only vague, uncertain answers which mean nothing to me. If you can enlighten me, I shall appreciate it very much.

Mrs. P. W. St. Amand

THE ANSWER

Judging by your name, Mrs. St. Amand, you should hardly be one to object to veneration of the Saints. Your husband's family must have some connection, at least by sympathy, with the great St. Amand, or Amandus, who was Bishop of Maestricht in the seventh century. His feast day is February 6. He has always been popular in the Low Countries, and is patron of brewers, innkeepers, and wine merchants. We sometimes spell his name Alan or Allen.

So may your patron Saint pray for us that we may reach an understanding on your problem. The matter is really quite clear in Catholic teaching; so you must blame me if I do not make it clear to you.

You really present two questions: (1) veneration of Saints, and (2) the honor we pay to their statues and pictures. I shall answer the first briefly, because you are chiefly concerned with the second.

Veneration of the Saints is a religious form of hero worship. Saints give us inspiring examples of all that we should be, or would like to be, in our efforts to imitate our Lord Jesus Christ. We are trying to avoid sin and acquire virtue; they did both in a remarkable manner. We are struggling to get to heaven; they blazed the rugged trail before us. They prove that the goal is possible; they have attained it.

The essential part of our religion is the adoration of God, our Creator, Lord and Master of the universe; and of Jesus Christ, the eternal Son of God, who became man. The Saints are close friends of God, intimately united to Jesus Christ in sharing His glory. It would hardly be polite for us to ignore them as we approach the throne of the Lord.

We worship God through them. We give Him glory by honoring His close friends. When we acknowledge them as Saints we honor the Savior who sanctified them; because they did not get to heaven under their own power; Jesus carried them there on the flood of His graces.

There is one slight inaccuracy in your question, which I would like to correct: we do pray to the Saints, not merely through them to God. It is as simple as asking your best friend to pray for you, when you know he is good at prayer. Your request goes directly to your friend; our request goes to the Saint. Each presents our pleas to God.

In moments of stress most of us find our personal prayers inadequate. So we ask our family or friends to pray for us.

214

Many pious persons search out the unlisted number of the Carmelite Sisters and call them in time of crisis; and thus get some intense prayers for their needs.

The Saints are our good friends, too. They were once human beings, pretty much like you and me. They know our problems and sympathize with our worries. They are close to us, because of our mutual closeness to Christ; they are united to Him in glory just as we are united to Him in grace. They were members of his mystical Body, as we are; now they have reached greater intimacy, without severing their spiritual bonds with the rest of us.

They are in a better position even than the Carmelites to make their prayers for us effective. They are closer to the source of all favors, right next to God.

Some of them have a listed number; the Church has let the whole world know that they are Saints. Others are tucked obscurely into the sublime folds of heaven's splendor; but they, too, can be reached. The good Lord puts us through to them. If heaven had no communication facilities it would be a poorer place than earth.

We do believe that the Saints are alive and alert; they love God and they love us who are striving to be friends of God. Some of them were our relatives or companions on earth. Some had a special place in the history of our redemption: like Mary, the Mother of Jesus; and Joseph, and John the Baptist, Lazarus and Mary Magdalen, and the Apostles. Others were valiant martyrs who died in imitation of their Master, great scholars who devoted their talents to knowing and loving Him, holy Popes and bishops, pious monks, and good, strong women who distinguished themselves in His service.

To adore the Saints would be silly and sinful. They are not divine, but merely human beings sanctified. But they are in union with the Divinity; and that is our goal, too. So it is sensible to regard them as models and to run to them for help. In that consists our devotion to the Saints.

And now about those statues! We won't single them out, but rather group them with pictures, mosaics, carvings, and icons, under the general name of images. We have them in our churches because we like them and have always been accustomed to them. They are beautiful and decorative; or at least we intend them to be so, even though they often fail to match this purpose. They add color and warmth; our churches would seem cold and drab without them. They often teach us bits of our religion, attract our attention to pious subjects, and aid our concentration in prayer.

Above all, images are an old Christian custom, going back to the days of the catacombs. In spite of a few rough days with the Iconoclasts, our religious ancestors always made use of images, even as we do, without worrying about idolatry.

Some abuses have emerged. Probably nothing exists on earth that man cannot misuse; and even the most sacred doctrines and practices of our religion are sometimes perverted to superstition, scandal, or injustice. But the teachings of the Church have always been clear on images. Usually popular practice has not been far out of line, though sometimes we must take into consideration the simple thinking of uneducated peoples to understand their practices. The sophisticated person often senses superstition in acts of trusting faith, while the pious peasant knows well what he is doing and is not far from the straight doctrinal line for all his simple thought and elaborate observances.

You propose the First Commandment as an argument against images, especially statues. Many Protestants call this the second Commandment; I will quote the pertinent parts of it from Deuteronomy in our Confraternity Edition: "You shall not carve idols for yourselves in the shape of anything in the sky above or on the earth below or in the waters beneath the earth; you shall not bow down before them or worship them." The words in Exodus are practically the same.

It is not at all sure that the Lord meant to forbid the carving of any statue. He prohibits those which would be used as idols. The Jewish people were always sensitive to dangers of idolatry, and yet they were not opposed to all statues or carvings. Many are mentioned in the Old Testament as either ordered or approved by the Lord Himself: the brazen serpent mounted on a pole, which healed the bites of the real serpents; the two lions beside the throne of

216

Solomon, and the twelve lion cubs which guarded the steps to the throne; the twelve giant bulls under the great basin in the Temple; the cherubim, winged bulls with human heads, which are often mentioned, used as decorations in the Temple, along with lions and oxen; and then, of course, the angels which were over the Ark of the Covenant.

So it seems that the Jewish people did go in for sculpture, although they abhorred idols. We do not read in the Old Testament of any statues of men; nearest to them were the human heads on the cherubim. Extreme Jewish opposition to statues developed late, about the time of Christ, when they objected to the golden eagle placed over the Temple gate by Herod, and persuaded Pilate to remove the statues of Caesar from Jerusalem.

Even if the First Commandment had forbidden all statues, there is no reason to believe that its prohibition would apply to Christians. In principle, the laws of the Old Testament were for the Chosen People of the Lord, given to prepare the way for the coming of the Savior. They lost their direct force when the New Testament fulfilled their promise and replaced them as a Covenant of God with His people. Of course, some of the Ten Commandments remain substantially in effect because they are a plain statement of the natural law: murder, adultery, theft, and perjury are wrong by the nature of things; they are contrary to God's plan for man.

The Apostles themselves, at the Council of Jerusalem, decided that most of the ancient ceremonial and religious laws did not apply to Christians. They did not have to be circumcised, or observe the Sabbath, or follow the dietary prescriptions, or adhere to the rituals of the Temple. Neither were they forbidden to become sculptors, although the making of idols remains always forbidden, as does the adoring of them.

The catacombs were cemeteries of the early Christians during the first three centuries; and they are extensively decorated. They are the cradle of Christian art; in them are early symbols of Christ and later paintings of Him, many pictures of saints, and a variety of biblical scenes.

We would know very little about this early Christian art

217

if we had not found it. The first Fathers of the Church make no issue of the subject; since images were widely used in their day, they were evidently taken for granted. It seems manifest that Christians simply adapted the art of pagan Rome to their religious needs. They apparently did it without any fear of idolatry, or any word of caution from those in authority.

The early Christians were not even afraid of figures of mythology, like Psyche, Eros, and Orpheus, which they adapted to their own religious meaning. They often used scenes from the Old Testament, like Daniel in the lions' den, Noe and the ark, Samson and the Temple, Jonas and the whale, and Moses and the rock. Among the early scenes pictured from the New Testament are the birth of Christ, the coming of the Magi, the Baptism of Jesus, the miracle of the loaves and fishes, the raising of Lazarus, and Christ teaching His disciples.

The catacombs did not lend themselves to sculpture, but we do have examples of Christian statues from the very early centuries, possibly from the first. These were apparently used only in the Western Church. Eastern Catholics were even more devoted to images; they used them in greater abundance and made more fuss about them, bowing and kissing, and burning incense and lights; but they wanted their icons flat: paintings, mosaics, and bas-reliefs.

This "image-worship" went on happily in the whole Church, unhindered and with little serious protest until the eighth century. Then the peace of the whole Church and the empire was violently disturbed by a fanatical wave of Iconoclasm, image smashing. It was led and directed by the emperor himself, and it was hard on all who clung to favorite icons.

There was probably some justification for the emperor's campaign. In the Eastern Church images had sometimes multiplied beyond reason, so that the inside walls of some churches were covered with icons from floor to ceiling. People took their pet pictures with them for protection on journeys; armies carried them like flags; and they were taken to the hippodrome for the races. They were in every room in the house and every store in town; they were on dishes, clothing, furniture.

There are indications, too, that sound doctrine was occasionally a bit jumbled. Some Christians apparently considered icons as gateways of approach to God and the Saints, or as channels of grace—almost as though they were sacraments. And many were seemingly convinced that God used icons as a means of working miracles.

Manifestations of devotion were also a bit excessive: lamps were burned before icons, incense was offered, hymns were sung in their honor, and bows and kisses were frequent. Most of these things are still done today in the Eastern Churches, both Catholic and Orthodox, without significant abuse. But in those days they were often exaggerated.

The fight of Iconoclasm is a long story, but we will try to make it short. In 726, the emperor ordered all images in the churches to be destroyed. The monks opposed him violently, and the people were almost in revolt against the smashing of their icons. It was a rough time, and it resulted in the Seventh General Council of the Church, the second Council of Nicaea.

In this ecumenical council—the last one accepted by all five Patriarchs—the doctrine of the Church regarding images was clearly defined and settled once and for all. It took some time for the action of the council to restore peace, but the ninth century marks the end of all serious controversy on this subject for traditional Christianity, both Catholic and Orthodox. And from then until the sixteenth century images of all kinds enjoyed wide popularity. They challenged the skill of the greatest Byzantine and Gothic artists and gave inspiration to the Renaissance. Statues, paintings, mosaics, and stained glass gave new beauty to the world and made religion warm and joyful.

Apparently the opposition of some Protestant groups is based on the assumption that statues and other images contribute to superstition. But Catholic authorities are as alert to dangers of superstition as any other group. They are familiar with these practices, have studied them, and are not alarmed by them; and only from time to time in the course of centuries have they found it necessary to correct abuses.

To sum it up, Mrs. St. Amand, we kneel before these statues because we can pray better there. They remind us of our Lord, to whom our prayers are directed, of His Mother, and His Saints, who inspire and help us. You have pictures of your husband and children around your home; we have images of the ones we love in church. They help to make our churches beautiful, for the glory of the Lord. And they do no harm at all; we have no tendency to adore them. Our statues have finely carved ears, but they can't hear a word. They haven't a brain cell in their hard heads. Only a fool would expect a statue to reach out a hand and shake the world, or even pat him on the head. But images can give us steady assurance that our Savior has strong hands, and that He keeps the world in them.

28

FREE WILL

THE QUESTION

I would like to send along a question. To me, a psychiatrist, it is important: it refers to the age-old question of Determinism vs. Free Will, and I am trying to find out why the Catholic Church considers and believes that man is endowed by God with the power to exercise free will and is therefore responsible for his actions resulting from choice.

The mind, and therefore one of its components, the will, is in its total functioning partly conscious and partly unconscious. To me, free will is equivalent to the conscious motives found in the ego. These conscious motives are in themselves very complex derivations of unconscious instinctual motives.

To me, a human act is determined or conditioned by a host of factors. The principle of causality in the field of human behavior seems to be indicated, with our actions determined more by unconscious than by conscious motivation—and one has no control of unconscious motivations. Is one's behavior determined by ethical values incorporated in the personality, and is it therefore one's responsibility?

H. Sinclair Tait, M.D.

THE ANSWER

In your letter, Doctor, I discern three questions or arguments regarding free will: (1) our reasons for believing in it; (2) the determining power of motivations; and (3) the effect of natural laws, like causality, on our free actions.

Our reasons for believing that man has a free will and is

221

responsible for his deliberate actions are derived from three sources: theology, philosophy, and immediate natural evidence.

In sacred Scripture it is clearly revealed that God will reward the good and punish the wicked. In various ways we are told that we will gain eternal life if we have faith, keep the Commandments, love God, and do good to our neighbor; and it is similarly evident that we will be damned to eternal pains if we are unfaithful to God, break His laws, or violate justice and charity.

We hold it equally certain that God is good and just. But it would evidently be cruel and unfair to punish a man for something he could not help. And rewards would be undeserved if we were not responsible for our own good acts. Without free will there should be no blame or credit; there might be a heaven, but there could be no hell.

It would be easy here, Doctor, to get off the track of your question and become involved in the theological problems of determinism, which result from original sin, the effects of God's grace and predestination. These are age-old questions, too, but not the ones which interest you.

Our second reason for believing that man is free results from our concept of man's nature. We hold that man has a spiritual soul as well as a material body; and freedom is a natural characteristic of spiritual things. Man is a rational animal, and the roots of his freedom are in the rational part of him. Of course, man is not entirely spiritual; so he is not entirely free. Determinism is a natural characteristic of material things. Man has a physical body and that body is subject to the physical laws of nature. But man's body and soul act together as a unit; so the freedom of man's soul deeply affects the material part of him, while his physical motivations strongly push and pull his soul.

Our third reason for holding man free derives from natural evidence: from the facts of our own personal consciousness, from man's universal conviction of freedom, and from the resulting moral attitudes and social conventions of all mankind.

My personal conviction that I am free is strengthened at

this moment by my sharp awareness that each phrase I write represents a decision, and often these decisions are made with much effort. I must make each one myself; I cannot wait for them to be thrust upon me. And when I am through I know that the result and responsibility are mine. If I should write errors critics will not blame motive forces or motivation tracts; they will blame me.

You will find it elementary, Doctor, to review our mental processes in reaching a decision. But I ask your patience while we think about deciding on a trip to New York. Our motives are many, and most of them are conscious: cost, inconvenience, pleasure, fatigue, separation from family, business profit, and recreation.

We might spend hours or days weighing these motives carefully; or we might jump to a sudden decision as soon as the idea hits us. As we weigh motives and balance them against opposite reasons we may find ourselves on the point of making one decision, then backing out and almost reaching another. We may end up sleeping on it, and we are likely to find our indecision painful. If we observe carefully we will find that not all motives are rational: feelings, emotions, moods, headache, and digestion may influence us; and sometimes we are led into decision by the power of suggestion.

In the long run, it would seem that the deciding factor is the focus of our attention. If we dwell on the pleasures of the trip and push all else to the back of our minds, we will surely go. But if we concentrate on the expense we may talk ourselves out of it.

All along, we know that the decision is our own, although we may seek to avoid it, to let someone else make it for us, or to leave it to chance. But if we do make the decision it is made freely; and we know that we could have made the opposite decision—and we can still back out of it, if we have not thoroughly committed ourselves.

Now my question to you is this, Doctor. How do you explain the complete and unquestioning conviction of freedom which we have at every moment of our debate and decision? You may say, as some do, that our decision is only a complicated conflict of impulses, working themselves in a roundabout way to an impulsive solution. Then how do you explain the keen conviction that we have an active, dynamic role in it and are responsible for the outcome? Is it an illusion? If it is, then it is an illusion common to all men, imposed upon them by nature itself. And I am sure that even when you have thoroughly convinced yourself that it is an illusion, you still suffer thoroughly from the illusion.

You probably deal with illusions and delusions daily in your work, but you do not postulate them lightly or needlessly. Would you then be content with the theory that all men, everywhere, at all times, are uniformly deluded regarding the freedom with which they seem to make their decisions?

Of course, the majority of our decisions do not result from careful and conscious deliberation. But generally, even in our spontaneous, horseback decisions we are convinced that we are free, and we blame ourselves that they are imprudent and ill-considered. Often when we review our sudden judgments we realize that we were swayed by motives which we did not recognize at the time. But swayed or not, the decision was ours—poor one that it was.

It is simply a plain and practical fact that in our daily lives we consider ourselves responsible and hold others responsible. Our moral convictions are based on a presumption of freedom. And in our social conventions we simply take it for granted that men are free in their deliberate actions.

Laws and punishments, honors and citations, blame and praise are based on the practical assumption of human freedom. Many people may hold a theory of determinism, but in their daily lives, with themselves and with others, they live, act, think, and speak as believers in free will. Our language portrays this belief, and anyone who uses the words "should" and "would," "ought" and "oblige," "duty" and "responsibility," gives testimony to man's common conviction that he makes his own decisions.

Often the same persons who deny free will are the loudest in their demands for unlimited personal freedom. They resent censorship, legal restraints, and social restrictions. They demand unlimited opportunity to enjoy the freedom which they deny that they have. They insist on doing what they choose while denying their ability to choose at all. If we were to suspect their unconscious motives we might compare them to the boy who wishes to eat his cake and keep it, too. They desire all the pleasures of sin while denying responsibility for it. We might call them determined libertines.

If the determinists should be right, the human race would furnish to a celestial observer a comic drama of deluded frustration: every human being, singly and socially, conscious of freedom of choice, convinced in practice that he is personally responsible and holding others responsible, and all of them simply helpless victims of uncontrollable motivations. Puppets with delusions of dynamism, they think that they manage the strings from which they dangle. And funniest of all, even the philosophers who know differently, and firmly hold freedom impossible, still act as simple and responsible as the savages.

In a way, Doctor, it seems strange that you, a psychiatrist, should doubt the freedom of the will, because the success of your practice must depend largely upon your everyday use of it. You do not treat your patient as though he were a complex set of reactions to stimuli; you treat him as a person.

Of course, you are primarily concerned with his motives and drives, which you try to diagnose and then help him to understand. But I am led to believe that one of the main goals of your psychotherapy is to build up responsibility in your patients. You help them to face reality, to avoid escape mechanisms, to outgrow childish attitudes, and to accept the responsibilities of a mature person.

After understanding their motives, they try to bring them under control, by substituting higher motives for them. But what good would all your effort be if your patients were not free to choose the better motives when they see them?

Also, I am certain that you depend very largely upon the co-operation of your patients. Do you consider this co-operation free or forced? I respectfully submit, Doctor, that if your patients are not free, then you are manipulating them as you would machines. Since they are not able to choose and so make something out of themselves, you are trying, in a complicated way, to make something out of them. You mold and fashion them into normality.

I know that you would not accept such a definition of your practice; and even if you did, you would be claiming for yourself the free will you deny your patients. You would be imposing your will on them, since you judge that they have no wills of their own.

Your second question, Doctor, has to do with motivation. You are in your own field here, and I would not dare argue with you. But I must point out that our notion of free will does not contradict any facts you may establish regarding motivation, either conscious or unconscious. Many people misunderstand our concept. The will is not an arbitrary faculty; it functions through the intellect, but it is deeply imbedded in emotions, inextricably bound up with man's physical nature, pushed and pulled by various forces, and probably quite unaware of the nature of many of its motives.

We do not claim that the will is omnipotent; we do not deny that you can find causal determination for many of its acts. But doesn't it sometimes surprise you?

We do affirm that we are active, dynamic persons; that our thoughts and actions are our own, not things which own us. Thoughts may at times overwhelm us, and desires may impel us to action, but we do the thinking, and the acts are our own. When they cease to be our own we are no longer held responsible. We are not normal—if you will tolerate that word.

The will functions through the intellect, and we cannot focus attention on motives of which we are unaware. So our will can deal directly only with conscious motives. Therefore, I freely concede to you, Doctor, that in the measure in which our motivation is unconscious we are not free. But do you not try by various processes of association and recall to bring unconscious motives into the area of awareness, and thereby make them subject to voluntary control? Is it not strange, then, that you who are professionally engaged in increasing the freedom of the will should deny its existence?

With many determinists it is difficult to argue, because they insist on defining their own terms in such a way as to

226

eliminate free will before we start. It is like tossing coins with a man who makes preliminary agreement: "Heads I win, tails you lose." To a determinist, if a man who is sorely tempted plunges into the revelry of sin, that proves that he was not free but was overwhelmingly motivated by his passions and his subconscious drives. On the other hand, if he resists the temptation and runs away from sin, that proves that he is so influenced by moral restrictions and social inhibitions that he is afraid to indulge his natural desires. Whichever way he turns, the poor fellow never had a thing to say about it; he was simply pulled or pushed.

Our concept of free will does not eliminate the pulling and pushing. It is aware of the tug of known forces, and admits the shove of unconscious drives. But it assures us that we are able to choose between conflicting motives, at least when we see them; and sometimes we deliberately scoot along with the pusher; sometimes give in to the pull.

Your third argument takes us back into the realm of philosophy. Just as we hold that man is free because he has a spiritual soul, so determinists say that man's actions are rigidly directed by physical factors because he is entirely material. They deny man's free will a priori; he just couldn't be free. And when the facts evidently contradict their theory, they either call these facts illusions or ignore them entirely. So we seldom find a modern book of psychology which treats of the will at all.

You say, Doctor, that the principle of causality must work in man's behavior. That implies that if you could measure all his motives you could predict his decisions with mathematical precision. So you must consider man a machine, totally subject to physical laws—a robot run entirely by chemistry, electricity, pressure, and heat.

To your law of causality some determinists have added the law of conservation of energy. They say that free will is impossible, because the process of choosing would add energy to one set of motives, thereby making them stronger than the opposing set. This energy would come from nowhere; it would have to be created by the will, and thus would add to the total energy of the universe. This conclusion directly contradicts our established laws of the conservation of matter-energy.

Such reasoning, again, fits only the robot man. It shows no understanding of man's spiritual soul. Spiritual things create no physical energy (except as God created all matter and energy in the beginning, and can do it again as He wishes). But spiritual things do have ways of directing physical energy and changing its quality; and in so doing they make the action of that energy unpredictable, reflecting into it their own natural freedom.

You are rightly concerned with causality when you study man's actions. It is your business to assess, evaluate, recognize, and understand his motivations. For practical purposes you do not touch his will any more than the surgeon whittles away at his soul. Your mechanical methods are, no doubt, particularly valid when you deal with subconscious motives. But your engrossment in your living, breathing robot need not eliminate free will from your concept.

You do need that free will if your robot is to become responsible.

29

NATURAL LAW

It is my announced purpose to give a simple explanation of the natural law, and I proclaim this goal though I know well it is impossible of attainment. If my presentation remains simple it will not really explain the natural law, but rather some flattened distortion thereof; and if it should adequately expound the natural law it will not remain simple. In this article I will speak often of the inherent nature of things: everything has an essence, and you cannot change that essence without making it a new being. And it is the essence of natural law to be complicated. If you give it a simple essence you make it something else.

Professors tell us that repetition is the key to successful teaching. So by rules of composition this will be a poor article. I plan deliberately to say the same thing often, with only slight variations of view or emphasis. And I propose, as one who is not a philosopher, to write an article on philosophy for people who are not philosophers.

It usually clarifies a discussion if we start it off with a definition; and if one definition helps make a subject clear, several should multiply its clarity. So I propose to define my subject from various angles.

The popular notion is that the natural law is inscribed in the hearts of all men, and this definition is based on excellent authority. In the words of St. Paul to the Romans, 2:12-16, we read that the Gentiles "show the work of the Law written in their hearts. Their conscience bears witness to them. . . ."

We must be careful of our interpretation of these words of St. Paul and of the conclusions we draw from them. Taken in a poetic or figurative sense they are a beautiful description of the natural law, which every man knows through his own reason; but we can easily derive from them notions quite the opposite of the natural law. We might conclude that each man knows instinctively the law of God in a sound and reliable manner. Our consciences read the writing in our hearts and we have no need of other mentor. Nothing could be more subjective or relative. Each man would find his law inside himself, and each would be a law unto himself. The natural law notion is that each man finds the law outside himself—in God's great world—and it is the same for every man.

The natural law is a moral law—a rule of right and wrong —which is prescribed by our own human nature when that nature is thoroughly known and understood.

It is the law which created nature teaches us, if we study carefully its organization, plan, and purpose.

It is the law of nature's God—that portion of the Eternal Law which has been manifested through creation.

It is the law of reason—the plan, purpose and will of God as we learn it from a careful study of created things, and especially of man.

Sometimes it helps to split a definition into parts:

The author—or lawmaker—of the natural law is God.

This law is promulgated in creation. God has a plan and all His creatures fit into that plan.

The existence and meaning of this law is known to us from experience and reason. By studying God's creatures we get to know his plan.

Subject to the law is every man.

The subject-matter of the law is the moral goodness of man's actions.

The content of the law is mainly some general principles of goodness, but the extent to which its precise prescriptions can be known with certainty is a matter of dispute, which we will discuss later.

The natural law is based upon some fundamental suppositions:

1. There is a God of supreme intelligence who created everything.

2. God had a plan in creating. This plan is a part of the Eternal Law, which is God Himself.

230

3. Every creature has an end and purpose to which it is destined in God's plan.

4. Some useful reflections of God's eternal plan are shown to us in the world He created.

5. Man is an intelligent creature of God, capable of recognizing God's plan in creation, if he will take the trouble to study it. It is not something man grasps at a glance. He must combine his individual efforts with those of his fellow men, and make wise use of experience and history, learning lessons from mistakes.

6. Man is a free creature, responsible for his own actions. God rules him by a moral law, which gives him rights and imposes duties, but does not force him against his will. Physical laws govern the material universe. Even animals are ruled by physical laws which we call instincts. Rocks and dogs attain their purpose in creation by laws of necessity. But man works out his purpose on his own responsibility, following a law of love and obligation. There are things he *ought* to do, but he is physically free to do them or not; if he does not do them he will fall short of the goal for which God destined him.

7. Man has rights as well as obligations. These rights are given him by his Creator. By nature he has right to all those things which are essential to the attainment of his goal in life.

8. Man is expected to learn his goal in life and to work toward it by his own intelligence and will. The natural law is a guide God gives him along the way.

Man is by nature a social creature. The state is needed to foster and protect his social living. So the state is a part of God's plan; its authority comes from Him and it must conform to His law. Its purpose is to protect and ensure man's natural rights, not to curtail or destroy them.

The authority of the state is a thing of right reason rather than of will. Laws oblige us, not because they express the will of the legislator, but because they fit into the plan of God— which includes the state.

The essential qualities of the natural law are universality and immutability. It is based on human nature, and in essence man is always and everywhere the same: a creature of body

231

and soul, having personality, intelligence and free will, made in the image of God and destined to happiness. And this law is known by man's reason, which is common to all races and all centuries.

However, our concept of the natural law will be unrealistic if we think it requires all men, everywhere, in every civilization and every age, to understand its detailed prescriptions in the same way. It has two great limitations:

1. The details of man's essence and purpose are not immediately and certainly apparent. The law of creation is not easy to read; it requires profound study.

2. Man's reason is limited and fallible. His long road to a complete comprehension of human rights and duties is strewn with the bloody debris of cruelties, oppressions, persecutions, and multiple injustices. And there is reason to believe that he is still some way from his goal.

The great value of the natural law is not that it provides a guide to the individual human conscience, but that it provides a reasonable foundation for all human laws—the immutable standards of right and justice to which all human laws must conform if they are to have force and validity.

The notion of the natural law is almost as ancient as human thought, and for the world community of the future it provides the only sound basis for unity and peace, with justice for all. It puts man's rights beyond the arbitrary will of the strong, and makes reason the immediate norm of rightness. I believe that there is much more of natural law thought in the Universal Declaration of Human Rights than its framers would ever admit.

Frequently we understand a thing best by looking at it in contrast with its opposites. The light of a candle shines bright in darkness, and red is strongest on blue or green.

For simplicity we might list the following notions as contrary to the natural law: positivism, subjectivism, relativism, pragmatism, and materialism.

To point up our contrast we might repeat the basic tenets of the natural law theory: Justice, right and goodness exist in the nature of things. Law is truth, in conformity with nature. Law is reason, which understands the nature of things

232

and the justice that is in them. Truth, justice, right, and goodness are as broad and unchangeable as the world itself. Being and obligation derive from the same source and are tied up in each other.

Our first contrast is materialism. Few people are so crass as to hold it bluntly in theory, but many follow it in practice. Its basic principle is: might makes right. It is the law of the jungle, the rule of expediency, the ethics of power. In opposition the natural law holds that certain things are right by their very nature, and we are in conscience bound to them whether we be strong or weak; other things are wrong by nature and we must avoid them, no matter how capably we may be getting by with them.

Subjectivism holds that the law is inside the individual, either written in his heart or elaborated in his brain. Right, duty and justice are strictly matters of his own conscience; they have no reality outside of him. In contrast the natural law, while respecting conscience as the immediate guide for each individual, holds that good and evil are realities outside man and can be known by him; and that it is the function of conscience to know and conform to reality.

There is another type of subjective morality which makes the virtue or evil of an act depend on the intention of the actor. If I am sincere, honest, and well-meaning I can hardly do wrong, or at least my wrong should not be imputed to me —and this is especially true if I act from motives of love and brotherhood. Natural law would hold that an act is good or bad in itself, and it is up to us to recognize its true nature. Our internal motives cannot change that nature, although they may, in our confusion, diminish our subjective guilt.

Relativism is the notion that morality changes from year to year, from place to place, and from person to person. Murder might be permissible on some remote and primitive island but it is wrong in the United States. Birth control was immoral in the nineteenth century but is virtuous today. Things licit for the king may be sinful for his subject. And so on. By contrast the natural law is universal and unalterable. Social conditions may change and demand diverse application of principles; concepts may be clarified so that ancient

233

notions are better understood today. But always and everywhere we deal with the same principles, which inhere in the nature of men and things.

Pragmatism puts morality to the practical test. Whatever works best for man and society is morally good. If birth control will solve the population problems of India then use it by all means. Any purpose so good makes any sound practical method morally right. The natural law will not permit a good end to justify immoral means.

The most inclusive and pervasive notion of law today is positivism. It fits the nature of things into law. Justice and right are what the law says they are. Law is will rather than reason—authority rather than truth. Men have rights because the constitution guarantees them; take away the constitution and the rights disappear without a trace; they have no reality apart from man's law. Neither does sin have a natural existence; it is what the law and social custom declare it to be.

In contrast to positivism the natural law theory holds that truth, justice, right and duty already exist in the nature of things before man's positive law is enacted, and that it is the function of man's law to declare these pre-existing facts of life and determine their detailed application to actual circumstances. It is the duty of the legislator to understand the realities of the natural law and to make his statutes conform with it. The positivist would say: "legal justice is natural justice; the law makes it so." The natural law man will say: "Legal justice must reflect natural justice, else man's law is vicious. The first requisite of sound law is right reason, rather than will."

These contrasts should make it clear that the difference between the natural law and all other theories rests on two basic premises:

1. The real and purposeful existence of man and the whole created world.

2. The reliability of our knowledge as reflecting the reality of things.

If I hold, as a basic philosophical theory, that the world in which I live has no inherent plan or purpose, then I can

234

never be a natural law man.

If I hold that man is not capable of knowing the plan and purpose of creation from his own observation and study, then I must find some other theory of law.

In other words the natural law has validity only in the measure it rests on (1) a sound metaphysics, and (2) a reliable theory of knowledge:

1. Metaphysics. The natural law concept supposes a firm and reasoned conviction that all existing things—including ourselves—have an essence, an inherent nature, which determines their goal and purpose in the plan of creation. Some people are convinced only of the existence of things and see no essential purpose in their being. Others are not quite sure that existence is real. Such people can never accept the natural law.

2. Theory of knowledge. Many modern thinkers are skeptical about the extent and reliability of our perception and understanding of things. Positivism is still popular; it deals confidently with things which are measurable and ponderable, or otherwise subject to scientific investigation; but it questions seriously the reliability of our abstract concepts. It is never sure of the essence or purpose of things. If you share such theory of knowledge then you can forget the natural law, because it supposes that we are able to really know, interpret, and understand the world in which we live. We are capable of errors, certainly, but when our abstract ideas are carefully checked and studied they conform reliably with reality. The essence of existing things is not entirely hidden from us; and the purpose of each thing is determined by its essence.

Our clearest understanding of the natural law would probably come from a study of its history: the varying notions of it held by philosophers, jurists, and moralists through the ages; the prominent role it has played in the development of the laws of most nations; and the sad effects of its rejection in some of the legal systems of modern times. However, such study would far exceed our scope. I shall attempt a sweeping summary.

The natural law is not an original or exclusive Christian

concept. It is derived from man's nature, which is the same the world over, and it is known by man's reason, which is common to all races. A few years ago on the campus of the University of Notre Dame the Natural Law Institute heard papers from separate representatives of various traditions—Jewish, Moslem, Hindu, Buddhist, and Chinese—tracing the independent development and influence of the natural law concept in these diverse civilizations.

Our own tradition of natural law had its beginnings with the philosophers of ancient Greece, and displayed its practical influence through the jurists of republican and imperial Rome, where Cicero was its greatest exponent. Aristotle is often called the "Father of the Natural Law," but actually Greece had better practical proponents of it before and after him, especially in the Sophists and the Stoics. His right to the title may be deserved because he gave us the sound basis of metaphysics and epistemology on which the natural law can repose securely.

The natural law attained its greatest development among the scholastics of the Middle Ages, and finds its clearest exposition in St. Thomas Aquinas. In spite of later weakening of its philosophical foundation it remained the preponderant influence in legal and moral thinking until the nineteenth century. But gradually in the course of these same centuries there was an attitude creeping in which we might call voluntarism—the very opposite of the natural law—and it slowly sapped our theory of meaning. Voluntarism emphasizes the will rather than reason. It begins with a misunderstanding of the integral nature of God; it tends to separate His will from His being. Things are wrong because God forbids them; they are right because He commands them. If He hadn't spoken we would have no way to question their morality.

The most extreme representatives of voluntarism have insisted on a literal interpretation of the Scriptures, and so have become extreme pacifists, vegetarians, and opponents of blood-transfusion.

The worst thing about voluntarism is that it has transferred its theory to the civil law, making the will of the legislator the norm of legality. Usually these notions have not been too noxious where the democratic process prevails; the principles of the natural law assert themselves in spite of denial, through the common sense of the citizens. But when voluntarism serves the dictator its effects are devastating. When the will of the strong man determines right and wrong the Devil's own work may well be done.

The natural law is a hardy perennial. Its life has often been threatened, but it has never disappeared from the scene of world thinking. Etienne Gilson has said that it always buries its undertakers. The nineteenth century saw its lowest decline, but in recent years it has shown signs of new life. Its decline was due to two factors:

1. Its philosophical foundations were undermined by positivism and similar theories which obscured man's nature and purpose.

2. Some proponents of the natural law had greatly abused its deductive processes. They made its evident principles the premises for intricate reasoning and remote conclusions; and it seemed to serve them well for purpose of rationalization. Opponents charged that if one's deductions were clever enough one could prove anything right or wrong, as might suit his aim and interest.

And this observation leads us to the much disputed question of the content of the natural law. One group, who might be called conservatives, hold that the value of the natural law lies mainly, if not exclusively, in its sound metaphysical viewpoint: the essential and unchangeable reality of good and evil, inherent in the nature of creation, and apart from the will or motives of man. Most will admit that it provides sound basis for deducing such firm and basic principles as the following:

1. Man has a natural obligation to do right and avoid evil.

2. All men are equal in nature before God.

3. Justice must be done. Each man should get his due.

4. Man has certain rights inherent in his nature and person; these rights come from God and are inalienable. No earthly power may justly take them from him.

The rights man has by nature are those essential to the

237

attainment of his goal in life. These surely include—in our present developed understanding of man, his nature and his purpose:

1. The right to life. You can't work toward your goal if you are dead.

2. The right to liberty. Man has his soul from God; not from any other man. His conscience is his own; even God won't force it. Of course liberty is not the absence of all restraint. Any reasonable view of man sees him as a social being; liberties must co-operate and not be noxious.

3. The right to property. A free man would be no better than a slave if he could not have things of his own. Man may idealize liberty, but he will fight as quickly for his property.

4. The right to self-expression. The power of speech, the ability to write, and the skill to convey ideas with brush or chisel are properties peculiar to man. They set him apart from the beasts; even these can be free and hold property.

5. The right to pursue happiness; nature does not guarantee its attainment.

Man has other natural rights, but these are basic examples; and the natural certainty of some other rights may be less evident. Even the ones we have listed have not always and everywhere been recognized, and are sometimes denied in our own day.

It takes little deduction to see that if one man has a right other men have a duty to respect that right. And it soon becomes evident that the prime purpose of the state is to protect that right.

Some fervent partisans of the natural law will try to apply its principles by simple rational process to the details of daily behavior. Deduction served Sherlock Holmes admirably, but the modern detective shows reasonable preference for careful scientific investigation. Many problems of modern morality are so complicated that they defy solution by pure deduction. In fact, some of them seem to defy solution by any process, and it is quite popular today to conclude that their morality is "ambiguous."

Our application of natural law principles to specific problems will be greatly aided if we call on the wisdom of mankind to guide us. Man has made his deductions bit by bit through the experience of the ages. We are fools if we scorn the sense and judgment of our ancestors and our current wise men and try to make our own isolated deductions.

We Catholics have another guide we must not ignore— even though the mention of it takes us away from the primary concept of the natural law. It is the Church of Christ, our teacher on earth.

We have strongly stressed that the natural law is not restricted to Christians or Catholics. It is universal. But Christianity has clarified two notions which give nature's law added meaning for us:

1. A personal God, from whose unlimited perfection all norms of goodness proceed.

2. The sacred nature of human personality. Man has a goal which transcends all other purposes on earth; so the individual man is the most important thing on earth; everything else exists for him—that he may use them for God's glory and his own spiritual fulfillment.

Catholic doctrine adds another notion: we know the natural law best when we learn it under the guidance of the teaching Church. Left alone there are many intricate moral problems we can never solve surely by appeal to reason alone. It is to help us with these that Jesus Christ remains with His Church to make it a reliable teacher.

History shows that the Church does not rush into every moral problem which presents itself and hand out pat decisions with arbitrary reliance on her infallible authority. Most questions are solved by the ordinary teaching methods of the Church; the guidance of custom, the studies of theologians, the writings of bishops and the sermons of priests. Every now and then, when it becomes really necessary, a Pope or general council will speak out in definite and official manner. And sometimes we can be sure of the details of natural law only because Jesus Christ continues to teach us through His Church—which does not make her own laws on the subject, but tells us clearly the eternal pronouncements uttered by God in the essence of His creation.

30

SEGREGATION

THE QUESTION

My question does not deal with Catholic theology as such. It concerns the practical application of what I believe to be Christian teaching. Because prejudice is a major factor in American life, integration of certain minority groups is a controversial subject.

One frequently hears or reads about "the Catholic Church's position on segregation" or "the Catholic Church's stand for desegregation of the Southern churches." But these are only passing references.

I have not found anyone able to elaborate or clarify what the Church's actual position is. Even my Negro friends are familiar only with the *fact* that the Catholic Church has taken a more positive stand against segregation than other segments of Christianity. What I want is a clear, factual, informative explanation of the Church's stand on segregation, especially in statements quoted from outstanding Church officials.

George Stenger

THE ANSWER

In the space allowed me, George, I can give you only a few of the quotations I would like to present on this tense and timely subject. There is a little book which gives hundreds of them: *The Challenge of Interracial Justice,* by Msgr. Daniel M. Cantwell.* I am using many quotations from it

* Techny, Ill.: Divine Word Publications, 1959.

240

here. And I might just take up my entire answer by quoting for you the statement of the Catholic bishops of the United States formally issued at their meeting in Washington, D. C., on November 13, 1958.

One of the clearest and most complete statements I know is found in *An Elementary Catholic Catechism on the Morality of Segregation and Racial Discrimination,* issued by Bishop Fletcher of Little Rock, Arkansas, for use in teaching the people of his diocese the basic truths of this agitated subject. It is privately printed and would probably have to be obtained from the bishop's office.

I am not trying to give you a bibliography on this subject, but anyone wanting to know the Catholic position should consult two books by Father John LaFarge, S.J., who has been our guiding light in this area for many years: *The Race Question and the Negro* and *The Catholic Viewpoint on Race Relations.*

It is helpful to keep in mind, too, that we have about forty-five Catholic interracial organizations in the country, working to promote understanding, justice, and charity in this troubled area of society. Several of them have publications which set forth Catholic teachings and attitudes. The one I know best is *Community.**

To get some system in my quotations I will group them under a few of the basic principles which they illustrate:

1. There is no room for racism in real Christianity. We believe that all men are created by God, are destined to adoption as His children, and are invited to the same intimate eternal union with Him in heaven. All of God's human children are equal in nature; each one has a spiritual soul, and the soul has no color; each one has received from his Creator the same natural rights as all others.

There is an essential unity of nature among all men; size, complexion, variations of bone structure and facial divergencies are all incidental to this intrinsic unity. Anthropologists may find it useful to classify men into ethnic groups on the basis of these incidental differences, but as far as Catholic doctrine is concerned there is no such thing as race; so

* Chicago, Ill.: Friendship House, published monthly.

241

any discrimination based on it is unreal and consequently unjust.

"Then only will it be possible to unite all in harmonious striving for common good, when all sections of society have the intimate conviction that they are members of a single family and children of the same heavenly Father" (Pope Pius XI, *Quadragesimo Anno,* 1931).

"As God's sun shines on all that bear human countenance, so does his law know no privileges or exceptions. Only superficial minds can lapse into the heresy of trying to confine God, the Creator of the world, within the boundaries of a single people, within the blood stream of a single race" (Pope Pius XI, condemning Nazi racism, *Mit Brennender Sorge,* 1937).

"The first of the pernicious errors, widespread today, is the forgetfulness of that law of human solidarity and charity which is dictated and imposed by our common origin and by the equality of rational nature in all men, to whatever people they belong" (Pope Pius XII, *Summi Pontificatus,* 1939).

"What colossal arrogance is involved and what infantile process of thought in the supposition that there are greater or lesser races among the children of Adam. The race of which it is our duty to be conscious is the entire human race" (Cardinal Cushing, address in Boston, 1948).

"It is the teaching of Holy Mother Church that every human being, regardless of race, color, or nationality, is created after the image and likeness of God [and] is entitled to individual respect and consideration" (Archbishop Rummel of New Orleans in a letter to the people of Jesuit Bend, La., who had refused to accept a Negro priest).

Osservatore Romano, the Vatican City paper, in a front-page editorial praised the archbishop for his firm stand.

"God created Adam and as from a common father all men came from Adam. The enlightened citizen must understand that he is a brother to the tribesman in deepest Africa" (Cardinal Stritch, sermon, New Orleans, 1950).

"God created men, and the entire human race comes from the same parents with equal rights" (Cardinal Cicognani, 1947).

"As a nation we began by declaring that all men are created equal. We now practically read it: all men are created equal except colored men" (Cardinal Spellman, quoting Abraham Lincoln, Harlem, New York City, 1951). The cardinal adds that our colored citizens, "like all Americans, must be free to exercise the rights given them in our Constitution."

Earlier, in 1949, Cardinal Spellman had stated: "The Church repudiates, as abhorrent to her very nature, the pernicious doctrine that men are born with the stamp upon them of essential racial superiority or inferiority. She recognizes no master race."

Among the six principal causes of segregation in Arkansas, Bishop Fletcher in his catechism cites "the false philosophy generally accepted that the Negro race is naturally inferior to the white race." And to the question, "What is the Church's stand on racism?" the bishop answers: "The Church condemns racism as contrary to its teachings that all men are inherently and naturally equal, and have the same dignity as children of God."

"To believe that one race or nation is superior to another in the Church, or before God, is heresy and should be condemned" (Bishop Waters of Raleigh, N. C., pastoral, 1951).

Father John LaFarge, S.J., sums it up by stating that "race" is a myth and "cannot serve as a practical basis for any type of human relationships" (*The Race Question and the Negro*).

2. All men are redeemed by Jesus Christ, called to be His brothers in the vital union of grace. Brotherhood in Christ ignores all racial barriers.

"Men may be separated by nationality and race, but our Saviour poured out his blood to reconcile all men to God through the cross and bid them unite in one Body" (Pope Pius XII, *Mystici Corporis,* 1943).

"To the question 'Who is my neighbor?' the Catholic Church makes answer: 'All men without distinction or exception'" (Bishop Fitzmaurice of Wilmington, pastoral, 1954).

"There is neither Greek nor barbarian, neither Jew nor

243

Gentile, neither white nor Negro; we are all brothers under the skin, brothers to one another and to one Elder Brother who lived and died for all of us" (Msgr. John M. Cooper, *Interracial Review,* June, 1949).

My old theology book, well-worn from seminary days, tells me that it is a matter of Catholic faith, defined by the Council of Trent, that Jesus died for all men. The Apostle St. John tells us that Jesus is a propitiation for our sins and "those of the whole world" (I John 2:2). And St. Paul agrees that God our Savior "wishes all men to be saved; gave himself a ransom for all" (I Timothy 2:4-6).

3. The Catholic Church insists upon strict justice as the basic relationship of man to man. The Golden Rule must rule. We must treat each man as we would want to be treated if we were in his place—and no chiseling or rationalizing!

"All men are endowed by their Creator with certain inalienable rights. These rights are conferred by God with equal bounty upon every human being. Therefore, in obedience to the Creator's will, each of us is bound to respect the rights of his fellow men. This is the essential meaning of justice" (pastoral letter of United States bishops, 1884).

"It is impossible for any good Catholic not to be on the side and in the forefront in the struggle for interracial justice, for all men are brothers" (Cardinal Spellman, 1951).

I am still tempted simply to give you in full the statement made by the bishops of the United States in 1958. Here are some pertinent excerpts:

Our nation now stands divided by the problem of compulsory segregation of the races and the opposing demand for racial justice. No region of our land is immune from strife and division resulting from this problem. In one area, the key issue may concern the schools. In another it may be conflict over housing. Job discrimination may be the focal point in still other sectors.

But all these issues have one point in common. They reflect the determination of our Negro people, and we hope the overwhelming majority of our white citizens, to see that our colored citizens obtain their full rights as

244

given to them by God, the Creator of all, and guaranteed by the democratic traditions of our nation.

The heart of the race question is moral and religious. It concerns the rights of man and our attitude toward our fellow man. If our attitude is governed by the great Christian law of love of neighbor and respect for his rights, then we can work out harmoniously the techniques for making legal, educational, economic, and social adjustments. But if our hearts are poisoned by hatred, or even by indifference toward the welfare and rights of our fellowmen, then our nation faces a grave internal crisis.

It is unreasonable and injurious to the rights of others that a factor such as race, by and of itself, should be made a cause of discrimination and a basis for unequal treatment.

4. There is another phase of justice which enters prominently into our racial problems. It is the relationship of the state, or government, to its citizens. It is called distributive justice, and it requires that the benefits of citizenship be distributed equally, equitably, and without discrimination against any group.

"A multiracial society can exist only where the different groups are permitted to live together in harmony, to cooperate in schemes for the common good, and to share the same political, social, educational, professional, and cultural facilities. Then, and only then can there be common interests and national unity.

"Nothing short of this concept of a multiracial society will have the approval of the Catholic Church" (pastoral, bishops of Northern Rhodesia, 1958).

"The natural rights of the Negro are identical in number and sacredness with the rights of white persons" (Msgr. Francis J. Gilligan, S.T.D.).

"We owe it to our Negro fellow citizens to see that they have in fact the rights which are given them in our Constitution. This means not only political equality, but also fair economic and educational opportunities, a just share in

245

public-welfare projects, good housing without exploitation, and a full chance for the social advancement of their race" (United States bishops, 1943).

"In the field of morality and particularly in the field of social justice and social charity Catholics should lead, not follow. Certain un-Christian attitudes have been tolerated by moral theologians 'for the time being.' The day of racial injustice has passed. The day of Christlike charity has arrived" (Archbishop Lucey of San Antonio, pastoral, 1954).

"A society based upon injustice has the seeds of its own dissolution within itself" (Cardinal Meyer of Chicago, pastoral, 1959).

5. Charity must enliven justice. It is not enough to treat our neighbor fairly; we must really love him as a brother, as we love ourselves. If we don't, let's face it, we are not truly Christian.

Jesus Himself taught us the meaning of love and brotherhood. Meditation on the words of the Master will show us that He prohibits discrimination among His brethren. His second Commandment is: "Thou shalt love thy neighbor as thyself." And in His story of the good Samaritan He makes it clear that "neighbor" is not restricted to race or nationality.

Pope Pius XII answered the question "Who is my neighbor?" by saying, "The neighbor is every man, the Negro of Central Africa or the Indian in the forests of the Amazon" (quoted by Archbishop Rummel).

"By this will all men know that you are my disciples, if you have love for one another" (John 13:35). Surely no race-hater can fit this norm of recognition. "That all may be one, even as Thou, Father, in Me and I in Thee" (John 13:35).

"As long as you did it for one of these, the least of my brethren, you did it for Me." Anyone who reads this from St. Matthew's Gospel cannot escape the evident conclusion that when we segregate Negroes we segregate Christ, and will end up on his left hand at the Judgment.

St. John makes pertinent comment on these words of Christ. "If anyone says, 'I love God,' and hates his brother,

246

he is a liar. For how can he who does not love his brother whom he sees, love God, whom he does not see?" (I John 4:21).

Pope Pius XI furthers the Lord's requirement of love in his encyclical on the priesthood. "That commandment enjoins a love which extends to all, knows no barriers nor national boundaries, excludes no race."

From another source: "The law of charity is the foundation of Christianity, and this law must reach out not only to individuals but to all nations, all races, and all classes" (Bishop Griffin of Springfield, Ill., letter, 1940).

6. Prejudice is a fertile source of sin: it quickly leads to rash judgment, varied injustice, and serious defects of charity. In advanced stages it leads to plain hate. We have a moral obligation to get rid of it.

"It is only too well known, alas, to what excesses pride of race and racial hatred can lead" (Pope Pius XII, 1945).

"There remains no other way to salvation" than that of repudiating definitely the pride of race and blood (Pope Pius XII, 1958).

"In the U.S. the struggle against inhuman and barbarous prejudice must be aided by all citizens" (*Osservatore Romano*, 1955).

"Northern prejudice is based more on ignorance than it is on a conscious, premeditated policy.

"Southern prejudice is not based so much on ignorance as on a deep, conscious, and deliberate dogma that all Negroes are inferior to all whites" (Father Joseph H. Fichter, S.J.).

"The prejudices, discriminations, and artificial conventions from which the Negro suffers are all based upon ignorance, ignorance of the moral law, ignorance of the principles of Christianity, ignorance of the fundamental facts of the whole situation" (Msgr. John A. Ryan, 1943).

Bishop Fletcher in his catechism says that racial prejudice is one of the principal causes of unjust racial discrimination. He calls the habit of racial prejudice a vice, which "is a habit inclining to moral evil." It becomes a sin when we "consent to (1) feelings of racial prejudice or hatred, or (2) deliberate thoughts, desires, words, actions, or omissions

247

which the vice of prejudice inspires." It can be either a mortal or venial sin. And a person is obliged to strive to overcome inclinations to racial prejudice. Its remedy is "the practice of racial justice and charity, both interiorly and exteriorly."

7. Segregation and various other forms of racial discrimination are uncharitable, unjust, unreasonable, and patently sinful.

"Can enforced segregation be reconciled with the Christian view of our fellow man? In our judgment it cannot, and this for two fundamental reasons:

"Legal segregation, or any form of compulsory segregation, in itself and by its very nature imposes a stigma of inferiority upon the segregated people.

"It is a matter of historical fact that segregation in our country has led to oppressive conditions and the denial of basic human rights to the Negro. This is evident in the fundamental fields of education, job opportunity, and housing" (United States bishops, 1958).

"The Church has always been energetically opposed to practices arising from what is called the color bar" (Pope Pius XII).

Archbishop Rummel of New Orleans, in a pastoral letter in 1956, condemned racial segregation as "morally wrong and sinful because it is a denial of the unity and solidarity of the human race and of the unity and universality of the Redemption and because it is basically a violation of the dictates of justice and the mandate of love, which in obedience to God's will must regulate the relations between all men."

Bishop Fletcher's catechism states flatly: "Segregation as we know it in Arkansas is immoral."

"When a Catholic fails to take a stand against racial intolerance or prejudice he is a slacker in the army of the Church militant" (Cardinal Cushing).

I could go on to give quotations on various types of discrimination: housing (Cardinal Meyer of Chicago made a memorable statement on this in November, 1959); on civil-rights legislation; fair-employment practice; sit-in protests;

248

segregated hospitals, churches, and public facilities—various critical phases of the current social unrest. But in the words of Bishop Waters, "It is our duty as Christians not only to love Negroes but to serve them, to help them. We need to help them to get better educational facilities, better opportunities for culture, better living conditions, better homes and families, better civic representation, and better friendliness in the community."

31
ARTIFICIAL INSEMINATION

THE QUESTION

I have been reading article after article over a period of time regarding artificial insemination, or what is referred to as "test-tube babies." Would it be morally right to legitimatize this practice, or must it be outlawed entirely in every type of case by reason of its being against the "natural law"?

I would like to know what the Catholic Church has to say on the subject, and what the actual moral and theological law is governing the practice, which is fast becoming a foremost problem of society.

Agatha Jolley

THE ANSWER

The Catholic answer is firm, clear, and definite, Agatha, and I could give it to you in a few words, but I think we will understand it better and see the reasons for it if I first outline the background of the problem and indicate in a general way the moral notions of those who favor it.

We all know, of course, that a new human life begins when a tiny male cell of reproduction, called a sperm, comes into contact with the much larger female cell called an egg, or ovum, and penetrates into its nucleus, so that the two of them combine into further cell formation—each contributing its due portion of hereditary qualities.

It is well known that not every married couple is able to have children, much as they may want them and try to have them. There are many factors which may cause their sterility, and in almost half such cases the fault, or defect, lies with the husband; the wife is entirely able to conceive and bear a child if only a live sperm could reach the ovum she produces at the right time. It is in cases of this kind that thoughts of artificial insemination are most frequent.

There are two types of such insemination, and they differ considerably in their moral and legal aspects. One is popularly designated as AIH (artificial insemination, husband). The semen of the husband is placed in artificial manner near the opening of the cervix. This method presumes that the husband produces live and active sperm which, for some reason, he cannot place in a natural manner in position for it to be effective. In such a case, should the wife conceive, her husband would be the real father of her child. No legal problems would be involved, and the morality of the procedure would depend on the methods used.

The type which is much more common is called AID (artificial insemination, donor). Either the husband produces no sperm, or it is inactive or undesirable. So some other man (usually anonymous, of course) supplies the semen, which is then placed in artificial manner—with a syringe, for instance—at the opening of the cervix. If the woman conceives and bears a child from such method, the donor is the real and natural father, even though he never saw the mother. The child may inherit his blue eyes, brilliant brain, and special blood type, even as it would from a father whose methods were more natural. One great difference is that the child will never know who its real father is; its mother will never know either; and the father will probably never see or recognize his child.

The proper handling of artificial insemination requires the help of a capable physician, usually an obstetrician or urologist. The usual simple method by which the donor obtains the semen is evidently immoral by Catholic standards. To ensure its effectiveness it must be used within an hour or so, unless special methods are used to preserve it, and the timing must be accurate as regards the woman's cycle. Modern medicine has several ways of determining the time of ovulation with considerable accuracy.

251

In recent years methods have been perfected of mixing the semen in a glycerol solution and freezing it at quite low temperatures. In this way it can be preserved for a long time, and "semen banks" can be built up so that clients may be served at the propitious moment. In one such bank I know of the semen of various donors is thoroughly mixed, so that when it is used for insemination no one on earth can know who will be the father. And if similar types of donors are used for the melange probably no future tests could ever indicate paternity. In this way legal problems are obviated.

One doctor who has had an extensive practice of artificial insemination insists that he will not touch a case unless both husband and wife are heartily for it. He is particularly opposed to the procedure when the husband has been talked into it, and agrees just to please his wife. He insists that both must be mature and have no moral qualms, and that the husband must calmly view the fact of his sterility in an objective, unemotional manner, without apology or excuse. Otherwise there is always the problem that the future child may be an uncomfortable accusation against his lack of virility, and that he may grow to resent it.

It is estimated that one couple in ten in our country is not able to have children. What are they to do? Grow old in loneliness and frustration? Seek an adoption? Advocates of AID point out the shortage of adoptive babies, the long waiting period, and the prospects that many couples will never receive a child, or, at most, will have only one to grow up spoiled and lonely.

Artificial insemination may give such a couple a child which is half theirs. It will inherit half its qualities from the mother; and if the donor is well chosen it might even resemble the humble husband. When the system works there is no reason they should not have as many children as they want by this method, maybe even using the same donor for all of them if he remains co-operative, or seeking a fortuitous variety by the mixing method.

Advocates of this procedure recognize that its legal status is at best ambiguous. Courts in different countries and in some of our states have given contrasting decisions; and

252

there are no statutes to guide them. What are the rights of the mother's husband? Is the child legally his? What are the rights and obligations of the donor? Could he be sued for damages by an irate husband, convicted of adultery—or even of statutory rape? Could he be forced to support his child? And what of the co-operating doctor? His procedures have no legal sanction, and a court might hold him liable for damages.

Such problems rarely arise, of course. Only a divorce action might stir them up. The entire legal question is avoided by secrecy, and the donor is protected by anonymity. Some scrupulous doctors have gone so far as to have the mother engage another obstetrician to deliver the child he has helped her to conceive through AID. This other doctor, knowing nothing of the background, can sign a birth certificate in good faith indicating the husband as father. More "mature" practitioners scorn such subterfuge and issue the certificate in normal terms, as indicated by the fact of the marriage.

The equivocal legal status of AID indicates its conflict with the traditional concepts of our society regarding legitimacy, paternity, and the inviolable unity of marriage. This conflict gives little worry to advocates of the method, who say that old-fashioned ideas will just have to catch up with the expanding frontiers of our brave new scientific world.

Before giving our moral evaluation of AID we might take a quick look at some of the proved or prospective possibilities of its extension. Even a pragmatic moralist must hesitate to endorse a principle which may readily lend itself to extensive abuse.

A few years ago it was reliably reported that a French woman had borne two children to her husband several years after his death. His semen had been preserved in a glycerine solution frozen at a temperature far below zero; and she had used it for her own artificial insemination. In itself, this is merely bizarre, but it opens the door for dreamy eugenists who hope to perpetuate the genes of a genius by careful use of his sperm to inseminate future generations.

Through ova transplants (putting the fertilized egg of one woman into the uterus of another) a "mother" might give birth to another woman's child. This may seem a bit fantastic, and I doubt that it has ever been tried; but we do know that it is a proven practice with animals. A prize cow can produce twenty calves a year by this method, allowing her lesser sisters to do the hard work of developing and delivering the offspring she has conceived, and which will inherit her traits.

Another method of achieving similar results might be to transplant the ovaries of one woman into another. Such procedure is only in the dream stage as regards human beings; transplanted organs are not generally compatible with their new host. But it has been done with dogs, and the resulting litters have the genetic characteristics of the female from which the ovaries came.

Another fantastic idea, not beyond the realm of future possibility, is that the ovum might be so altered by chemical process that it could become fertile without a sperm, and the resultant child would inherit its characteristics exclusively from the mother. She would be in effect its "father," too. Provident planners have a name all ready for the process: auto-adultery.

We know that the bull has practically disappeared from prize herds of cattle; his place has been taken by a syringe— and by a remote, carefully selected donor, who will sire many thousands of calves. Will the brave new world similarly select a few Adonic geniuses to improve the breed of the human species?

Ways have been found to alter genes of heredity; and in some experiments directed mutations have been handed on to dozens of subsequent generations. Who can say that similar methods will never be used on human beings? After all, DNA, the basic constituent of the gene, is now being synthesized in laboratories.

But the culminating fantasy has already been made a partial reality. Not many months ago we read about an Italian scientist who was trying to grow human embryos in his laboratory: real test-tube babies. He obtained live ova from women, fertilized them with male sperm, provided carefully contrived conditions and nourishment, and then watched the little fellows grow. Of course, he was not able to duplicate all the environment of the uterus; so his experimental children became little monsters and he had to kill them—in early embryonic stages, of course. Theologians, hearing of these procedures, expressed such violent disapproval that he discontinued his experiments.

Your mention of the natural law is very casual, Agatha, but the explanation of this basic concept of the Catholic moralist is very complicated. I will indicate some of the fundamental premises of the natural law.

It presumes that there is a God, the Creator of all things.

It supposes that God has a purpose in His creation, that He is a reasonable being who does things according to some plan, and that He did not create the world out of perversity, just to satisfy a cynical sense of humor.

It supposes that we are rational human beings, able to study God's creative purpose as it is manifested in the nature of things, and able to figure out with a measure of accuracy His plan for His creatures.

As applied to Christian morality it presumes that God has given us a revelation which confirms and corrects our natural understanding of our purpose, and points out to us our proper route through life, and the rules of the road.

It takes for granted that we are free people, able to make decisions and to know and choose between right and wrong. It does not forget our known weaknesses or the proved limitations of our freedom; but it will not accept ideas of determinism which make us totally dependent on factors of heredity and environment, so that our destiny masters us.

The basic principle of natural morality is that those choices are good which advance us toward the goal of creation; and those actions are evil which make us deviate.

When the natural law concept is used by a Catholic moralist he always keeps in mind a further postulate, which you may not be willing to accept. Jesus Christ has given us His Church as teacher and guide in helping us decide more obscure applications of the basic principles of morality.

Let me put all this in other words. I accept a rule of reason as my guide to right and wrong. I believe that God created me

255

for a purpose: His glory and my own eternal salvation, goals which are inseparable from my neighbor's rights and welfare.

I believe that God has given me a nature designed to achieve this purpose, and that I must use my reason to understand my complete nature: as man, as creature of God, as good and loving neighbor, as a member of organized society, as a part of Christ's Church, as priest, husband, wife, father, mother, laborer, or merchant.

I do not mean that I crawl into a vacuum and there deduce detailed rules of conduct from general principles. My conscience, my practical perception of good and evil, is largely formed by parental teachings, by the knowledge and traditional attitudes of my society, by individual example and my personal experience. But if I am alert I keep checking it against the realities and purposes of life, especially in the light of revealed truth and in consultation with the teaching authority which the Holy Spirit constantly guides.

Even when I follow the guidance of the Church on a particular problem my morality is still a rule of reason. The Church simply points out to me, more certainly than I might perceive unaided, the nature and purpose of things. The Church acts as a teacher of morality, not a maker of moral rules. She does have her own positive laws, by which she makes specific and often arbitrary application of general prinicples. But there is nothing arbitrary or volitional about her teaching of the natural law; she merely interprets and verbalizes reality.

Our moral principles on human procreation come from two fundamental concepts. The first envisions the sacred nature of marriage as a part of God's plan for man's happiness and sanctity. The other recalls the direct role of God in the creation of the individual human soul.

We believe that marriage is a contract and status designed by God, that its rights are permanent and exclusive, and that its basic purposes are twofold: the procreation and education of children, and the mutual happiness of husband and wife through their love and co-operation. In most arguments Catholics are kept busy trying to convey an understanding and acceptance of the first of these two purposes of marriage and to show how the direct frustration of it is immoral, as in birth control. In this problem of artificial insemination they must rather defend the second purpose and point out that marriage is not a mere scientific laboratory for the procreation of children or for the artificial improvement of the species. It is rather a union of love and fulfillment, of desire and satisfaction; and the rights it gives are exclusive of all intrusion, even by use of dispassionate instruments.

It is firm Catholic teaching that almighty God is directly involved in the procreation of each human person. The spiritual soul of the baby is not transmitted by its parents. It is not the natural product of special genes. It is the loving work of the Creator: a new entity, a distinct personality, destined to know and love God for eternity. It is for this reason that the human embryo cannot replace the guinea pig.

Now, I have not presented all the principles which relate to the morality of artificial insemniation, but I think it best to sum it all up by quoting from two talks given by Pope Pius XII on this subject. The translation is my own, and I am using only excerpts. The first talk was given to a convention of Catholic physicians in October, 1949, in French; and the second to a group of Catholic midwives, in Italian. You can find them in the *Acta Apostolicae Sedis* (the official publication of the Holy See).*

1. The practice of artificial insemination as applied to man, is not exclusively a biological or medical problem. It involves morality and law.

2. Artificial insemination outside of marriage must be plainly and flatly condemned as immoral. The Holy Father here points out that one of the purposes of marriage is the education of children, their security and legitimacy. And here I might mention, Agatha, that about three years ago a Protestant minister in England startled Sunday-supplement readers by advocating artificial insemination for poor lonely spinsters, who should not be deprived of the joys of motherhood. His outburst was a recoil against a forceful condemnation of AID by the Archbishop of Canterbury, Dr. Geoffrey Fisher.

* Vol. 51, p. 560; Vol. 53, p. 850.

3. Artificial insemination in marriage is equally immoral when it is done with the "active element" of a third party. Only married partners have mutual rights over their bodies for the procreation of a new life, and these rights are exclusive and are not transferable.

4. Principles of the natural law are recalled: the fact that the desired result is obtained does not justify the means. The legitimate desire of a married couple to have a child does not prove the lawfulness of artificial insemination as a means of realizing that desire.

5. The use of certain artificial methods to facilitate the natural act of marriage or to enable it to attain its desired results is not necessarily forbidden.

6. To reduce the married life and the conjugal act of husband and wife to a purely organic function for the transmission of sperm would be to change the domestic hearth into a biological laboratory.

7. The conjugal act is by its nature a personal thing, the simultaneous and immediate co-operation of the spouses, the expression of their mutual gift to each other, and in the words of Scripture their union in one flesh. This is much more than the mere union of the sperm with the ovum.

32

GAMBLING

THE QUESTION

I just finished reading an article on the origins of bingo. It interested me, but I could not find any explanation for its acceptance by the Catholic Church.

I would very much enjoy having this topic discussed in your column. My main question is: "Does the Church base its argument on Scripture, or on tradition?" The question, of course, concerns all types of gambling.

Loren R. Ellwein

THE ANSWER

Let me assure you, Loren, that you could be a good faithful Catholic and still detest bingo. Some pastors find it a practical way of raising money for their churches, schools, and charitable works; they think it is less painful than the direct method of extracting revenue from reluctant and sensitive purses. But even in places where bingo is legal many loyal Catholics consider it a corny bore.

Popular critics of Catholicism would make you think that the Church is officially in favor of gambling, that she is the secret patron of sharps, shysters, and shills, and that she is a sideline promoter of the fast buck. In truth the history of the Church shows a long tradition of opposition to gambling; it was frequently forbidden by Canon Law from very early times, and often under severe penalties, even of excommunication. The Council of Elvira was held in Spain about the year 306. Apparently it sought to relax the severity of existing laws against gamblers. If they repented their crimes they

259

could be restored to communion with the Church after one year of penance.

The Fourth Lateran Council, in the thirteenth century, forbade clerics even to be present where games of chance were played.

Canonists often interpreted the Church laws strictly in this matter of gambling. Even when the letter of the law forbade only dice, it was understood to mean all games of chance, and even games of skill when they were played for money.

The Council of Trent, in the sixteenth century, urged the observance of the old canons against gambling and strongly forbade the clergy to take part in "unlawful games." It was up to each bishop to decide which games were unlawful in his diocese; and some bishops were very strict. There were places where games like croquet and football were forbidden to the clergy, along with dice and cards. There was generally much dispute about the propriety of chess; and St. Peter Damian once openly rebuked the Bishop of Florence for playing chess in public.

Our modern Canon Law makes no explicit mention of gambling for the layman, but it still forbids priests to take part in games of chance in which money is openly exposed and at stake. And our modern moralists set forth some strict rules, required by justice, charity, piety, and various other virtues, if gambling is to be lawful.

The current American impression that the Church favors gambling results from the average Catholic's reaction to the rigorism of prudery, the righteousness of the Pharisee, and the virtuous scowl of the Puritan. We believe in discipline, austerity, and asceticism, but we cannot stand the forbidding frown of those who see intrinsic evil in the happy things of God's good world.

In all history the heresy most violently opposed by the Church was that of the Catharists, better known as the Albigensians. Their basic tenet was that God's material creation was essentially evil, and that all physical pleasure should be avoided. The Church found these notions so intolerable that the Inquisition was the result.

Catholic teaching is strict in matters of morality; the

Church often draws the protests of the world because of her strong stand on divorce and birth control and various phases of sexual morality. But by nature and philosophy the Church is liberalist and optimist. She is liberalist because she stanchly upholds man's individual liberty. Against recurrent tides of determinism, she firmly insists that man has a free will; and against diverse forms of positivism she strongly maintains that man's natural rights come from God and cannot justly be alienated by any power on earth.

The Church is optimistic in her conviction that God is good and His creation delightful, and that all of God's creatures can be used for His glory, that there is nothing inherently evil in any of them.

The Church has learned well, from her twenty centuries of human experience that man is perversely capable of using any of God's creatures for evil purpose. The grape and the dice can join with the lyre and the lyric to lead men to sin. But the Church has never found the fault in the enticing creatures themselves, but rather in man's misuse of them. Beauty is good although it can lead man astray. Truth is good although it can confound man's mind.

With this attitude of thought firmly ingrained, the Catholic is quick to recoil when prohibition suppresses man's traditional drink and when blue laws ban his normal pleasures. He knows as well as anyone that wine can make him drunk, and that drunkenness is sin. But he insists upon his right to quench his thirst pleasantly, as a free and responsible man. He knows that dice can lead to dishonesty; but he insists on his natural right to enjoy an innocent game without bother from reforming busybodies.

Catholics have no serious argument with sociologists who point out the public evils of gambling: graft and gangsterism, dishonesty and delinquency. We offer our support to sensible efforts to control these evils by law, to regulate and suppress as the common good may demand. But when the police step in on our private little game of penny ante we resent it as an infringement of our natural rights and freedom. And we protest, even though our opposition may seem to line us up with the hoodlums.

261

If reformists did not antagonize us by presenting false attitudes of freedom and sin, we Catholics would go along with them heartily in their condemnation of the abuses of gambling: the graft and corruption, the cheating and conniving, the passion and penury. The trouble is that they want to forbid our sound bet on a football game, and prevent our friendly session with the boys in the back room.

We simply believe, in our optimism, that it should be possible to suppress the abuses of gambling without stamping out the proper use and fun of it. And we know, in our realism, that no police force is strong enough to stifle in man his normal urge to take a chance, or that thrill of suspense that he gets when the stakes are high and the chips are down.

History shows that the desire to bet is a native trait of man. Nor is it merely an evil of fallen man; Adam took a fateful chance while his exalted nature was still intact. He lost miserably, but his experience has never greatly discouraged his offspring. They still want the thrill of daring and risking, when the hope of winning is needled by the fear of losing.

The ancient Lydians are given credit for inventing games of chance, well before the time of Croesus; probably they only adapted them from older games of the Phrygians and Egyptians. In early years the Olympic races were run for valuable prizes; only in later times did honor and tradition make the simple garland a challenge in itself. And Homer tells us that the suitors of Penelope were seated on a cowhide playing some gambling game while they waited their fate.

The Romans were such avid gamblers that the republic had to enact stringent laws of suppression; all kinds of gambling were forbidden except during the revelries of the Saturnalia. During those days of debauchery the pitched penny could go quite unnoticed.

The Romans had regular dice like ours, with six even faces, and they used to throw them from a cup onto a special table or a polished floor. But they also had more complicated dice, called "ankle bones." These too had six faces, but no two were equal in size or shape. Usually only four sides counted, because the other two never came up, any more than a flipped coin will stand on its edge. But still when four dice were rolled from the cup, thirty-five different combinations were possible. Best of all was the "throw of Venus," when each of the four dice came up with a different face.

In medieval times games of chance were rampant, often mixed with gallantry and skill, as in the tournaments. But dice remained the favorite. One popular game was called "tables," or "counters," which was played with pawns resembling chessmen.

Because of the wide prevalence of games of chance in feudal times we find civil statutes in many countries forbidding, permitting, or regulating gambling in its various forms. Some of the laws provided severe penalties. For instance, at Brescia a statute prescribed that gambling houses should be torn down, literally. English common law did not forbid gambling, and it closed gaming houses only if they became public nuisances. However, as early as the fourteenth century, statutes began filling this gap, and they became stricter as Puritan influence came to the fore. At one time or another practically everything has been forbidden, from "faro" to "ace of hearts." The greyhounds and horses have often been banned, along with football, bookmaking, and lotteries.

In the United States, laws usually followed the English lead, with frequent tendencies to greater severity. Many states forbid slot machines and punch boards; bingo, dice games, and roulette; betting on races and football games; and all forms of lotteries, even those for charitable causes.

And still gambling goes on. It has to hide out and go under cover, but it finds a way. It develops guilt feelings, but suppresses them with bravado. Usually our laws seek to suppress gambling as a source of graft, a breeder of gangsters, and a tool of syndicates. But sometimes we find that the hidden menace, lurking behind bribed officials, is worse than the patent problem, rightly licensed, regulated, and controlled.

Our Church would have us respect those laws against gambling which are rightly enacted for the common good. If they are sound and fair, designed to suppress abuse, to protect society from gangsters, and to remove from youth the solicitations of vice, they bind us directly in conscience, so that we are guilty of sin before God if we break the laws of the state. However, some of the simpler laws may rely entirely on the police for their enforcement, obliging us to behave as decent citizens, but creating no direct obligation in conscience. This is particularly true of those laws whch seem to proceed from the meddling bluenoses and infringe needlessly on our personal liberties.

Regardless of the laws of the state there are certain rules of morality which must be followed in any type of gambling or betting; otherwise it is a sin.

It must be honest and fair. It is not right to bet on a sure thing, or to deceive your adversary about the odds. It is wrong to take advantage of youth and inexperience, to match skill against simplicity. And it is worst of all to cheat: to mark the cards, load the dice, stack the deck.

Any kind of bribery is wrong, whether of public officials or of basketball players. The "Black Sox" were morally reprehensible; and those who knowingly bet on their fixed games were equally bad.

Gambling should be a recreation, not a career, a relaxation, not a cause of emotional turmoil. You should neither gamble to live nor live to gamble. If gambling becomes your master, you are a sinful slave. The compulsive gambler is like the alcoholic; he should never draw the first card, nor take the first look at a form sheet.

The time spent in gambling must not be taken from duty. A game gets out of line when it takes a man from his family, distracts him from attention to his work, slows his zeal for better things of life, or injures his health because of loss of sleep or air or exercise.

The stakes must not be dangerously high. It is unreasonable to risk one's total fortune on the turn of a card, or to stake all future hopes on the black or the red.

The money wagered must be our own. It must not be needed for dress or food, or the solvency of business. And, above all, it must not be needed for the health, comfort, and security of one's family.

The passion of the game must be reasonably restrained.

264

The heat of the contest should not embroil the participants in fighting, quarreling, and various ill feelings.

Bad companions must be avoided. Too often, places of gambling are foul joints where delinquents hang out. Through the entire course of its colorful history gambling has been associated with various vices: especially drinking, swearing, fighting, loafing, thievery, and prostitution. In the thirteenth century the city of Bologna tried to regulate gambling by licensing only four houses in the city; but soon these four had to be closed because they became centers of immorality and debauchery.

However, in this matter we must not put the primary blame on gambling. Often it is only a by-product of the other vices: something to do while getting drunk or awaiting an assignation. Take away the gambling, and the other vices will remain unmitigated.

An insidious evil of gambling is the effect it has on man's thinking: on his attitude toward life. Tense watching of the dice can separate a man from reality and inspire him with the heady hope that a living can be earned without working. It can seduce him to fatalism: to the belief that success is a matter of chance, fortune a smile of whimsical gods, and salvation a turn of the wheel.

But after listing all the evils and restrictions, Loren, we must still face the fact of the gambler's instinct. Thank God, there is a bit of it in all of us. This world offers little of value without some risk. The man who shuns all danger is a coward. The courageous man calculates his risks, and enjoys the thrill of them. He does not live for them, but he firmly hopes to live through them.

The mature gambler knows how to win with consideration for others, and how to lose with regard for reality. He knows his odds and takes them with eyes open. He is not a daredevil who uses bluster for courage, nor a baby who whines when snake eyes stare at him. He has enough conviction to back his knowledge, courage to stake his skill, and spirit to lay odds on his judgment.

The lawmaker courts futility if he seeks to suppress in man his normal urge to take a chance when the stakes are good and the odds are fair. The good God who made us placed deep down inside us a certain thrill in suspense, an intoxication with danger, which we should never try to escape, but rightly use and control.

Risk is rightly thrilling, fate is fascinating, and luck is luring. It may not be possible to discern all the emotions involved: the bravery and fear, the hope and dread, the greed and prodigality. But in their best mixture they are powerful and exhilarating; they give life its zest, effort its spur, and man his masculinity. The timid man seldom forges ahead; and the one who fears to gamble will never have the thrill of a win. He may console himself that he will never lose either; but he probably has little to lose, and worry will kill what fun he gets from hoarding what he has.

33

BULLFIGHTING

THE QUESTION

Last Sunday four of us went to the bullfights. Afterward, while we were discussing the sport, I asked my wife, who is a Catholic, what the attitude of the Church was toward bullfighting. I was frank in saying I thought it was strange that it was popular only in the Catholic countries of Spain and Mexico, and of South America. I should think the Church would oppose inhumane treatment of dumb animals. It is a painful "game" for the bulls, and, in some cases, the horses.

My wife was the only Catholic in the group, and she did not know the answer. She suggested writing to you about the Church's attitude in regard to bullfighting.

Robert Shackett

THE ANSWER

You live on the Mexican border, Robert, so you know more about bullfighting than I do; but we should both admit to a problem when we try to give a moral evaluation of it. We don't really understand or appreciate it. For instance, you call it a sport, and most North Americans would consider it such; but the Spaniard says it is an art, and should be judged by artistic standards.

We would consider a Spaniard presumptuous if he were to come to our country, go to one football game, and then criticize the game forcefully. We would be especially offended if he seemed to question the whole moral fiber of a nation which would permit such gross cruelty of man to man for no clearly discernible purpose. We would tell him to try to learn the game, to appreciate its skills and its strategy, and to consider how it builds character, courage, and strong bodies eight ways.

It is not surprising that the Spaniard is a bit impatient with Anglo-Saxons who know nothing of the bullfight except the blood and panoply, but who proceed with supercilious righteousness to condemn it as insensate cruelty and primitive barbarity. We are facile in condemning foreign vices, but complacent about our familiar domestic sins.

Bullfights take place in a plaza, where there is always sun, sand, and an enthusiastic but critical crowd. With much ceremony, fanfare, and showmanship, a number of bulls, usually six, are killed in the course of an exciting afternoon. The procedures are formal and traditional, with much color, fancy costumes, and lively music. The men who participate in the bullfights are called *"toreros"*; and the stars of the show, who finally kill the bulls, are called "matadors." The routine by which the bull is allowed to demonstrate his strength and courage, is tired and weakened and set up for the kill, is all determined by definite rule and custom. The various maneuvers by which the *toreros* show their skill, grace, and daring are called *"suertes,"* and they culminate with the sharp plunge of a knife into a vital part of the bull's neck, with elegant dexterity and hopeful precision.

The basic idea of the bullfight is a display of man's valor, skill, and graceful mastery against an animal's power, ferocity, and instinctive courage. It is a modern refinement of man's primitive pursuit of wild beasts for food, from fear, as an enemy, or for the thrill of the chase. So it gives expression to basic instincts, and to the *torero* it gives that satisfaction which comes from the conquest of fear. Man has always received a thrill from his challenge of danger; and those who lack courage tremble with fascination to see it displayed.

We are likely to find cruel, shocking, and senseless a rough and dangerous sport with which we are not familiar. But actually we Americans have imported violence more vicious than the bullfight right into our living rooms and made it pap for our children. The same people who condemn the Spaniards as barbarous may thrill to the distant delight of a TV boxing match, in which some punch-happy old pro is beaten into insensibility for the entertainment of beer-guzzling spectators. But even this vicarious violence is mild compared to the repetitious versions of mayhem and murder which fill our synthetic westerns and spark our spurious police thrillers.

We trace proudly the history of our spectator sports, back a full fifty or even a hundred years. Bullfighting has been in vogue for a millennium. The Iberian peninsula was infested by wild bulls in early days, and men fought them with the weapons they had available.

The Moors particularly liked to hunt them on horseback, and later it became a test for the valor and skill of the medieval knight.

Church authorities have often frowned on bullfighting, but their efforts to suppress it had little effect. In the sixteenth century, Pope Pius V issued a decree which provided severe penalties for both the performers and spectators at a bullfight and for princes who permitted such spectacles to take place. But a few years later Gregory XIII mitigated the penalties for everyone except the clergy, and Clement VIII limited the ban to holy days. In modern times it seems that there is no Church law against bullfighting, except that in many places the clergy may be forbidden to attend.

But your question, Robert, is concerned with the morality of the bullfight; and for the Catholic moralist the primary concern is the risk taken by the *toreros*. Is a man justified in exposing himself to such danger? Pius V apparently considered the risks unjustified in his day. But it seems that experienced bulls were often fought in those days: bulls which were wise to the tricks of the *torero* and could not be counted on to react by instinct. They were dangerous, and many fighters were killed. The Church withdrew its condemnation only after the rules had been changed to exclude experienced bulls from the ring. Today no matador would think of fighting a bull which had experience in the arena.

It is the common opinion of moralists today that the risks are not great or immediate enough to make bullfighting immoral. The skill, dexterity, and teamwork of the *toreros* com-

269

tiquity, with many adherents today in some parts of the world. If human souls inhabit the bodies of animals, then we must treat those animals with the same concern we would have for our fellow man.

The second error has less profound roots. It is mainly sentimentality. It is the morality of feeling: we are sad when we see an animal suffer; so it must be a sin to inflict pain on a poor, helpless brute. One of the extreme representatives of this school was Cowper, who wrote: "I would not enter on my list of friends the man who needlessly sets foot upon a worm." What would he think about those wholesale "murderers" who spray fields with DDT?

The extremists of this sentimental clique spend their time berating "vicious" doctors who practice vivisection in an effort to combat cancer or to save children from pain. In strict logic, they would as soon see a child suffer as a white mouse. And their legislative lobby presses for laws requiring anesthetizing of pigs before sticking them in butchering.

Some sentimentalists even become vegetarians; thus they will in no way condone slaughter of animals. And some have been known to will their property to pets.

In the measure that rational thought influences these tenderhearted people, their basic fault is in ascribing rights to animals as though they were persons. It is Catholic teaching that only persons have rights. You and I have received rights from God, because we need them to accomplish the purpose for which He created us. We have them because we are intelligent and free, because we are capable of responsibilities which correspond to the rights. They are rooted deep in our very personalities. If someone uproots them he harms us as persons.

Man's purpose is to serve God: to grow in the knowledge and love of God by making use of the rights the Creator has given him. All other created things are made to serve man. They fulfill their purpose by helping man to serve God, by helping man to achieve the complete development of his human personality in union with God.

Since animals have no rights, we have no duty toward them. But we do have a duty to ourselves, our neighbors, and God. These duties determine the treatment we should give animals, which may belong to us or our neighbor, but, in any case, are all created by God to fit into His plan of things. We must treat them the way God intends.

To ourselves we have a duty of practicing virtue: kindness, mercy, affection, generosity, calmness, patience, strength, and self-control. If we are to develop these virtues effectively we must practice them constantly. Our personalities are integral; the various facets of our character must fit into a consistent whole.

We cannot be sure of our mercy to men if we are brutal to animals. We are not creatures of pure reason, able to discern calmly and act logically in all things. We are creatures of emotion and habit, of vice and virtue. If we are brutal to animals we train ourselves to be cruel to men. If we become angry at animals we lose our own self-control.

Our duty to animals is a part of our duty to God. All lower creatures, including animals, are subject to man and created to serve man's welfare. But they fit into God's plan for the world, and we are obliged to treat all things in accordance with their nature, as given them by God.

Animals have a sentient nature, capable of suffering, a trait they have in common with ourselves. We may use them freely for our reasonable wants and welfare, but we may not rightly abuse them. To inflict pain wantonly is not to satisfy a reasonable human need, but rather to serve a vicious perversion. So when man treats a brute cruelly for no sound purpose he does wrong, not because he violates any right of the animal, but because he misuses God's creature. He acts contrary to the plan of creation and the design and nature of creatures.

One of God's greatest perfections is mercy; it shows in His care of all His creatures. He lets us share in His dominion over things; we should also share in His providence over them— His love and care and mercy. Such awareness of God's love for His living, sentient creatures inspired St. Francis of Assisi to love the birds as his brothers.

34

PERSECUTION

THE QUESTION

I am a Jew by birth and by belief. I fled from Germany to America about twenty-three years ago, and I know that so many good Catholics helped Jews in their desperate situation. Especially, nuns and priests endangered their own lives in order to save human beings; and last but not least the great leader of Catholicism, your holy Pope, did a marvelous work in Europe for the sake of Jewish people.

But how can it be explained that in the medieval times the Catholic Church in Spain and in other countries was so hostile to the Jews and considered them as second-class citizens and made their lives so miserable? I don't put any blame on the present Catholic generation, but I would like to have a historical explanation and would be glad to hear your opinion about this.

Dr. Enrst Appel

THE ANSWER

Your letter, Dr. Appel, indicates that you and I would agree on the subject of social abuses: as members of modern society we should feel shame for our own delinquencies in justice and charity, but we should avoid guilt feelings and resentments about the abuses of former generations. We cannot alter the facts of history, and we should not seek excuses for the crimes of the past. We should rather study past mistakes calmly, that we may profit by them. If experience is the best teacher, then history should be the mentor supreme.

To understand the treatment of Jews in medieval times we should (1) try to solve the age-old puzzle of anti-Semitism, and (2) attempt to appreciate the medieval mentality.

How it all began is really a mystery, but the story of anti-Semitism stretches through twenty centuries and relates in many sordid chapters man's reluctance to mature in his jumbled concepts of equality and brotherhood, of human rights and dignity. It tells in terms of cruelty and suffering of our plodding, half-hearted efforts to develop legal institutions to protect the rights of man, and shows the effects of ignorance, prejudice, fear, and hate when they are directed at our brethren of a different tribe, race, creed, or nation.

Even today, prejudice does not present a pretty picture. There has been progress, but it is only partial, and we resist mulishly each further step. We see isolation based on fear of foreigners, segregation resulting from anxieties about race, and various restrictions because of bias against religions. Habitual injustices are held to be right, and established social inequalities are represented as the will of God. As we survey the history of bigotry we may console ourselves that we are not as bad as our ancestors, but we leave no legacy in which our children can take pride.

There seems to have been no definite anti-Semitism before the time of Christ. The Old Testament tells of much hatred, fighting, and oppression. The Hebrew people were often under the domination of greater powers. But this was the ordinary fate of a small nation in those harsh times.

However, it is not true to say that anti-Semitism is entirely a by-product of Christianity. It began in the Greco-Roman world following the Dispersion, and its first manifestations are seen before Christianity became a social influence. Some rather obscure writers, like Apion, gave it strong impulse, but even men like Seneca and Tacitus were involved in it. These writers told of ritual murders, donkey worship, civil disloyalty, and strange and vicious practices which have formed the fictitious background for the anti-Jewish prejudices of medieval and modern times. I understand that the first pogrom took place in Egypt in A.D. 38.

In general, during the early centuries of Christianity the

Jews suffered no special civil disadvantages, and by the ninth century they formed an outstanding commercial class. But by the end of the Crusades their inferior position was inexorably established. They were excluded from the craft guilds and forced out of commerce by social pressures. To survive, they had to become moneylenders and collectors of taxes. There was opportunity for them in moneylending because Church laws against usury kept Christians out of the business. And as tax collectors they were the expendable tools of grasping governments. When the people started grumbling too much about excessive taxes, the state would put the blame on Jewish "extortionists," and the unrest would be assuaged with a pogrom or by the expulsion of Jews from the country.

The laws of many countries deprived the Jew of civil rights, bound him by various restrictions, and made him dwell in a walled ghetto. Legal and social pressures combined to make him live by his wits or his hard labor at a subsistence level. The trade guilds followed the craft guilds in excluding him from their monopolistic membership. So in the world of commerce the Jew had to become a peddler or a middleman. The transition from barter to finance gave him a partial reprieve from oppression and opened a new area for his acute skills. But his position in the world falsely etched his image in the Christian mind as a rapacious Shylock deviously defrauding the guileless Gentile.

Pogroms were frequent, often stirred by catastrophe or plague in which Jews were made the scapegoats. The popular mind pictured them as Christ-killers, deliberate unbelievers, desecrators of the Eucharist, and children of the Devil. It was symptomatic that people blamed the Black Death on them in the fourteenth century, and that they were banished from various countries as malignant targets of divine wrath.

Medieval Christians probably believed that zeal for the faith was good reason for persecuting Jews. They called the Jews perfidious because they refused to believe truths which had been made evident to them; so they were guilty and deserved to be punished. But hidden behind this righteous excuse were all the ignorance, credulity, and crude emotions that lie behind most intolerance, such as:

Fear: sometimes it was physical; in popular image the unknown Jew was vicious. More often it was a transferred insecurity, an anxious defense of privilege, or a superstitious bulwark to faith.

Prejudice: knowing so many frightful fabrications that the plain truth cannot get a hearing.

Ignorance: charity never has more than a sentimental chance until we give it fact to feed on.

Credulity: primitive people show an avid readiness to accept forgeries and believe fantastic tales, especially those of crime, cruelty, cunning, and conspiracy.

Scapegoat: there is always a need for something or someone to bear the burden of those many hostilities, resentments, and frustrations which convention will not permit us to heap on the brethren of our own group, who are actually to blame.

Glorification of conformity: the Jew committed the crime of being different. He observed the Sabbath, followed dietary laws, and maintained a stubborn solidarity of race and family.

Xenophobia: the medieval world had none of our modern facilities for communication, travel, and world knowledge. Even we of the space age tend to suspect the foreigner in our midst, as well as the one beyond the border. The Jew in the ghetto was a foreigner and a stranger, even though his ancestors had been natives of the city for generations.

Avarice: when the guilds excluded Jews from their membership they must have seen commercial advantage from one corner of their corporate eye. And when a government expelled them from the country their property could often be confiscated.

Pride: the modern world has much of it. The Nazis really thought they were better than the Jews. And many white people are smugly convinced that their race is superior to that of the poor Negro whose father was recently a slave.

I could go on and on with this list of the real causes of prejudice. My point is that intolerance and persecution, wherever you find them, are mostly the products of the vicious side of man's nature and reflect the mores of his civilization.

They may be intensified by fanatical ideologies, but they are never the logical result of any sound religion, and certainly not the legitimate product of Christianity: the religion of love, patience, and mercy. Understand me well; I am speaking of ideals and doctrines, not trying to deny that our long persecution of the Jew had deep religious motivation, and was in fact often aimed at forcing conversion on him.

Certainly there is nothing about anti-Semitism, or any other form of prejudice, which can be justified by Catholic doctrine. We cling firmly to the truth. We insist that it is an objective reality, immutable and important. We cannot be indifferent to it, or permit error to be a substitute for it. We are zealous that everyone should see it, embrace it, and love it. But we know that it must never be imposed on anyone.

Faith is free; force it and it is no longer faith. It is twice free: it comes freely from God as a gift, and it is embraced freely by man's mind and will. It is man's response to God's word and love; it implies man's giving of himself to God. And a gift must be free, else it loses its value.

We do have an obligation to believe, but that duty comes from God, is imposed by truth, and operates on our free will. No human law can enforce it. The sincerity of a man's conscience is one of the greatest values on earth. Force used to bring assent is a crime against sincerity as well as freedom—against both truth and conscience. A forced faith does not please God and it makes a hypocrite of man.

The Church has the duty, given her by Jesus Christ, to bring truth to all men, but she must do it in a way to inspire its acceptance in faith. She must respect the honesty of man's intellect and the freedom of his will. If she were to use force or threats she would destroy the very faith she seeks to implant. Laws and social pressures may force external conformity; they can never produce faith.

When we read the message of Jesus in the Gospels we find more emphasis on love than on truth. St. Paul combines the two, telling us that we must "practice the truth in love." We must love truth, and love those who receive the truth. We love truth poorly if we try to jam it by force into an unwilling mind, where it will be secretly despised; and we have a false

278

love for our brethren if we try to rob them of their freedom and sincerity in the interest of truth.

If we love truth we will hate the error opposed to it, but we will not let our hatred extend to the honest man who is in error. Really our intolerance springs less from an honest love for truth than from a selfish desire to vindicate the superiority of our own convictions, and to shore up our own troubling doubts.

Certainly then it can never be the role of the Church to force faith; but even less is it a function of the state, however uniformly Christian or Catholic. The duty of the state is to seek the best welfare for its citizens, and this can never be attained by forcing them into conformity against their convictions—or by persecuting them for failure to conform in matters of religion.

In fairness to the medieval mind, I should point out that people of those days were convinced that the state was a solidly Christian community. Jews were not part of such a community; so they were not good citizens. They were intruders, to be tolerated, at best.

The Reformation did not improve the status of the Jews; they were often caught in a squeeze between the fervor of Protestantism and the reforming zeal of Trent. But the humanists raised some strong voices in their favor, and here and there improvements were made. General emancipation began in the eighteenth century and was favored—legally at least—by the revolutionary movements in America and Europe. But progress has been slow. The Dreyfus affair stirred France to new hatreds. In Germany, racism and nationalism prepared a base for Nazi fanaticism. In England, no Jew was allowed in Parliament until 1858 and in Russia someone counted 650 laws against Jews in 1888.

The picture has never been attractive, but medieval man with all his cruelty never came close to the ghoulish genocide of our own century. The Nazis made the ancient pogroms look like picnics. But anti-Semitism has never been exclusively religious. In medieval times when religion was the predominant social factor, intolerance was expressed in religious terms. But even then it was largely racist, economic, selfish, and psychological. It always springs from man's lack of maturity, understanding, and love. For the Christian it means that he has never grasped the full meaning of the Master's basic teaching: that we love our neighbor as ourselves.

Tolerance is a matter of charity. Maybe the first Christians understood that term; at least they loved one another. But it has taken the rest of us a miserably long time to mature in our comprehension of Christ's teaching. The story of the Good Samaritan is one of the best known of our Lord's parables, but its racist, nationalist, and religious import seems to have escaped us. It was for a purpose that Jesus cited as perfect neighbor a despised foreign heretic. We chatter about loving our enemies, and we fail to love foreigners who are our friends, to say nothing of our near neighbor who has other facial features or religious customs.

Love seeks the best good of the loved one. If we love our neighbor fully we want him to know the truth; it is for his good. But if we really love him we will never destroy the freedom of his conscience.

I am not trying to preach to *you*, Dr. Appel, but to admit *our* faults as Christians and to explain the reason for them.

It would be well for all men of the Western world to remember that our society has been formed from ideas that are basically Jewish. Pope Pius XII said that spiritually we are all Semites. So when we are anti-Semitic we are also antispiritual.

35

TOLERANCE

THE QUESTION

I would like to know why it is considered a sin for a Catholic to attend a church other than the Catholic Church. This, to me, is most unfair. I can see no harm in it, after attending your own, that is. Every church is the house of God, even though the teachings may differ.

When I hear a Catholic say it is a sin to go to another church I can only think that the Church is afraid of losing her people. If one is a true believer in his religion then he will not go astray. If he is not, then he doesn't belong there anyway. (By this I mean that if he is not a true believer in the Catholic faith, he should not be a Catholic.)

I have been to a Catholic church, Baptist, Lutheran, etc., and to my own Greek Orthodox church. I feel that I am a better and more intelligent person for it, because it is both educational and interesting to see the worship of others. It has not harmed my own personal beliefs one bit, and has helped me to understand others better.

V. Rentas

THE ANSWER

Miss Rentas, you would understand the Catholic position if you would thoroughly consider one of the basic teachings of the Church: that historically, and with explicit intent and purpose, Jesus Christ established a Church, and only one Church. He expects all men to be members of it, to worship God in it, and to be instructed and sanctified through it. He

281

remains with it, lives in it, and acts through it. It is His own mystical Body: a spiritual extension of Himself which embraces all of us, its members, into sanctifying union with Him.

Now I don't expect you to agree right off that the Catholic Church is the one and only Church established by Jesus Christ; that He wants everyone to belong to it; and that it is the only institution He put on earth for the salvation of men. All I ask is that you appreciate that this is our belief, and that we are very definite and firm about it.

Our conviction comes from our understanding of the teaching and sanctifying purpose of our Savior; from a study of His life, example, and words; from His choice and training of the Apostles and the various powers and commissions He gave them; from His special selection of Peter as head of His Church; and from His repeated prayer that all might be one in Him. It is based on the history of the early Church as found in the Acts of the Apostles and the writings of the early Fathers. And it conforms also to our understanding of man and his spiritual needs.

From this conviction that we have the only true Church of Jesus Christ results a direct implication which must be unpleasant to you, and to anyone who belongs to another church. In the words of Christ we find no evidence that He established or wanted a variety of denominations. And we cannot find it historically reasonable that a church which came into existence a thousand or fifteen hundred years after the time of Christ could be His own authentic establishment.

Catholic teaching on this point is generally regarded as arrogant. We would be better accepted if we would drop this narrow notion. The trouble is that it is an essential part of our understanding of the mission of Christ in the world. It is through the Church that He teaches us in a reliable manner the truths of revelation. It is through the Church that He unites us to Himself in sanctifying embrace. And it is through the Church that He wants us to worship God in union with Him, and with the Sacrifice He gave us.

I emphasize this doctrine because in it is the reason for our attitude towards participation in the services of other churches. If all churches were equally true, all in similar manner a part of the mystical Body of Christ, then I would agree thoroughly with the implications of your question, Miss Rentas. We should broaden our experience, run around to various services, seek out the best sermons and most inspiring music, and finally affiliate with the congregation which we find most congenial and helpful.

On the other hand, the person who accepts our doctrine of the one true Church is rather overwhelmed by the aggressive indifferentism in the world.

It is aggressive because its adherents are not content with being indifferent themselves; they insist that everyone else should be indifferent, too. They are far from indifferent with people who refuse to be indifferent. They attack our firm position, claiming that they represent liberalism, tolerance, and intellectual alertness as opposed to the stubborn obstinacy of our prejudiced minds.

Our unwillingness to have anything much to do with the religious services of other churches is largely a protection against this encroaching indifferentism. If I were to run around to other churches, taking part in their worship as the spirit moved me, I would certainly give external approval to the basic principle of indifferentism: that one church is as good as another. And it would not be long until I absorbed that same spirit myself; and it would dig insidiously at the roots of my Catholic faith.

Seldom would we find in any Christian church a method of worship which is objectionable in itself. We all worship the one true God, and we express our love and adoration in song and prayer. In your own church, Miss Rentas, you share with us the true Sacrifice of Jesus Christ and His grace-giving sacraments. I have deep veneration for your sacred liturgy; it brings Jesus to your altar and recalls in effective manner His redemptive death on the cross. But I do not join you in it because I would thereby give seeming approval to the sad separation of your Church from the one your forefathers adhered to for centuries.

I could more easily enter into the worship of your Church than that of Protestant denominations. You have carefully retained all the essentials of the worship designed by Jesus Christ. They have discarded many parts—or even all of it—

and have substituted methods of their own. These methods may be good and inspiring, but my acceptance of them would endorse another type of indifferentism: the notion that man-made services are as good as those given us by Jesus Christ in His death agony on Calvary.

I am perfectly free to join with my Protestant friends in private, or unofficial prayer—in family devotions or civic invocation—as long as my joining does not encourage religious indifferentism in them or in myself. I may not let it be interpreted as giving my approval to their church or to their officially designed methods of worship.

One point I must make clear: our conviction that we belong to the one true Church does not make us immediately intolerant or even intolerable. Catholic doctrine has great respect for the sincerity of the individual conscience. The attitude of a Catholic who understands his faith should be governed by his neighbor's integrity. Good faith may, in the mercy of God, often produce the same sanctifying effects as the true faith.

Even though salvation be only through the one true Church we do not thereby imply that either you or our Protestant brethren are individually deprived of sanctity or of the means of getting to heaven. Your honest good faith unites you in implicit desire to the one Church of Christ, through which salvation comes.

As long as you have that good faith, Miss Rentas, you as a member of the Orthodox Church are in a particularly sound position. You retain almost all of the teachings of Jesus Christ, together with the incalculable spiritual advantages of the Mass and the sacraments. You have them in all their original form and efficacy, just the same as we have them, and they will sanctify you, just as they do us, when you receive them sincerely and devoutly.

Our Protestant friends also retain many of the essential spiritual things which Jesus gave us. Among these are belief in the one true God and in the three divine Persons; faith in Jesus Christ our Savior, the eternal Son of God; the example of His life and the inspiration of His teachings; Baptism to confer divine life; and a spirit of love and repentance to obtain forgiveness for sins. We know how upright and devout many Protestants are; we know that the graces of Jesus Christ will work wonders in their souls.

So the true Catholic must be tolerant, filled with love and understanding for those whom he believes to be in error. He must not equate error with truth, but he must respect convictions. He must never try to force a conscience, impose beliefs, or deprive of personal rights because of honest error. He must hold every man to be sincere until evidence proves the contrary—and even then his love must fail not.

But your question isn't really about tolerance in general, but about the precise point of our taking part in non-Catholic religious services. The Church has a definite law on this point, and I will give you my own translation of the Latin in which it is expressed in Canon 1258 of the Code of Canon Law.

"It is not permitted for the faithful to *actively* assist in any way or to take part in the worship of non-Catholics.

"Passive or merely material presence may be permitted as a civic duty or courtesy, for a serious reason, which is to be judged by the bishop in case of doubt, in the funerals, weddings, and similar solemnities of non-Catholics, provided there is no danger of abuse or scandal."

Laws are formal and often forbidding statements. The practical interpretation of this law depends on many factors. For instance, its application is much different for us who live in communities which are predominantly Protestant than for people in strong Catholic countries. We have much more reason to attend various religious functions. Our neighbors, friends, and relatives are involved in them. If we refused to attend we would give offense; and there is seldom danger that our attendance will be misinterpreted.

Certainly no Catholic in our country should hesitate to attend the funeral of a non-Catholic relative, friend, or business associate. It is a gesture of sympathy, respect, brotherly love, and civic solidarity.

In most places in our country a Catholic need not hesitate to accept the honor of being pallbearer in non-Catholic services. I say in most places, because a few dioceses may have special regulations, or local circumstances might change the aspect of things.

We can be almost as free in our attendance at a marriage —as long as it is the proper union of two non-Catholics who are free to enter into it. The marriage of divorcees presents a special problem; and generally no Catholic should attend such a ceremony.

Marriage is a less sensitive occasion than a funeral, but family relationships and friendship impose social obligations which cannot be ignored. However, the problem of being a member of the wedding party is a bit complicated. In various places there are diocesan regulations on the subject, and these must be observed. The law says that the bishop is to decide in case of doubt; and naturally some bishops are stricter than others. My own opinion inclines to leniency, especially where relatives and close friends are involved. But I advise that a Catholic should not follow my general opinion; he should consult a local priest.

Some time ago I personally attended a ceremony of ordination in an Episcopal church. The new priest was the son of a close and long-time friend. His father did not think I was reneging on my conviction—often expressed in banter—that Anglican orders are invalid. He knew I was not suddenly forgetting the Catholic "intolerance" of which he had often accused me. But he was much aware that I was joining in the joy and pride of his family.

Suppose me to be in danger of death in one of the iron-curtain countries. I cannot find a Catholic priest. I am conscious of sin, unsure of my contrition, and aware of the need of the sacrament of Penance to complete my forgiveness. In such circumstances I would call on one of your Orthodox priests and ask him for that sacrament.

These examples are presented to show you that we are not as intransigent as we are often thought to be. We are simply careful to avoid giving encouragement to religious indifferentism, or seeming approval to doctrinal error. We are not insensitive to the religious fevor and sincerity of our neighbors, nor do we approve of Catholic ghettos in which we would shirk our civic and social obligations as good brothers, friends, and neighbors.

36

CHRISTIAN UNITY

THE QUESTION

Many true Christians are praying for unification of all Christians. How are Catholics instructed to pray for this intention? Do they feel that everyone will be made to bend to the Roman Catholic Church?

Naturally a Protestant true to his conscience cannot believe all that the Roman Catholic Church teaches, just as Roman Catholics don't accept all that Protestants do. However, I, for one, and most Protestants I know, earnestly believe and pray that sometime in His own time and way God may reveal how a unity can be accomplished without any true Christian of any denomination suffering a loss of a truly spiritual conscience. This certainly must have divine help. The unified Church may not necessarily be called the Roman Catholic Church, but undoubtedly will include the true Christians of your Church in the One Holy Christian Church with Jesus Christ as the head.

Are Catholics and Protestants praying for the same thing?

Nancy Guild

THE ANSWER

Since you sent your question to me, Nancy, you have probably read in the *Catholic Digest* (Dec. 1960) the six ground rules proposed by Dr. Robert McAfee Brown as a guide for religious discussions between Protestants and Catholics. I think that Dr. Brown had your problem in mind when he devised his sixth rule. It is frankly evasive of the ultimate obstacle to union, which you foresee, but it can be abundantly fruitful if we have sufficient faith in God's providence. It reads:

"Each partner (Protestant and Catholic) must recognize that all that can be done with the dialogue is to offer it up to God. What happens as a result of the dialogue must be left strictly in his hands. If something is to issue from it, He will see that something does."

Dr. Brown is a Protestant minister and a professor of theology at Union Theological Seminary in New York. His ground rules are an excerpt from a book *An American Dialogue*. He wrote the first half of this book and Father Gustave Weigel, S.J., professor at Woodstock Seminary, wrote the second half. The other five rules are that we must: (1) trust each other's good faith; (2) know our own religion thoroughly; (3) try honestly to learn about the other person's religion; (4) be humble and penitent for our guilt in the present separation; and (5) frankly face the issues, both those which should unite us and those which keep us apart. But we must not be impatient for tangible results, and all our efforts must be inspired by prayer.

Dr. Geoffrey Fisher, the former Archbishop of Canterbury, implied a similar attitude in a public statement he made in preparation for his friendly visit to Pope John. "We can travel quite a long way together before coming to the barriers which divide us and which no doubt will divide us for a long time."

Your question, Nancy, hints at the basic difficulty which would surely discourage us desperately if our reunion were to be achieved by human efforts alone. We have totally different concepts of the Church of Christ, and there seems to be no way to reconcile them.

We Catholics believe that Jesus Christ established a visible, enduring organization of which He is the head and the source of spiritual life. It has weathered the schisms and heresies of the ages, has received many scars and bruises from its enemies and from the sins of its own members, but it remains the same mystical Body of Christ, without essential change. So for us the quest for unity is and can only be a reintegration of everyone into this existing Church. Naturally our Catholic prayers for unity will often reflect this basic concept.

Protestants in their ecumenical efforts generally try to avoid any preliminary definition of the Church, but their prevailing attitude, as reflected in the World Council of Churches, is that the One Holy Church is something not now existing but to be designed, built, and embraced with a measure of compromise by everyone. So Protestant prayers for unity will naturally reveal this attitude, which shows itself in your own letter.

And yet I don't believe that we need to pray against each other. We are both praying that the will of God be done; and we know that ultimate unity must be His will, however it is to be attained. Jesus Himself gave us the example at His Last Supper when He prayed "that all may be one, even as Thou, Father, in Me, and I in Thee: that they also may be one in Us" (John 17:21).

One significant effort at united prayer is the Church Unity Octave, observed from January 18 to 25 each year. It began under Episcopalian auspices, but soon became Catholic in its general acceptance. Just recently its prayer has been revised and its purposes restated so that it will permit more general Protestant participation. But even if we don't say precisely the same prayers, we should all pray for the same purpose: unity in Christ, according to the will of God.

Protestant interest in unity has grown rapidly during the last thirty years. The World Council of Churches is its strongest and most hopeful expression. Mainly because of our different doctrine about the nature of the Church we as Catholics have not been able to enter actively into its membership and deliberations, but our interest in it has gradually increased and we have become more confident of its sincerity, more sympathetic with its purpose.

The cause of Christian unity has been closely associated with the coming Second Vatican Council ever since Pope John XXIII first announced his plans for it. We should not hope for immediate, concrete results. It will be primarily concerned with Catholic problems; Protestants will not take an active part in it; but the very fact that the Pope has established a secretariat to maintain contact with other churches is a sign that he hopes to lay a foundation for future progress.

Probably the most significant current effort toward unity is the dialogue, about which Dr. Brown, Father Weigel, and many others, both Protestant and Catholic, have recently written. It is something which concerns theologians primarily, but all of us can enter into the spirit of it, pray for its success, and prepare ourselves so that any results achieved at a higher level can seep effectively into our own lives.

The dialogue proposes an intellectual and cultural exchange between different religious groups, especially Protestants and Catholics. It proposes a co-operative study of the Scriptures; greater familiarity with patristic writings and with those long centuries of Christian tradition which we all have in common; a calm and objective reassessment of the Reformation, its causes, conflicts, and results; a deeper understanding of doctrinal agreements and differences; and a reciprocal appreciation of values inherent in our diverse traditions, customs, and attitudes.

In other words, it is the purpose of the dialogue to make us understand each other better, so that we can love each other more and thus prepare ourselves for the effective work of God's grace in our souls. This grace alone can bring us to unity.

Pope Pius XI approved this purpose very simply in a speech which he gave in 1927. "For reunion it is necessary above all to know each other and to love each other." Love without knowledge is feeble sentiment. Knowledge without love is sterile; it will never sanctify.

Even though we are not theologians, you and I should participate in the dialogue and in all similar efforts at reunion. I don't mean that we should launch a campaign of talking religion with our neighbors. Such talk can occasionally be useful when we know what we are talking about, when we are calm and charitable, and are not trying to win an argument. But generally our participation should be an honest effort to expiate our past sins and those of our ancestors by practicing the opposite virtues.

We all agree, I am sure, that our present variegated disunion is not the will of God but the result of our sins. Pope Adrian VI in 1552 frankly acknowledged that God was permitting His Church to be persecuted because of the sins of Catholics—from the Pope on down. We have not always imitated his humility, but many of us are seeking it today in truth and honesty. And Protestants, too, are readier to admit the excesses of the reformers.

Here are some of the virtues we might practice, in contrast to the past:

1. Our most scandalous historical crime is that we have fought each other so bitterly, wasting energies, dealing in atrocities, distorting truth, and destroying love. We should now join our forces to fight our real enemies: sin, suffering, secularism, and the atheistic forces of Communism.

2. In the past we have striven to prove each other wrong. Our forces have been concentrated on arguments, apologetics, and polemics. And sometimes our language has not been nice. We should now try to work together to see the truth and understand it. Instead of arguing religion, we should study it. Instead of defending it, we should practice it.

3. In the past—even the immediate past—we have not always told the truth about each other. We have distorted history, twisted doctrines, and spread calumnies. We should now unite zealously in the cause of truth, plain, bald, and unbiased.

4. We have blamed each other for the Reformation and religious wars, for persecutions and restrictions on religious freedom, for prejudice and political scheming. We should stir up that humility which will permit us to admit our share of the blame on each point—and when necessary remember the admonitions of Jesus that we turn the other cheek and walk the extra mile.

5. Often we have been unable to see any good in each other. We may like each other as friends and neighbors. But to me your Protestantism seems illogical and strictly negative. To you my Catholicism is despotic, formalistic, and superstitious. We should search for the real values we both possess.

This point calls for a few examples. If I know Protestantism I will see in it an active participation of the laity in public worship; a use of the vernacular which makes public prayer more meaningful; a genuine reverence for the Bible as the Word of God; an appreciation of grace as a free gift of the Redeemer; a tradition of moral uprightness with special insistence on the social virtues.

If you know Catholicism you will appreciate the deep faith and strict faithfulness which her doctrines inspire; the sacrifice and dedication of her Religious Orders; the traditional beauty of her liturgy; the effective consolation of her sacraments; the intimate personal appeal of her Saints.

6. We have often been suspicious of each other personally. Our Catholic attitude has been influenced by the fact that we were once a small, persecuted minority in America, and that we have had to struggle against opposition to attain equality. We see Protestants as prejudiced, reducing us to inferior status.

Protestants, on the other hand, seeing the Church as an authoritarian, monolithic anachronism, refuse to believe that American Catholics honestly love liberty, revere the Constitution, and respect the rights of all men.

We must learn to ignore our inborn prejudices and to trust each other. The better we get to know each other the more we will find that most of us are sincere, honest, devout—and humanly fumbling.

7. As we come to know each other more thoroughly in the spirit of Christ, we will come to love each other as brothers of Christ. Each of us will see in the other the sanctifying image of the Savior. We Catholics will come to realize that most Protestants, because of their Baptism and their good faith, are much more united to us in the Church than would appear at first glance. And Protestants, in turn, will realize that we are not arrogant enough to exclude them from the hope of reaching heaven.

Need I go on, Nancy? If I take the flat and forceful stand that unity will be achieved when all heretics submit, I block the way to all progress. If you insist that the old Church of Christ is corrupt and irreformable, that human hands must shape a new one based on compromise, then I see no use of going further with you. But if we both agree to seek truth honestly, to love each other as Christ taught us, and to pray fervently with trust in His providence, God only knows what success may be achieved. Our Lord assures us that "things that are impossible with men are possible with God."

37

SECULARISM

THE QUESTION

In our Catholic papers these days I find two sharply contrasting attitudes about the degree of participation we should exercise in the world about us: in reading secular magazines, in co-operating with secular universities, in leading or taking part in civic campaigns and activities. Some people seem to think we should escape into a sort of Catholic ghetto, made up of parochial school, Catholic press, Catholic social, professional and labor organizations, trade only with Catholic business men, consult only Catholic doctors or lawyers, and generally remain aloof from non-Catholic activities of all kinds: educational, civic, political, and social.

To me it seems we should be good Americans as well as good Catholics, good neighbors without thought of religion, race or nationality, good honest politicians and business men, letting our Catholic faith and morality exercise its influence through our example.

(Name withheld)

THE ANSWER

You will recognize, my friend, that I have strongly edited your question. That is why I do not print your name. But you do rightly indicate a broad diversity of attitude, polarized by two ideals: (1) personal faith and sanctity, removed from dangers of error and temptation, and (2) a charitable influence for good in the world, with courageous combat against error and temptation.

294

Which should be the proper attitude for the strong and conscientious Catholic? I am not merely straddling a fence when I answer that both polarizations must be maintained. For most of us outside monastic life—restricted personal involvement is apt to become selfish, sterile, and static. But on the other hand, our outward influence will be vain unless we have first built sound faith and solid sanctity into our own characters.

There is a tendency for us to inject offensive names into our controversies. The person who tends to isolation is labeled a bigot—intolerant and narrow-minded. The person who tends to participate may be called a liberal, as though it were an evil name, and accused of secularism.

Religious thinking can have differences of orientation and emphasis without being heretical or dangerous. And if we are not always tolerant of these differences we can at least be exact in our indictments.

In controversy we should be careful of the terms we use. I am a secular priest; but I would not like to be accused of secularism. The fact that I live and work in the world—rather than in a monastery—does not necessarily mean that I am worldly.

It might be well for us to consider just what is meant by secularism; it can be a system of thought and conviction, but more often it is an attitude of life which makes the material world the center of all our aims and interests, and thus excludes God.

The philosophy of secularism is directly opposed to religion. It is first cousin to atheistic Communism. If you were to drain off from Communism its peculiar social and economic theories you would have secularism in its most radical form.

Religion is the bond between God and man. Secularism has no need of such bond because it ignores God and thinks only of man.

Secularism holds that man is a creature of the world, and that his only practical goal in life is the happiness he is able to attain here on earth. It is closely allied with either atheism or agnosticism, and is directly opposed to Catholic thinking, which holds that man is a son of God, that his first vocation is holiness, and that life's true goal is beyond this world. No earthly pleasure has value in comparison with heaven's happiness.

Most of us, as Catholics, are not in immediate danger from secularism as a philosophy; its errors are apparent to us. But unless we are careful we are likely to get caught up in the prevalent attitude and spirit of secularism. We live surrounded by it; we absorb it unconsciously; and we may be carried away on the buoyant wave of it until we suddenly find ourselves floundering in its depths.

Secularism as an attitude does not fight religion; it merely dilutes it. And it is doubly deceptive because the ingredients it uses to thin out spirituality may seem half-religious themselves: urbanity which resembles charity, and makes religion polite and refined; broad-mindedness which looks like tolerance while it gradually softens conviction; and intellectualism which can make religion sophisticated and snarl the simplicity of faith.

As Christians become infected with secularism their early symptoms are quite innocuous: ardent effort, driving ambition, mundane knowledge, and temporal success. But then gradually the glitter of their immediate goals blurs the clarity of life's true purpose. As the disease progresses they lose their sense of sin, except for those antisocial sins on which the world frowns. And gradually they become so wrapped up in the enticements of God's beautiful world that they forget it was God who made it.

Not only does secularism dilute our personal religion, but it gradually alters our social relationships. Man's innate dignity and goodness come from God. The Christian loves his fellow man as a son of God and a brother in Christ. The worldly man loves as his fancy leads him and hates when his emotions recoil.

Sound religion recognizes the fact that all man's natural rights come from God and are inviolable under God's law. Secularism is likely to recognize rights only as they fit into personal convenience and social utility. We have let our religion be much diluted by worldly attitudes when we look with favor on discrimination, segregation, oppression, or any other type of social injustice.

When secularism invades the Christian family it robs it of its sacred character and supernatural purpose. It discards God's plan for the home and substitutes the enlightened planning of modern marriage. It mitigates all the divine rules about pleasure, procreation, and permanency. It enthrones TV in place of hearth and shrine; leaves education strictly to the school and religion to the church; and then wonders why delinquency becomes its frequent product and divorce its tragic end.

Possibly the saddest effect of secularism is in education, and there it has taken its firmest hold today. In our country of many conflicting religions we had to leave the subject of religion out of our public schools as a matter of compromise and expediency. And now we find this practical necessity becoming an accepted philosophy: God has no place in education. And we see unsuspecting acceptance of the encroaching claim of the state that education is its exclusive right. Parents are pushed out of the picture, and the presence of the Church in education is tolerated with displeasure.

In the world of business, industry, and finance, secularism is in its native environment. This is the realm of the world, and worldliness flourishes naturally. Money, profit, interest, wages, and the products of industry and agriculture: these are the goods of the world. Only the naive businessman regularly thinks of these worldly goods as belonging to God and intended to serve His glory. Secularism would never put abstract considerations of justice and charity ahead of the profit motive.

Secularism excludes God completely from the factory, store, and office. These are not the places for Him. He belongs in church.

From the beginning of its history Christianity has manifested two extremes in its attitude toward the world. There have always been religious isolationists who rejected the world and all its trappings. And there have always been religious integrationists who stressed the influence that religion must have on the world if it is to accomplish its mission in the world. Most of us are somewhere in between, trying to live in the world without becoming too worldly.

Some isolationists have become escapists; and many of them have achieved great personal sanctity. If you must be an extremist I would strongly counsel this course. Follow the hermit into the desert, the monk into his monastery, or the nun into her contemplative cloister.

The trouble with escapism is that it is not a practical course for the average person. It requires a special vocation. Most of us must live in the world and face its problems. We must tear a living from the stingy clutch of the world, find companionship with the men of the world, and contribute our share to the good of the world.

Both isolationists and integrationists can find support for their positions from the words and actions of our Lord. His life on earth does not give us a simple black-and-white answer to all problems; His teaching and example were rather designed to fit men in all positions in life. He personally accepted the responsibilities of secular citizenship. He paid His taxes; directed that Caesar should have his due; and was clearly abreast of His times. He was interested in fishing, sowing, and harvesting, in the work of the shepherd, the publican, and the vintner. And above all He lived among men and loved them, men and women of all kinds and various nationalities.

Yet Jesus warned us often and strongly that we must not seek the things of this world; that God and His glory come first; that we should not be concerned with what we eat and wear; and that the poor are really the blessed ones, along with the meek, humble, and persecuted. The greatest example of violent zeal which Jesus gave was in driving the tools of secularism from the Temple.

The example of the early Christians might encourage the isolationists. They went underground; they worshiped in secret; they scorned the world even to solitary penances in the desert and death in the arena.

But the integrationists can cite in their favor the example of later centuries, when Christians emerged from their isolation, took over the empire, absorbed the barbarians, took the faith valiantly to new lands, and completely transformed Western culture: its law, art, thinking, and behavior.

Much of our Christian acting and thinking is in conflict with that of the world. And we must keep it that way, or we become worldly. Two courses are open to us: we can retreat in fear and escape the world's influences; or we can face the world and fight its evils, throwing the full force of our Christian conviction into changing it. We can ignore the world and let it drift on its merry way; or we can so live that the world will be a better place for our neighbors to inhabit.

The vocation of each individual is personal. Some are called to the cloister; some must live in the world. Those in the cloister can strengthen us by their prayers and give our activities spiritual effectiveness; but it is certain that religion will never play a dynamic role in the world unless it comes out into the open. It must invade the home and the school and the market place. And effective invasion must be led by those who know the real problems of the modern home, who are experts in education, and efficient in the world of business.

It is easy to be frightened into escapism when we view the shocking impact of modern culture on Catholic thought and life. In standing up for his faith the Catholic must confront skepticism, naturalism, and agnosticism. In upholding his unworldly ideals he runs straight into the pragmatism of modern morals. He finds truth confronted by relativism, and his freedom challenged by determinism. If he tries to uphold marital morality he finds himself confronted by a social and economic system which is geared to defeat his efforts; and he is derided by threats of overpopulation and the humane advantages of parental planning. His family fidelity is shaken by frequent divorces; and his spirit of sacrifice is made to seem foolish in the midst of the indulgence about him.

But in spite of the dangers, and because of the intensity of the combat, religious men must stand up to the world with courage. If they all retreat into the desert the ideas and attitudes of the world will thrive unopposed, and soon will become strong enough to invade the desert itself.

Our modern secular culture is strongly repugnant to Christian principles, but it certainly outshines the pagan culture of the Roman empire. Yet early Christians—once they had sunk their roots deep in faith and sacrifice—did not flee the dangers. They moved in and took over.

Religion must light the way, or culture will grope in darkness. Religion must provide the motives, or culture will go around in aimless circles. And we cannot simply put the light on a remote pinnacle, or post the motives above the altar. We have to take them effectively into the midst of the world's frantic scramble. If Catholics do not become intellectuals the thinking of the world will never be Catholic. If religious men do not become scientists our sciences will never develop a conscience or be directed to spiritual purposes. If religious men do not enter business and politics we cannot expect Christian ideals to appear in these areas spontaneously.

If we are to live effectively in the world, we must keep up on secular things. But if we are not to become secularists we must keep the religious viewpoint. We must keep the double lens of our stereopticon. We see the third dimension if we keep our view in focus.

38

APPARITIONS

THE QUESTION

Who was Simon Stock? As a Baptist layman, I find little difficulty understanding and accepting most Catholic doctrine, but the Blessed Virgin's appearance to St. Simon and her presentation of the scapular to him seems as incredible to me as Moroni's visit to Joseph Smith.

I know there must be a satisfying answer, and I am looking forward to hearing from you.

O. W. Hickey

THE ANSWER

You express yourself forcefully, Mr. Hickey. However, the Blessed Virgin's appearance to St. Simon Stock is not a matter of Catholic doctrine, and you could be a good Catholic without believing it. But if you were a Catholic, it might be advisable for you to be less vehement in your repudiation of this popular legend; otherwise you might shock pious souls and give the impression that you reject all apparitions.

By calling the scapular story a popular legend I may myself grate some devout sensibilities. But at least I emphasize two important points: (1) that it forms no part of God's revelation to His Church; (2) that its authenticity is not based on the best historical evidence.

The Church was established by Jesus Christ to teach His Gospel, and He promised that He would remain with her always to see that she taught it faithfully and accurately. We believe that she is infallible when she teaches those things

301

she was founded to teach: the truths of revelation which she received from God, and which are found in the Bible and in the Apostolic tradition of the Church. This official or public revelation of God ended with the Apostles, and nothing has been added to it since.

God may, if He wishes, make additional revelations to private individuals, and apparently He has done so at various times. But these are made for the individual who receives them and for those who may accept his personal word about them. You and I can be thoroughly critical of their authenticity and reliability.

The Church could never require that we accept them with divine faith. The most she asks is that we keep an open, unprejudiced mind: that we be willing to accept evidence for what it is worth, and not put arbitrary limits on God's power or His personal concern with the affairs of men.

Now, what are the historical facts about St. Simon Stock? He was one of the first superiors general of the Carmelites and the one most responsible for their firm establishment in Western Europe. He was an Englishman; his election as superior general took place in 1247; and the apparition to which you refer is supposed to have taken place at Cambridge on Sunday, July 16, 1251.

At the time, Simon was deeply concerned about the welfare of his Order. It had been established on Mt. Carmel in Palestine about a century earlier. Under harassment of the Saracens its monks were leaving the Near East and trying to establish themselves in Europe. But they were not well received; other Religious Orders and the secular clergy opposed them strongly; and there was danger that they might be suppressed entirely.

Simon's great devotion to the Blessed Virgin, patroness of the Carmelites, helped him in the midst of his problems. She is said to have appeared to him and given him assurance that his Order would survive and prosper. Thus encouraged, he went to the Pope, Innocent IV, and obtained a letter of protection, enjoining other Orders and the secular clergy from interfering with the Carmelites.

The first account we have of this apparition dates from

1291, forty years after it took place. It tells only of the assurance given to Simon regarding his Order. Another forty years later, a certain Johannes Grossi wrote that the Blessed Virgin had also assured Simon that those who faithfully wore the Carmelite habit would be protected from eternal damnation. It was not until 1642, almost four centuries after the event, that all the alleged promises regarding the scapulars appeared in their present form.

Critical historians are not much impressed by documentation of this kind. Neither are they impressed by the general reliability of early Carmelite writers, who were more concerned with tracing the legendary origins of their Order than with an accurate recording of events. So we may well be skeptical as to whether the Blessed Virgin ever appeared to Simon Stock at all, and even more skeptical as to whether she gave him all those promises about the scapular. But regardless of the authenticity of its historical origins, the scapular devotion is entirely consonant with Catholic beliefs and practices. The Church has found it useful in promoting piety and confidence in the Mother of Jesus. So she has given the scapulars hearty encouragement.

By implication, the question concerns much more than St. Simon Stock and the scapulars. What about apparitions in general? Many modern ones, like those at Lourdes and Fatima, are much better attested and documented. What should be our attitude toward them?

As a Catholic, you could not take the attitude of rejecting all apparitions as impossible or incredible. You would quickly find yourself at odds with important parts of the Bible. Recall a few of the well-known apparitions narrated in the Old Testament. Very often it was God Himself who appeared in some created form; first to Adam and Eve when He told them not to eat the forbidden fruit, and then later when He cast them out of paradise. He appeared to Cain after the world's first murder; to Noe many times, telling him how to build the ark and what animals to put into it; to Abraham, Jacob, Isaac, and, in a special manner, to Moses, in the burning bush and on Mt. Sinai. He also appeared at different times to various prophets in the course of centuries.

303

Sometimes angels were delegated to make the appearances: for instance, to Agar when she was running away from Sarai; to Lot at Sodom; to Balaam, in such manner as to frighten the ass he was riding; to Josue at Jericho; to Gedeon under the terebinth tree in Ephra; to David, to Elias, and to the three Hebrew boys in the fiery furnace. Tobias had an interesting series of close associations with an angel.

The New Testament also gives details of many apparitions, some of which had an intimate part in the history of our redemption. The archangel Gabriel appeared to Mary to announce to her that she was chosen to be the Mother of the Savior. All who know the Christmas story remember the apparition of the angels to the shepherds, when they sang, "Glory to God in the highest, and on earth peace to men of good will." An angel with countenance like lightning and raiment like snow announced the fact of the resurrection to Mary Magdalene and the other Mary.

We might also discuss the special nature of the apparitions of the risen Savior during His forty days on earth before He ascended into heaven. But we do not wish to equate these with the various appearance of the angels, who served as messengers and agents on many occasions; for instance, to Zarchary in the temple; to St. Joseph in dreams at Nazareth, at Bethlehem, and in Egypt; to the Apostles, to liberate them from prison; and more impressively to St. Peter, to liberate him again.

The various apparitions described in the Scriptures probably differ in their physical and psychological nature, but they all have this in common: that their reality is attested by the authority of God. We cannot discard them as fantasies or fables without rejecting the inspired Scriptures.

It is quite different when we are dealing with apparitions not narrated in the Bible. Our knowledge of such events comes to us from ordinary human testimony and from documents which are not sacred. We may be as skeptical as sound reason and historical criticism require. We rightly sift the testimony and challenge the documents. We examine the character and psychic traits of the alleged visionaries, their motives and general virtues, their tendencies to hysteria or hallucination, to exalted imagination or gullibility, and to excessive emotion or exaggeration.

The Church herself is exactingly critical when she finds it necessary to investigate alleged apparitions. Bernadette at Lourdes and the children at Fatima met opposition and skepticism from priests and bishops almost as strong and suspicious, if not as relentless, as that from materialists.

The Church's official investigations are made by a tribunal established by the bishop of the place where the apparitions are alleged to have taken place. Tribunals of this kind are precise and formal in their procedure, exacting with regard to evidence, critical and competent in their evaluations. Experts are consulted in the various scientific fields involved, and theologians are alerted to check deviations from orthodoxy. Even if you discount the special protection which the Holy Spirit gives to the Church, you would have respect for her findings in these inquiries, simply because of her judicial and scientific care.

More often than not the Church's careful investigation will result in her rejection of the alleged apparition as unreliable, or even in her condemnation of it as a fantasy, fake, or fraud. You may be sure that she will condemn any reported revelations which are not in accord with sound Catholic doctrine, which encourage superstitions, or which do not promote sound piety and morality. And she will reject any such phenomena if they are based on questionable testimony or give any indication of hysteria or other psychic disturbances.

You may remember the blaring headlines of a few years ago which proclaimed apparitions of the Blessed Virgin at Necedah, Wisconsin. The alleged appearances were carefully investigated by the Bishop of LaCrosse, and on the basis of his findings all public demonstrations and devotions connected with them were discouraged or suppressed. The hysterical fervor of many enthusiastic devotees gradually died out. This is typical of many such cases which the Church does not find worthy of credence.

You may well be asking yourself, just why the bishop

bothers investigating these matters at all. Why is he particularly concerned because some individual claims to have received visions and revelations? Well, usually these things cause wide publicity; people gather in great crowds; there is wild speculation, credence, and denial; and various types of devotion develop. Then in the interest of religion it is the duty of the bishop to see what is going on.

He is required by Canon Law to watch lest superstitious practices develop or devotions be introduced in his diocese which are at variance with Catholic faith or out of harmony with Catholic tradition; and he must even consider the possibility that such novelties might be inspired by the profit motive (Can. 1261, Code of Canon Law). Without his approval no books or pamphlets may be published which tell of new apparitions, revelations, visions, prophecies, or miracles, or which introduce new devotions (Can. 1399, Code of Canon Law).

Sometimes, after long and careful investigation, the Church does give her approval to popular belief and devotion resulting from an apparition, as she has done at Lourdes and Fatima and at various other shrines throughout the world. Now just what does that mean, and to what does it oblige us as Catholics?

First of all, she never gives any infallible decision about the authenticity of an apparition or the reliability of private revelations. Usually the approval is made on the local level, by the bishop, and is more negative than positive, more permissive than supporting. In effect, the bishop tells his people that he finds nothing incredible or repugnant to religion in this alleged apparition and that they can believe it if they wish. He may even indicate that he is rather sold on it himself, and may permit or encourage pilgrimages to the place considered sacred, allow a church to be built there, and let publicity run its course.

Sometimes the Holy See is more directly involved in the approval. Pope Pius XII has given strong encouragement to the devotion to the Immaculate Heart of Mary which resulted from Fatima. And he certainly gave wholehearted, official endorsement to the centennial celebration of the apparitions at Lourdes. He wrote a letter to the whole world on the subject, and sent his official representative.

The Holy Father was evidently delighted to see eight million pilgrims converge on this shrine which resulted from apparitions of the Immaculate Mother of Jesus to a little peasant girl named Bernadette. He knew that these pilgrims to Lourdes manifested a strong faith and fervent devotion, never hysterical or superstitious, but always sound and fundamental in the best Catholic tradition.

Remarkable miracles are regularly alleged to take place at Lourdes, and it is clearly evident that every day God's grace brings courage, patience, understanding, and resignation to those who suffer and are not healed. And acts of charity and edification are constant.

Sometimes the Church goes so far in her approval as to establish a feast day and a special Mass commemorating the apparition. She has done this for Our Lady of Lourdes, on February 11; there are many others. Sometimes she grants indulgences to encourage the devotions which result from the apparitions. And very often she has canonized as Saints the persons who had the visions. When she gives such thorough approval, to what are we Catholics obliged?

Even by celebrating the feast of Our Lady of Lourdes, canonizing Bernadette, and writing an encyclical, the Church does not impose upon us as a matter of faith the authenticity of the apparitions at Lourdes. Yet any Catholic would certainly be arbitrary, prejudiced, proud, and disrespectful if he were to reject them out of hand and without sound factual information. The Church's approval requires that we be sensibly respectful of the fact that the entire matter has been meticulously investigated and critically evaluated, at first hand, by wise, competent, and conscientious men. It requires that we be wisely humble.

Very often the Church's attitude toward apparitions is determined by the fruits of goodness they produce. St. Paul gives prime example that an apparition can set a man on the road to sanctity (Acts 9:3 ff.). There are many similar episodes in the lives of the Saints, and St. Bernadette of Lourdes is a recent example. The Church did not canonize her because she had visions, but because the impact of those visions impelled her to practice virtue and become a Saint. Likewise, whatever the original facts of Lourdes, there is an evident, daily, enduring fact of Lourdes which leads millions of men to greater faith and devotion, love and confidence, prayer and resignation, an alert awareness of God's personal care of us, and a more ardent practice of virtue.

So we might say that the Church's centennial approval of Lourdes was more because of the fruitful fact of Lourdes than because of the initial facts which her careful investigation found credible and proper. The same is doubly true of St. Simon Stock and the scapulars. The Church has long been aware of the spiritual value of the scapulars; so she strongly approves the fact of them, even though the story of their origin can not be firmly tied to facts.

You might be a good Catholic, and have no special interest in Lourdes or Fatima or any other particular shrine or apparition. The miraculous medal might offend your aesthetic taste or the scapulars irritate your skin. You would not need to feel that there was any defect in your faith or fervor; but neither should you feel critical of more impressionable souls. The Church does not impose these special devotions. She merely permits or recommends or encourages them for those who find them helpful.

39

PSYCHIC PHENOMENA

THE QUESTION

I have been told by Catholic friends that prognostication of the future is considered by the Church to be the work of the Devil.

For several years I have had a scientific interest in psychic phenomena, owing to some unexplainable personal experiences. I would like to know what the Catholic Church believes regarding the work of such places as Duke University in the fields of parapsychology, psychokinesis, etc. What is its stand on telepathy? On people who are proved experimentally to be psychic?

Does the Catholic Church approve research that seeks to determine whether the mind is in itself a sensory organ as well as an interpreting and directing mechanism?

Does the Catholic Church believe that just as God has gifted some people in art, music, athletics, memory, and so on, He has also gifted others with special senses to—so to speak—break the space-time barriers?

Mrs. John Piroz

THE ANSWER

Your question, Mrs. Piroz, opens up a wide field for discussion. A few years ago most of us were following with half-skeptical interest the noisy and noisome events which gravely disturbed the peace of the Hermann home at Seaforth, Long Island. Newspapers told us vividly about bottles which popped their corks and jumped off shelves; about

309

statues which flew about the room, and a bowl of flowers which hopped off its table; about a skidding phonograph, and a toppling bureau.

I do not know that they have ever solved the mystery of those bewitched bottles, the nimble statue, and the errant furniture. Apparently the strange activities have subsided and interest has waned. But at the time everyone had a theory. Some were sure that they discerned the frantic antics of a poltergeist, a noisy spook who makes a nuisance of himself with senseless pranks. The more scientific-minded looked for downdrafts from the chimney, sonic booms from aircraft, faults in the earth, underground streams, or atomic effects from outer space.

Among other investigators on the scene was an emissary from the Duke University parapsychology laboratory. I have never heard that he propounded any theory about those particular events, but his visit made the alert public quickly conclude that the bowls, bottles, and bureaus were made to bounce by psychokinesis, the power of mind over matter. At Duke University it is called PK, and it is based on the theory, apparently borne out by observation, that some people can influence objects without touching them.

This drama of Long Island was merely one widely publicized example of a plethora of phenomena generally called psychic, mystic, or occult, which are often considered by the popular mind to be supernatural. The world's literature is filled with fantastic events of this nature, and they are part of the whole fabric of folklore. Homer's heroes consulted oracles and consorted with the dead; medieval men tortured witches and lived in terror of vampires; and in modern times spiritism has tormented souls of the dead until they apparently came back from the nether world to rap tables and exude ectoplasm.

Man has always been fascinated by mysteries, and he has always lived enmeshed in them. The sun and the moon, the stars and the storms filled him with wonder and fear. Life intrigued him and death threatened him; disease and dangers lurked always near him; and eternity was ever ahead. He needed explanations, and often he sought them in unlikely

310

places. Gradually he has untangled many of his mysteries, but he has never been resigned to the patient acceptance of others which will not be resolved as long as he lives. He lashes out at the enigmas which taunt him, and not being able to solve them with sensible theories he resorts to the fantastic.

A quick glance at man's history would seem to indicate that his imagination works more readily than his intellect; that he is credulous before he is critical, superstitious before he becomes scientific. His flighty efforts to learn things beyond human ken and to do things beyond mortal powers have resulted in a weird litany of arcane and esoteric sciences, occult arts, and mysterious phenomena.

There must be a hundred words in our language to denote various phases of man's fancy for the fantastic. They run the alphabet from "animism" to "witchcraft"—yes, even from "astrology" to "zetetics" of the zodiac.

In his efforts to learn hidden things and to see into the future, man has consulted oracles and ouija boards, tea leaves and crystal balls. He has tried out fortunetelling and clairvoyance, theosophy and necromancy, second sight, soothsaying, and spiritism. He has mixed strange brews and philters, juggled divining rods and dowsing sticks, studied palms and skulls, read portents in the stars, analyzed automatic writing, consorted with varied spirits, and made pacts with the Devil.

Man's imagination and superstition have peopled his world with ghosts, goblins, and ogres, with witches and vampires, spooks, hags, and crones, as well as with wily dwarfs and happy little fairies. He has found his favorite stories best believed when they are quite incredible, as long as they mix horror with mystery, fantasy with fear, and monsters with midgets in such vivid fashion as to make brave men tremble at noises of night, and to frighten little children out of their wits.

Finally, man's overpowering desire to perform miracles has produced fakirs and conjurers to vie with witches and sorcerers. Their long history of levitation and bilocation, of faith healing and ghost walking, have ended up in prosaic

311

suggestion and psychokinesis.

The Church has had to contend with these various forms of superstition and occultism throughout her history. By her constant opposition to them she has gradually stamped them out, but never succeeded in uprooting them; they spring up like spores.

The advancement of learning and science has aided the Church in her fight against phantoms and fetishes. As man learns more about the world he lives in he finds it more marvelous but less frightening; when he knows natural causes for phenomena he need not search for spirits to explain them; and as his attitude becomes more scientific he is less credulous and imaginative.

Of course, the Church has always accepted the world of spirits. God is a Spirit; He created the angels as spirits; and some of these angelic spirits made devils of themselves. Man has a spiritual soul, and the spirit in him lives on after the death of his body. Spirits are powerful things, after the manner of God, who is all-powerful. And spirits, both good and bad, can no doubt exercise direct influence on the material world. After all a Spirit created the material world, a Spirit keeps it constantly in existence, maintains its order, and makes it run. Spirits other than God can inject themselves into the affairs of the material world only in the measure that the good Lord permits, and we are not able to compute that measure.

The interaction of spirit and matter is evident in man. Our spiritual soul gives us life, co-ordinates our bodily functions, and makes use of our brain to think. Certainly, then, it is not unreasonable to imagine that spirits may be able to influence material things in other ways—even though it seems beneath their dignity to go around rapping tables and making bottle caps pop.

The Church's main concern in matters of this kind is that we avoid superstition, which is religion out of gear and running wild. Religion is the Church's business, and she does not want to see it abused.

It is the primary duty of the Church to see that God is rightly worshiped. Superstition interferes with that duty.

When we consult an oracle, or the Devil, or the souls of the dead about things only God can know we attribute to them divine knowledge; and we may do the same with fortune-tellers or a crystal ball. When we try to obtain favors from the fates or the fairies we attribute to these mythical creatures powers which are supernatural, and rightly belong to God.

The Church has a long history of condemning witchcraft and ordeals, black magic and the evil eye. Half a century ago, when spiritism was the fad, the Church was very forceful in forbidding Catholics to have anything to do with it. There was a lurking suspicion that the Devil had a hand in such doings, and at best the medium's trance seemed an improper means of probing mysteries beyond the grave.

In general, the Church would like us to be critical, sane, and sensible. She would not inhibit man's imagination or curtail his dreams, but she would prefer that he distinguish fact from fiction. While she strongly condemns superstition, she is benignly tolerant toward pious beliefs and practices which seem an aid to Christian devotion and present no threat to faith. She has had to warn us hundreds of times about purported apparitions which on investigation proved to be eidetic images or hysterical imaginings. But when a vision seems sane and sound she leaves us free to make our own judgment about it, and to accept it as it helps our piety.

Persons at the parapsychology laboratories at Duke University are engaged in scientific study. The Church has no quarrel with them; they seem to be patient, careful, and honest in their experiments. They strive to be objective in their evaluations and reserved in their conclusions. The Church is probably more kindly disposed toward them than are their fellow scientists in more materialistic fields.

The Church has a maternal love for science; she has watched it flounder in some of its early theories, like a child learning to walk; and she has seen it fall flat on occasion when it tried to soar into the realm of philosophy. But she is happy with the knowledge man has gained by his experiments, observation, and study. Knowledge is an attribute of

313

God Himself, and man resembles his Creator when he shares divine cognition.

Although the Church has a maternal interest in science, the laboratory is not her own workshop; she gives her blessing to scientists and lets them carry on their experiments. However, she is concerned with those scientific theories which seem to protrude into her own field. And since parapsychology studies the nonmaterial part of man, that part which we call the soul, it is to be expected that there should be some common points of interest.

One reason the Church is well disposed toward the investigations at Duke University and other parapsychology centers is that scientists in this field put a refreshing emphasis on the spiritual part of man. It is the accepted custom in other sciences to ignore the soul. Hardly anyone goes to the trouble of denying the soul; it simply is eliminated from consideration, since it cannot be weighed, measured, or dissected.

This ignoring of the soul gives a strong tint of materialism to all scientific investigations. There is constant danger that the practical daily habit of ignoring spiritual things in the laboratory and clinic may lead to the elimination of higher things from man's total thinking: from his philosophy and his attitude toward this life and eternity.

Parapsychology brings the soul back into the laboratory, where effort is made to control and observe its activities. In their recent book *Parapsychology—the Frontier Science of the Mind,* Drs. J. B. Rhine and J. G. Pratt, of Duke, maintain that the established data of their studies logically constitute "an experimental refutation of the mechanisic philosophy of nature that has become well nigh universal today in all the sciences." They contend that it is this challenge to mechanism which makes other scientists slow to accept them into the fraternity. And they take pride in the boost they have given to religion by bolstering one of its basic tenets.

At the same time, our good parapsychologists reveal an inadequate concept of supernatural religion. They congratulate themselves that their evidence for the spiritual in man has permitted science "for the first time" to give support to religion. They think that otherwise, throughout all history, religion has receded before the findings of science, giving up its doctrines and altering its concepts to fit the new knowledge obtained by experimentation.

When I try to give a direct answer to your first question, Mrs. Piroz, I encounter the first point of apparent serious conflict between the theological concepts of the Church and the philosophy on which the Duke professors base their theories. You ask whether the Church does not consider prognostication of the future to be the work of the Devil. Actually, we consider that the Devil himself does not have certain knowledge of free future events. God alone knows what man may decide in making use of his free will. Of course, God can let the Devil know, if He wishes, and He can also let man know. And both man and the Devil can make some educated guesses.

Rhine and Pratt propose the theory that man's soul is able to operate without dependence on space and time. We might concede their theory, as regards space; but we consider independence from time to be an exclusive attribute of God. They admit frankly that their theory is likely to bring them into conflict with established concepts of causality and free will. If my power of precognition tells me naturally and with certainty the future decision my neighbor will make, then his decision is not really free, or not really subsequent, or else I share divine knowledge, or something equally confusing.

However, spontaneous evidences of some sort of precognition have remained constant and frequent throughout man's history, from the oracles and prophets of ancient times to the fortunetellers and crystal gazers of our own day. If scientific investigation of extrasensory perception, ESP in the language of parapsychologists, can cast any light on this age-old problem, more power to the investigators. And I would not be greatly concerned that they use some wobbly working theories.

You present another question which I have not touched directly. I am sure that the Church would raise no barriers

315

to investigation of the possibility that man's mind can acquire knowledge of external reality in other ways than through the senses—or can influence physical objects in other ways than through the muscles. It is our traditional concept that everything in the mind has come there through the senses; but, on the other hand, we are not inclined to restrict the unknown potentialities of the soul. In matters of this kind traditional concepts can be adjusted, if necessary. And there are certainly many things which these old concepts do not completely explain—clairvoyance, for instance, and telepathy, and psychokinesis—and our haunting old friend, precognition. These things certainly deserve investigation.

As to the possibility that some psychic individuals may be equipped with special genius for ESP and PK, it sounds reasonable, and might explain many strange phenomena, like second sight and premonitions—and poltergeists! On the other hand, some people may be more credulous, sensitive, and impressionable than the rest of us. Personally, I crave no power of seeing visions or making tables hop.

40

THE DEVIL

THE QUESTION

In a recent discussion with Catholic friends of mine several statements were made that amazed me. I was told that in cases of demon possession a priest would be called in to perform a ritual or ceremony of some kind to expel the evil spirits. Now, isn't this a bit fantastic in this day and age?

I was also informed that several Catholic priests had written books on demonology, vampirism, and witchcraft. I must admit this sounds just as fantastic to me. Is it permissible for a Catholic to read and study such things? Please enlighten me in this matter.

Frank Browley

THE ANSWER

In this day and age, Frank, we tend to be more critical and less credulous. That attitude is good. It helps to eliminate superstition, foolish fears, and the burning of persons accused of being witches. But we must be watchful that our skepticism does not intrude upon our faith, and lead us to doubt the truths revealed by God. Our modern enlightenment may well keep us from seeing the Devil in every dark corner, or behind every quivering bush; but it should not lead us to doubt Satan's existence or his powerful influence on fallen man. These are truths clearly taught us in the Scriptures.

We pride ourselves today on being scientific. We seek natural explanations for even the most occult phenomena.

Often we find proved natural causes; at other times we devise theories which are satisfying in their probability; and for the rest we maintain that calm reserve which confidently awaits an explanation while research plods its patient frontiers.

But we must be very careful that our scientific attitude does not lead us into the materialism which denies the spirit in man or the supernatural in the universe, which scorns any realm of knowledge higher than that of experiment and mathematics.

We had best be slow to scorn the fantastic. We live in the midst of it; sustain ourselves with it through the problems of reality; frequently induce it with opiates and alcohol; and let it guide our lives with its illusions. We often distract ourselves for hours with fantasies: in daydreams, books, and periodicals; on the screen, radio, and TV—by no means excluding the commercials. Where would the modern housewife be without the fantasies which sell soap? What would she do with the children without their fantasies of space, time, and violent death? Modern fantasies are as frequent as the medieval; they are simply emasculated. The fantasy of witchcraft held mighty drama; the maraudings of the vampire, stark terror.

Do you really think the Devil has taken a long vacation? Maybe his working hours are shorter because he has so many human allies to do his work for him. Why should he work overtime when modern man seems so capable of damning himself without satanic help?

The Devil is simply anonymous. Active as ever, he does his work behind the scenes. He knows that modern man does not believe in him, and he likes it that way. We do the Devil's own work for him when we deny that he exists. If we were to see him clearly face to face and know him for what he is, then with God's grace we could vanquish him.

In one phase, at least, this day and age is the Devil's own. Falsity is the outstanding trait of his diabolical nature. Our Lord pointed this out: "There is no truth in him. When he tells a lie he speaks from his very nature, for he is a liar and the father of lies." And we have seen modern men, and

318

particularly the leaders of modern men, develop this devilish attribute to artistic perfection in the "big lie" of propaganda and diplomacy.

We know that in other days and other ages benighted people imputed to the Devil personally and directly every unaccountable evil event—and in those times many things were unaccountable. But we moderns have our avid credulity aroused by something like *The Search for Bridey Murphy*. Maybe we have only changed the area of our gullibility. We are fascinated by mystery and morbidly enticed by the sensational.

My sharp comments on this day and age do not answer your question. In my own experience, I have found few Catholic priests who are interested in demonology. In the seminary they studied it briefly as a minor part of the tract about the angels. They have no doubt about the Devil's existence and his potent, all-pervading influence in the affairs of men. But for practical purposes they incline to the modern custom of ignoring him. Their most recent championship bout with him was that waged by the Curé of Ars a century ago.

However, leaving the priests out of it, you are correct in intimating that the Devil has staged a comeback in modern literature. Maybe we should not call Dostoevski modern, but Gide certainly is, and Bernanos; and on lower literary levels thousands of books and articles have been written by sundry authors on various phases of the occult—in this day and age.

Vampirism is hardly to the point. Even when they created their darkest medieval terrors, vampires were not believed to be devils. They were persons who were dead, but not dead enough, whose graves were not able to contain their restless souls.

Witchcraft is much to the point. Witches consorted with devils and bewitched their victims by Satan's powers—or so it was popularly believed. And the Devil probably had his own special fun in inspiring the popular fear, hatred, and persecution of his henchmen. However, if I am to answer your question, I must get down to the Devil himself and not be distracted by his outmoded diversions.

That Satan exists no Christian can reasonably doubt. The
Scriptures are full of the Devil—from Genesis, where he
takes the form of a snake to slither Eve unto her fall, to the
Apocalypse, where he is bound by a chain for a thousand
years and cast into the bottomless pit. The Apocalypse gives
us our fullest account of Satan's fall and banishment from
heaven. Isaias gives us one of his many names: Lucifer, the
day star—because of his original brightness. Our Lord seems
to refer indirectly to this original fall when He says, "I saw
Satan like lightning falling from heaven." Certain texts seem
to indicate that the sin of Satan may have been one of pride,
or of wanting to be like God; and II Peter 2:4, and Jude 1:6,
among others, refer to his punishment: "Dragged down by
infernal ropes to Tartarus . . . tortured . . . kept in everlasting
chains under darkness."

From the time he tricked our first parents to their fall,
the Devil has been active in the evils of men. St. Paul refers
to this influence of the "most wicked one." He advises us
to put on the armor of God (truth and the gospel of peace,
the breastplate of justice, and the shield of faith) that we
may "be able to stand against the wiles of the devil." And
Jesus recognized the power of Satan in the affairs of men so
much that He called him "the prince of this world."

Because of our co-operation with the Devil in evil we will
be punished along with him: "Depart from me, accursed
ones, into the everlasting fire which was prepared for the
devil and his angels."

To sum up Catholic belief on this subject: Demons do
exist; they were created by God as angels, endowed with
His grace, and invited to love Him and enjoy the happiness
of His home in heaven forever. But motivated by pride, ambition, envy, or some other sort of angelic temptation, they
rebelled; and hell was created as a place of their punishment.
There they stubbornly persist in their rebellion and hatred
and do all that they can to lead men away from God. Their
influence over men is great; they cannot directly attack our
intellect or hinder our freedom of will, but they can present
all manner of temptations and solicitations to us, as the
serpent did to Eve, and they can even take control of our

imagination and bodily reactions, and thus exert indirect influence on our higher faculties.

In the work of our Redemption, Satan was the direct and immediate adversary of Christ. The Redeemer had been promised to crush the head of the serpent. He began His public ministry by personal conflict with the Devil, and He ended it with effective triumph over him in that victory of the cross which liberated all men from their bondage to the "prince of this world." "To this end the Son of God appeared, that he might destroy the works of the devil."

No one who believes that Jesus Christ was the Son of God can doubt that there were genuine cases of diabolical possession during the days of our Lord. Anyone who knows the Gospels is familiar with the many cases in which the Devil was driven out of afflicted souls by Jesus and by His Apostles whom He sent out explicitly for this purpose. By His divine power Jesus instantly restored those poor people to normal health, but their cases are distinguished very definitely from His cures of those who were merely sick.

Jesus vindicated for Himself the power of casting out devils—emphasizing that He did it by the power of God, not by that of Beelzebub. He cited this power as a proof that He was the Messias, and He used it frequently during His ministry. He gave it expressly to His disciples, and indicated that it would be one of the distinguishing marks of their ministry after His death. The Apostles made use of this power often. (Acts 19:13-16, indicates why the Church is very careful about permitting a priest to use the rite of exorcism; unworthy ones may well end up "tattered and bruised" from their encounter.)

If you remain unconvinced about possession and exorcism in the time of Christ it would be well to look up some of the dramatic cases which are described in detail: the man in the synagogue whose devil admitted that Jesus was the Holy One of God (Luke 4:33-35; Mark 1:23-26); the Syrophoenician woman whose humility obtained the help of Jesus for her daughter, whom he healed at a distance (Mark 7:25-30; Matt. 15:21-28); the young man in the land of the Gerasenes, whose devils—named Legion—went into a herd of pigs and impelled them violently to their death in the lake (Luke 8: 26-39); and the boy healed just after Jesus came down from the Mountain of the Transfiguration (Mark 9:13-28). It was on this occasion that Jesus explained to His Apostles the need for prayer and fasting in driving out devils.

In view of all this evidence we Catholics believe that men can be and have been possessed by the Devil, that exorcisms are possible by divine power, and that Jesus gave this power to His Church, which has exercised it constantly throughout the centuries, generally with great care and prudence. We cannot treat these Gospel stories as mere superstitions, legends, or rumors. And we cannot believe that Christ would expressly encourage popular superstitions by pretending to drive out devils when he was really only curing poor epileptics or neurotics.

The Church does have a special ceremony for exorcisms. It is found in the Ritual, but it can be used only by special and explicit permission of the bishop. The priest who uses it must be pious, prudent, and upright in his entire life; he must be mature in age and venerable by reason of his office and dignity. He is advised to go to Confession before beginning his work and to proceed in it with charity and humility. He is advised to review his theology, and not to believe readily that a particular case is one of possession.

Certain norms are given for discerning possession, like a person's carrying on intelligent conversation in a language he has never known, revealing distant and hidden things, and manifesting powers that are clearly above nature. It is recommended that the general picture be considered, rather than to take one indication alone—and this is particularly applicable in these days of speculation about extrasensory perception, telepathy, and clairvoyance.

I have no way of knowing how many cases of possession there might be in this day and age. Probably not many. I have personal knowledge of only one alleged case and I have never tried to verify the facts, although they were told me by a personal friend who was present at the exorcisms. Father Joseph de Tonquedec, S.J., one of the best authorities on the subject, is quoted as saying that in twenty years of

investigation he has never come across a case of real possession. Undoubtedly many of the phenomena which were once believed to result from possession are now recognized as symptoms of hysteria, neuroses, and catalepsy, or may result from natural powers now being studied in para-
p

we find remarkably fewer cases of possession
t ancestors seemed to find does not necessarily
r ler generations were entirely wrong. It may
s at the Devil operates differently today; pos-
but diabolical influence is everywhere, mani-
d, crime, prejudice, and falsity—and even in
being elusive he is more effective. If we
n down we could eliminate him. If we could
on him we could crush him. But if he can keep
his identity or reality, he will sneak up on us
us doing his work for him.

nd age we should be neither superstitious nor
al, neither fascinated by the occult nor ob-
tery, neither obsessed by a fiery-eyed dragon
r dubious of the world of spirits. We should
a natural explanation of every phenomenon,
perts in pertinent sciences, but not reject the
spiritual intervention. The Devil may be hard
an to swallow, but without him we can never
nd Christ the Redeemer. Whom was He fight-
no adversary? Was He crucified to crush the
ead of an imaginary serpent?

41

THE SECOND COMING

THE QUESTION

Here is my question. "Why do we not hear more from the Catholic expositors about the Second Coming of Jesus?" I know from literature I have read that Catholics who teach the Bible do believe He is coming again. The Second Coming is such a joy and hope to look forward to. I am not a Catholic.

Mrs. Henry Seib

THE ANSWER

Your question, Mrs. Seib, recalls to me an experience of my years as hospital chaplain. Once while visiting a mental ward I was backed into a corner by a wild-eyed lady with a loud, intense voice and gesticulating arms. She proclaimed herself the "Herald of the General Judgment"; and I did not argue. She looked the part, and I was willing to admit her claims if only she would let me out of my corner.

But the arms flailed too widely. She had read her Scriptures thoroughly and learned her verses well. So I had to listen with waning patience and growing anxiety to various frightful fulminations and threats of disaster and doom, which were sure to come on the world because blinded clerics like myself would not hearken to God's herald and prepare for the fatal day which she was sent to announce.

I hope I do not offend you by this reference. Your question has nothing wild-eyed about it. But possibly my friend, the "Herald of the General Judgment," may give a hint why the

324

Church does not greatly emphasize the Second Coming in her general preaching. We try to put stress on those points of doctrine which will do the most practical good for souls, and we tend to pass lightly over those mysteries which often confuse or frighten the average layman, or lead him into fruitless speculation or superstition.

It is true that Jesus taught clearly His Second Coming. We believe it and we teach it without question; but we are not inclined to dwell on it: there is so much that is vague, mysterious, and uncertain about it. We are not sure of its time, manner, place, or circumstances; and there is wide field for imaginings and fears. Through centuries of experience the Church has found it much more salutary to emphasize the more immediate and comprehensible realities of death and individual judgment for each one of us.

The Church learned this lesson early in her history. Jesus made it fairly clear in His teachings that no one—not even the angels in heaven, but only the Father—knew when the end of the world would come. But the early Christians often misinterpreted His words, confusing His prediction of the destruction of Jerusalem with His warnings about the end of the world. And the idea became quite general that the end would come very soon—almost any day—and people tended to take a negative attitude in their preparation for it. Instead of making long-range plans with emphasis on leading a holy life and spreading the kingdom, many of them tended to sit back and wait in dread and fear, looking anxiously for the signs Jesus had foretold.

Other early Christians had even worse notions on this subject. They were called millennarians or chiliasts. They expected the millennium: Jesus would come back to earth again and establish here a glorious kingdom in which His happy subjects would live joyfully for one thousand years. Some of the millennarians were heretics, but many of them were otherwise orthodox Christians, even great Saints.

Jesus had always preached a spiritual kingdom; His reign was not of this world. But this notion was foreign to many of His fellow Jews of that day. They were disappointed in Jesus. They had expected the Messias to restore the glory of Israel and establish a triumphal kingdom with Jerusalem as its capital.

Most of these earthly-minded contemporaries rejected Jesus; but they had heirs to their attitude among His followers. In His first coming the Messias had failed to establish the worldly kingdom which had been expected, but He would surely do it the next time He came—and He had promised to come again.

Not all misinterpretations of Christ's word died out after the early years of Christianity. Each century has seen a succession of "Heralds of the General Judgment" pointing to signs, screaming threats, and naming dates. The prophets of one century are not deterred by the failure of their predecessors. Predicted dates have come and gone, but each new prophet thinks that his date will be the true one; this time it will really happen.

One of the deep impressions of my childhood concerns such a prediction of the end of the world, given much publicity in our newspapers. I do not recall the details, but the prophet was leader of a sect in Illinois—the Zionists, I think. He had two basic doctrines: (1) that the world was flat, and (2) that it would come to an end on a near and definite date. Even then I had heard the story of Columbus and was reasonably sure that the earth was round; but I was a bit relieved when the sect leader's predicted date passed without catastrophe. And only now do I learn that the world is really a bit pear-shaped.

Just as I began meditating on your question, Mrs. Seib, I ran onto a newspaper article telling about a wild rumor in Paraguay that the world was going to end on a specific date. The rumor created panic in one village near Asunción. Three persons died of heart attacks. Many sold their homes, apparently with a confused notion that they might take the revenue with them when the end came. The only missing feature of this panic was suicide. Usually when frantic people fear the end of the world some of them will desperately hasten their own end by violence.

Fears of this kind are not sensible or salutary. They do not make Saints—only fanatics. And the Paraguay incident

326

is repeated often in various forms in different parts of the world. Even while I was composing this answer to you, Mrs. Seib, I received another question of similar nature. Let me quote it as an example of the stories that go about.

"Recently someone told me about a Padre Pio who prophesied that the third world war would have occurred by the first snowfall of 1960, would last seven days, would be followed by a short period of peace and the end of the world. What comment have you on this? Has the Church made any pronouncement on such prophesies?"

Now, I have great respect for the pious Padre Pio, and I greatly doubt that he ever made any prediction of this kind. That "first snowfall of 1960" betrays the rumor; they never have snow in southern Italy where Padre Pio lives. And in one part of the world or another I am quite sure the first snowfall of 1960 was on January 1. The world has not yet come to an end.

The Church does not wish to encourage the anxieties which result from speculation about the end of the world. So she teaches the word of Christ about His Second Coming —as she must teach all His words; but she tries to emphasize that we know not when it will be nor what may be the manner of it. And she constantly insists that it is much more practical for each of us to consider our own individual end rather than to soar into fearful fantasies about cosmic transformations.

The last things—the ultimate end and destiny of each of us and of the world in general—form an entire area of theology called eschatology. In it we study about death and judgment, heaven, hell, and purgatory, the end of the world, the resurrection of the body, the Second Coming, and the General Judgment. This study falls naturally into two branches: (1) the last things which await each of us individually; and (2) the last things which will happen to the world in general. The Church, in her teaching and preaching, emphasizes the individual features as being more practical and understandable.

Death. As far as I am personally concerned, in a practical way, the end of the world will come when I die. And much that Jesus said about the end of the world applies precisely to my individual death. It will come like a thief in the night; I know not the day nor the hour. I must be prepared and vigilant.

The particular judgment. Again for practical purposes, as far as I am concerned individually, the Second Coming of Christ will take place immediately after my death. He will be my Judge then and there; and this particular judgment will be final and irreformable. The General Judgment will not alter it: only proclaim it and portray its justice.

Heaven. The kingdom of Christ is spiritual and eternal; it will be a place of complete and lasting happiness. We will live in union with God, share His home, partake of His goodness, and bask in His love. And heaven will be available to each of us immediately after death, if we love God thoroughly and are filled with His grace.

Hell. For those who do not love God—or who love evil things more—the coming of Jesus in the particular judgment may be catastrophic. Hell is for those who ask for it. We choose it when we reject God's goodness; and the just Judge will not deprive us of the full consequences of our choice.

Purgatory. Often we recede from our choice of hell and repent of the sin which damned us. The merciful Lord forgives our guilt and restores us to His love. But the sin still leaves its mark; and nothing defiled can enter heaven. So if one's penances have not healed his wounds, purgatory must complete the job.

Often, too, our choice of evil is not so thorough and decisive as to reject God. We choose only bits of badness which we try to reconcile with goodness. When death and judgment find one in such a state, that is, with venial sins on one's soul, that person is a candidate for a place of purgation where God's great love will enflame his coolish love, probably in painful process, as true love must sometimes operate.

Purgatory prepares us for heaven when we are almost, but not quite, ready. It burns off the blemishes of sin, and activates our faculties for the enjoyment of supreme happiness.

The judgment of the individual comes at his death; the judgment of the world comes at its end. Jesus describes the General Judgment in vivid terms, sometimes frightening, sometimes consoling. It will be the moment of truth for all creation. Men and things will stand out as they really are, for all to see and understand. Fakes will be fathomed, deception will disappear, false fronts will fall, and goodness will be so glorious that everyone will value it at its full worth.

About the cosmic fate the following facts are clearly presented to us:

The physical world—or at least this earth—will be destroyed or completely transformed. It is intimated, at least figuratively, that this destruction will be by fire, and that a new world will emerge from the embers. It is not quite clear what purpose this new world will serve.

With the emergence of a new world will come a glorious restoration of the complete human nature and personality of each one of us. The resurrection of the body is one of the great mysteries of Christianity, but a fact clearly taught by Christ and His Apostles. From the time of our death until the resurrection only our souls will be alive—and our souls are not the whole of us. We will not be living human beings, but only living souls. And then at the resurrection we will be our total selves once more, but human beings adapted to the life of heaven—or to the half-life of hell.

In the General Judgment, which will follow the resurrection, everyone will see and appreciate the justice and mercy of God. We are told that even the sins of the Saints will stand out, but not to their shame; rather, to make them all the happier for God's mercy, grace, and forgiveness.

The good will be separated from the wicked. Jesus describes it as a rather orderly scene. He will come on the clouds of heaven with power and majesty, and like a shepherd culling his flock He will put the sheep on the right and the goats on His left; and the criterion for selection will be the practical love we have shown for Jesus by being kind to our neighbor.

If you find it consoling to think about the Second Coming then let your thoughts wander as they will. Jesus definitely

329

promised that He would come again. But if you find it frightening to think about the end of the world, then keep firmly in mind that no one really knows when it will come; and there is no sound reason to think it will be soon. We are pretty sure that this old world has been rolling along for a few million years; and it looks as if it should be good for a few million more—unless we get careless with atom bombs!

The Scriptures mention various events which are to take place before the Final Judgment. Hardly any of them have yet occurred.

The gospel of Christ will be preached in the whole world.

Henoch and Elias will come back. They never did die; they will be the real heralds of the General Judgment.

A great apostasy will take place. St. Paul used this argument to console the Thessalonians. They should not be terrified, as though the day of the Lord were near, because this revolt has not yet happened.

The Antichrist will have his day—the man of sin, the son of perdition. Every vicious character down the ages from Nero to Hitler has been imagined as the Antichrist.

There will be extraordinary disturbances of nature: wars, pestilence, famine, and earthquakes. "The sun will be darkened, and the moon will not give her light, and the stars will fall from heaven, and the powers of heaven will be shaken."

There will be a general conflagration.

The trumpet of the resurrection will sound loud enough to awaken the dead. It is believed that Gabriel will do the blowing.

The "Sign of the Son of Man" will appear in the heavens. This is believed to be the cross of Christ, which may show itself in wondrous light.

But even when you think you have seen all these signs, don't yet be frightened. It is probable that you have read into natural events your own interpretation. Don't be a herald of the General Judgment. Leave that job to Henoch and Elias.

42

THE RESURRECTION

THE QUESTION

Catholics pay homage and offer prayers to a departed
soul, bring his body into church for funeral Mass, and so on.
What of persons who die in airplane crashes or mines where
their bodies are never recovered? What of them on resurrection day?

Rosemary Diorio

THE ANSWER

Just to keep the record straight, Rosemary, the prayers
are offered *for* a departed soul and the homage is paid to
God. But your basic problem is one of many objections which
have been proposed through the centuries against the Christian belief in the resurrection of the bodies of the dead. The
only answer to all these questions is that the resurrection
will be accomplished by the direct, unlimited power of God.
He had no trouble creating our bodies when He first breathed
life into them; He should have no difficulty reassembling
them when He is ready to give them new and eternal life.

The resurrection is a mystery, just as creation and life
and eternity are all mysteries. We can never fully grasp it
or explain how it is to be accomplished. We cannot imagine
it or describe it in natural scientific terms. But that is no
reason to reject it; on similar grounds we would have to
reject all mysteries, and then little or nothing would be left
of our religion.

We accept the fact of the resurrection because of the clear

and explicit teaching of our Lord Jesus Christ, and because of the evident reflection of His words in the teachings of the Apostles, especially St. Paul. These words in the New Testament are so obvious and definite that the doctrine of the resurrection has been explicitly believed and taught by the Church from the beginning. It did not need to be gradually clarified and defined like many other doctrines.

And yet, though few doctrines have been more clear and consistent through the centuries, probably none has been more questioned, denied, and ridiculed by non-Christians and by occasional heretics within the Christian family.

Naturally, all who deny the immortality of the human soul ridicule the resurrection. What would be the sense of a risen body floating around through space, with no soul to give it life?

It may seem silly to you and me, but from ancient times various groups of people have considered our material bodies as putrid prisons in which our glorious spiritual souls had unfortunately been confined. Those people saw death as the eternal liberation of the spirit, free to enjoy the pleasures of heaven; and surely no body would ever rise from the grave to imprison a soul anew.

A similar notion in more extreme form inspired successive groups like the ancient Manichaeans and the medieval Albigensians. They held that all material things are by nature evil, proceeding from some satanic creative power. Spiritual things are good, the work of God. So man on earth is the center of constant conflict. His spirit must conquer his evil flesh and thus attain its reward. In God's holy heaven there will certainly be no evil body to fight with the saintly soul.

In modern times we are more familiar with those denials of the resurrection which proceed from materialists and rationalists. They label the resurrection an ancient superstition, scientifically unsound. It is a part of their general denial of things spiritual.

If we have occasion to argue with people who deny the resurrection we must not make the mistake of trying to prove it to them by reason, and least of all by science. It is not at all a natural thing which can be established by logical proofs. It is a supernatural thing which we can know only by faith. If the person with whom you are talking does not accept the word of God through Jesus Christ, then you might begin at some other point to help him see the soundness of revelation. Only in the measure of his faith in the message of Christ will he accept the fact of the resurrection.

I do not mean to imply that Christians alone believe in the resurrection. You cannot prove it from reason, but like all matters of faith it does make sense. Your human personality is made up of a union of soul and body. Your soul separated from your body is not you—only an imperfect and incomplete part of you. If you are to live for eternity in perfect happiness, doesn't it seem fitting that you should live as your complete self—as a human person, not as a deprived spirit?

Here on earth our bodies and souls work together in all our deeds, both good and evil. The body cannot commit sin alone; neither can the soul; even in its thinking it must use the brain. My acts of virtue are mine—not my body's or my soul's. With God's grace my good acts are credited to me as a person made up of both matter and spirit.

We Catholics emphasize the fact that even the most spiritual and supernatural features of our sanctification are joint experiences of body and soul. Grace comes to us through the waters of Baptism poured on our heads. Penance is performed in affliction of the body, shared fully by the soul. And in acts of sin, which cause the loss of grace, the body often seems to take the lead.

Why then should only the soul be rewarded or punished? Shouldn't the body get its share? Shouldn't the complete person reap the consequences of what the complete person did?

The doctrine of the resurrection of the body simply supposes that man lives in eternity as man, not as a ghost, or a half-human spirit.

Christian belief in the resurrection of the body is closely connected with the Incarnation and with the resurrection of our Savior. Since God took for Himself a material body, we have great reverence for our bodies. Since Jesus obtained grace for us through the sufferings of His body, shouldn't that grace have an effect on our bodies?

Since God raised up the body of Jesus after death and then took it up to heaven, we believe that He will do a similar favor for our bodies, which are sanctified through the death and resurrection of His Son. This is the frequent theme of St. Paul: because Christ is risen we will rise also to be with Him.

Furthermore, death is the result of sin. If there had been no sin there would be no death. But the effects of the Redemption are greater than those of sin. So as a result of the Redemption death will be conquered—in the resurrection.

Only the fact of the resurrection is a matter of faith. It does mean, of course, that our risen bodies will be our own—not new ones created for the occasion—not scrambled or exchanged ones. But the doctrine does not tell us the precise nature or manner of this identity. Our risen bodies will be greatly transformed and spiritualized so that they can live in heaven—or in hell. What is involved in this transforming process? We don't know, although theologians have speculated about this for centuries.

Traditionally, most Christian teachers have insisted on some sort of physical identity of the risen body with our present earthly body. And yet they insist, at the same time, that the risen body will have no real, tangible, physical characteristics, except this identity. It will seemingly have no weight, or mass, or subjection to physical forces. On the contrary, it will be immortal (while all physical things change) and the bodies of the Saints in heaven will be impassible (capable of no suffering), agile (not subject to space restrictions), and subtle (it was subtility which permitted the body of Christ to enter the room of His Apostles even though the doors remained closed). And those who are old and feeble—as well as the immature—are given hopeful assurance that they will rise in the prime of youth.

These theological speculations are interesting to those who like to deal in imponderables. I think they all come down to this: in the resurrection our identical personalities will be restored; we will have the same body and soul we had on earth, but our bodies will take on many of the characteristics of the soul and participate in its more perfect spiritual life.

Insistence on physical identity today becomes mechanistic and gruesome if we put it in terms of the reassemblage of identical atoms.

The truth is that the resurrection is a supernatural process; when we try to explain it in natural, scientific terms we can make it seem ridiculous. Your problem of the lost and disintegrated body would really present difficulties if the resurrection were a mechanistic search and sorting of particular atoms. But the only point which really concerns me is that almighty God, who created all things physical and spiritual, knows a way—simple to Him—of restoring my complete human personality for eternity, along with the complete personalities of all those whom I have loved here on earth.

I believe we may avoid confusion on the subject of the resurrection of the body if we outline our belief in the various things which happen to us after death. First comes the violent separation of soul from body. Then the soul, which is by nature immortal and cannot die, goes directly to judgment. We know not the nature of this individual judgment, but we believe that it is immediate and final and that God's justice and mercy will obtain in it. We do not expect a formal arraignment before a solemn tribunal; neither will St. Peter check through the books to total up our debits and credits. Rather, there will be within us a surging awareness of the divine life in our souls, or a despairing realization of the irreparable absence of that life.

When we come to the particular judgment, if we love God completely, without impediment, we will be joined to Him immediately in the love of heaven. If we come to Him without love—with a distinct preference for evil things—we will go to hell without pause. But there may be many of us at that decisive moment who love God essentially, but not completely. There are defects in our love, and these must be repaired in purgatory, a place of final preparation for heaven.

We have no opportunity for repentance after death, but the sanctifying grace of Jesus Christ can still work its purifying effects to remove stains of sin and supply defects in our love. We may suffer in this process of preparation for heaven; at least we are grievously detained from our ultimate happiness.

But it is only temporary, and our final salvation is assured. There is only one exit from purgatory and it leads directly to the eternal embrace of God's love.

I emphasize this subject of purgatory because it is often less understood than our notions of heaven and hell, and because it has direct application to your question, Rosemary. At the funeral of friend or relative we do pay respect to the body of the deceased, as a sign of our love for the person of which that body was an essential part and as an indication of our belief that the same body will rise again to re-form that same personality. However, we seldom pray to the departed soul, but rather for it. We do not hope to alter the justice of judgment, but we believe that if that soul should be in purgatory our prayers can be helpful to it, since God's graces are given in response to prayer.

All the respect we may pay to the deceased body, our taking it to church, and our care in burying it, will not help it to resurrection. Eventually it will disintegrate; its organic elements will enter into new life, probably even help to form a new human body. Our embalming, entombing, and monument building will not make the work of resurrection any easier for the infinite power of God. He can just as easily restore the identical body if its constituent parts are scattered over a consuming ocean by the force of crash and explosion —or if they are spread through the atmosphere by transforming fire.

For long centuries of earthly time our souls will be in heaven or hell (or maybe for a time in purgatory) while our bodies go through the altering processes of all physical and organic things. Then ultimately will come a great change in cosmic creation. We generally call it the end of the world. Maybe it might better be called the beginning of a new world. Anyway, it is at that time that our bodies will be brought to life again by reunion with our living souls, and it is at that time that we will see Jesus Christ coming on the clouds of heaven to show forth the justice of His judgment to all men. Then purgatory will cease to be, heaven will be complete, and the monotony of hell will change only to renew remorse.

Set in Old Style No. 1
Format by Terry Pace
Manufactured by The Haddon Craftsmen, Inc.
Published by HARPER & BROTHERS